Parks for Life
Moving the Goal Posts, Changing the Rules, and Expanding the Field

Will LaPage, F

*Essays on Applied Ethics
for Parks and Recreation in the 21st Century*

Parks for Life
Moving the Goal Posts, Changing the Rules, and Expanding the Field

Will LaPage, Ph.D.

Essays on Applied Ethics
for Parks and Recreation in the 21st Century

"We believe that the outdoors is a statement of the American condition."
—*President's Commission on Americans Outdoors, 1987*

Venture Publishing, Inc. *State College, Pennsylvania*

Cover Photo: The Tree of Life (1854) by Hannah Cohoon, Andrews Collection, Hancock Shaker Village, Pittsfield, Massachusetts. Reprinted with permission.

Trademarks: All brand names and product names used in this book are trademarks, registered trademarks, or trade names of their respective holders.

Production Manager: Richard Yocum
Manuscript Editing: Shannon B. Dawson, Michele L. Barbin

Library of Congress Catalogue Card Number 2007921652
ISBN-10 1-892132-67-2
ISBN-13 978-1-892132-67-3

To the idea,
the reality,
and the promise
of parks.

Contents

Part Three
EXPANDING THE PLAYING FIELD 173

Acknowledgments

The idea of Parks for Life is hardly original. I am grateful to my fellow commissioner, Charles Jordan, of the President's Commission on Americans Outdoors, 1985–1987, for his many reminders during our discussions that parks are for much more than fun and games. Since 1993, IUCN, the World Conservation Union, has had an active program of Parks for Life focused on 15 regions around the world. I am indebted to the broad view of parks, as essential to the community, the economy and to preserving national patrimony that is overwhelmingly apparent in each of the countries that I have visited as a representative of our government. For their willingness to read and comment on an earlier version of the manuscript, I am indebted to my colleagues Ken Olson, Cem Basman, Larry Mink and Tim Merriman. My editors at Venture Publishing, Shannon Dawson and Michele Barbin, deserve enormous credit for patiently coping with my purple prose. To my wife, Susan Cockrell, who insisted that these essays be published, goes all of the credit for motivation. Most importantly, to our children and grandchildren, *Parks for Life* is itself an acknowledgment that deferred stewardship is the superhighway to an encumbered and diminished park legacy.

About the Author

Will LaPage is an international consultant for park system administration, funding, and partnership building. He has worked with the U.S. State Department and the U.S. Agency for International Development, providing assistance to national park systems in eastern Europe, Central America, and the Caribbean and has worked with outdoor recreation planners in South Africa. From 1985 to 1987, he served on the President's Commission on Americans Outdoors, and from 1984 to 1994 was director of New Hampshire's state parks and historic sites. Dr. LaPage is the first recipient of the Theodore and Franklin Roosevelt Award for Excellence in Park Research and has authored over 100 research reports on outdoor recreation trends. He has taught courses on the issues and ethics of park management at the Universities of New Hampshire, Maine, and Wyoming and was a senior lecturer in parks at Colorado State University from 1994 to 1996. Dr. LaPage is the 2006–2007 Reynold Carlson Distinguished Lecturer in Parks at Indiana University.

Prologue
Opening the Floodgates of the Possible

Politics is the art of the possible.

—Otto von Bismark

When we Americans think of our parks, we think first of recreation and, in distant second place, we may think of conserving their splendor. After all, our parks are already protected, aren't they? We are far less likely to reflect on parks as the economic engines that they are for tourism or on the jobs they generate. For less than a handful of us, the word *park* will express the significance of America's most successful export—one of its best ideas—adopted by scores of nations in every part of the world. Equally unlikely is an automatic appreciation of parks for the lives they have changed; or a recognition of parks as sources of inspiration for great works of art, literature, music, and incubators of national and state pride. We take our parks for granted, yet we would surely be impoverished without them. The real tragedy is that we could do infinitely more, if only we were to ask it of them: providing vital services for peacemakers, health promoters, community builders, and problem solvers for a dynamic society in a dynamic world.

Can we really afford our limited view of parks? Declines in attendance across the National Park system are met with answers rather than questions. Yes, society is changing, and park relevance may indeed suffer from that change. But isn't the real question: What have parks done to expand their relevance? Parks for Life is a challenge to our state parks and federal recreation lands to step outside of their traditional scripts, ignore their borders, and help society address a more holistic set of problems. America today bears only a shadowy resemblance to the heyday era of these public lands, and yet we continue to look for traditional answers to perpetual underfunding of park operations and decades of token support for preserving these lands unimpaired for others. The continued marginalizing of our public parklands makes it difficult to see that the road to real solutions is the one that winds through exciting new challenges—*the one less taken.*

Persistent crowding at our public parks is perhaps less an indicator of slipping relevance than it is a failure to grow at anywhere near the rate of society's demands. Perhaps those decades of supposedly *loving our parks to death* are finally taking their toll. Who wants to visit a tired, overused, old park when there are fresh exciting alternatives as handy as the Internet? The multibillions in deferred maintenance on these lands is irrefutable proof that we are not a nation that comes even close to loving its parks to death. And, a policy of *no new parks until we can take care of the old ones* is little more than a sham, a *wait-and-see* attitude, hardly a commitment to *stewardship before growth*, when not a penny is added for stewardship.

The thesis of Parks for Life is that there is only one way out of the whirlpool that our parks find themselves in: They can, and must, be seen as social necessities, providing benefits far beyond recreation and preservation—far enough to encompass every aspect of our lives. Such a holistic view can only come from within the park profession, and will require a major change in the dominant park management paradigm, along with the ability for critical self-analysis and a willingness to discard ineffectual philosophies.

Shifting from a paradigm that is essentially transactional, an implicit contract between a park's management and visitors, to one that is transformational has been halfheartedly under way for decades. The introduction of visitor centers, nature interpretation, and park outreach programs demonstrate widespread recognition of the need for better park appreciation and a higher quality of visitation. Such programs, limited as they are, connect with only a small minority of visitors. Recent innovations in transforming visitor impacts, such as Leave No Trace, Tread Lightly, and Carry In–Carry Out litter reduction programs, are adopted by an even smaller proportion of visitors. Although most of our big park systems are well along in years, they still do not share a coherent set of best management practices, a professional creed, or a holistic view of how they can best interface with their communities for mutual sustainability.

It would be inaccurate to suggest that our major public park systems are in a state of denial about their potential. However, an almost total preoccupation with surviving as underfunded recreation providers year after year inevitably pushes that potential off the drawing boards. The inability to develop that potential is not just a failure of parks. We all own the parks, so we share alike in their potentials and their failures.

Failure may sound like an overly harsh call; yet, how can we not conclude that it is a *failure of holism* that artist-in-residence programs are such a rarity in our parks, and scientists-in-residence are all but nonexistent? Is it not a *failure of park spirit* that every major park does not have a sister park in a Third World country? Isn't it a *failure of vision* that every park is not a vibrant extension of our schools and classrooms? Isn't it a *failure of humanity* that we have not intensely focused on parks for peace by designating parkland on the borders of nations? Isn't it a *failure of pride* that parks haven't assumed a leadership role as models of environmental management? Isn't it a *failure of understanding* that we allow parks to be closed because of a lack of funding or staffing? How can anyone appreciate a closed park? Isn't it a *failure of a sacred trust* that we haven't been able to resolve the perennial deferred maintenance problem? And isn't it a *failure of desire* that we haven't yet matched the reality of parks with the vision of their founders? In fact, isn't that really the test of professional success? After all, those founders weren't even certified professionals!

Parks for Life offers no blueprint for the future; it intends, rather, to provoke the possibilities. The unavoidable conclusion is, however, that if there was ever a need for our parks to make a bold stroke, the time is now. There would appear to be no better way to frame that bold stroke than with the concept of partnerships—partnerships of every possible kind with every conceivable aspect of our lives. These are not partnerships as flesh on skeletal budgets, but partnering because, quite simply, it is a better way of managing the public's assets in a democracy. These are not partnerships that have been thoroughly sanitized and bureaucratized, but partnerships that retain their beautiful diversity. These are not token partnerships for dressing up the annual report, but real collaboration designed to double and quadruple paid staff hours, to increase the transparency of decision making, and to challenge complacency. Lastly, these are not just partners because of what they can do for parks, but because of what parks can do for them. Until we are willing to move the goal posts, change the rules, and expand the field of players, the full benefit of a partnering ethic will continue to elude us, including its powerful symbolism of a people partnering with their land, permanence partnering with change, and diversity partnering with oneness.

Professional attempts at unleashing the enormous potential of parks have been an ongoing, almost incidental, process of scattered innovation and slow adoption. Parks for Life is simply a call to open the floodgates of the possible. How many more blue-ribbon commissions, high-level reviews, class-action suits, whistleblowers, and parks-in-peril exposés will it take before we commit to the absolute necessity of Parks for Life as the best medicine for park health, public health, and community health? Parks change lives every day. Just imagine the collective power, the latent unused power, suddenly available to every park professional working with a holistic mission of Parks for Life!

Think about the assets of our parks, the best, most spectacular, most inspirational landscapes in America. These are assets that can produce a *Grand Canyon Suite* or a "Rocky Mountain High," or our most successful national export—assets owned by the American people and dedicated to their pursuits of happiness and fulfillment. Don't you think such assets, and such pursuits, are capable of something infinitely larger than a few hundred million visits each year? Shouldn't the return on those assets at least capture a few of the transformations that the land so generously dispenses, such as despair into hope, sickness into health, strife into peace, callousness into caring, indifference into pride, arrogance into humility, and confusion into understanding?

Is it conceivable that stewardship only happens in response to perceived value? Is it possible that in attempting to make stewardship the means rather than the end result, we have failed to capitalize the value of these lands beyond their limited utility for recreation alone? And, isn't it highly probable that a massive infusion of partnerships will provide the critical added value to truly make them Parks for Life?

Part One
MOVING THE GOAL POSTS

The players in the game of parks have been moving the goal posts ever since the first park was dedicated. In response to never-ending pressures for land, park crusaders have fought against incredible odds to ensure that our park systems grew apace with the growing demands of communities, states, and the nation. While citizen advocates were growing the parks, dedicated stewards within our park systems were risking jobs and careers in the protection of existing parks against special interests. The record of accomplishments by the winners of the Stephen Tyng Mather award for courage in protecting the national parks is barely the tip of the proverbial iceberg of dedicated professionals in every state and federal agency. Every one of them has proven to be a master at moving the goal posts—extending the definition of a park professional. Now, we not only need to adopt these standards but we also need to widen them to embrace a much broader set of goals—goals that speak to parks for all of life.

Parks for Life:
An Emotion-Based Park Ethic

There can be no transforming of darkness into light and apathy into movement without emotion.

—Carl Jung

Science does not create public parks. Science can tell us that parks are good for us, good for our environment, our economy, and good for many of the creatures with which we share the planet. Science can provide us with some useful clues for managing parks to maximize some of these benefits, but if we wait for science to create parks it will be too late. Emotion creates parks—and because parks are always at risk, emotion is a powerful tool for protecting existing parks. Parks are continually threatened by competing land interests, neglect, mismanagement, underfunding, occasional overuse, massive under-appreciation, and by being taken for granted.

Parks are Earth's bandages in the absence of a land ethic. Sometimes parks are tourniquets for hemorrhaging and irreplaceable ecosystems. We repeatedly, and mistakenly, have seen park establishment as an end, rather than as a beginning, or a demonstration or model of what could be—a small step toward the land ethic that Aldo Leopold argued for more than a half-century ago.

Parks are one of the most popular concepts ever to be adopted and promoted by any society. The rallying cry, "Parks are for People," tells only part of that story. The list of benefits provided by parks vastly exceeds that which appears in their annual reports. Healthy, progressive societies have a holistic view of their parks—a view that is fostered by an ethic connecting parks with all aspects of life, health, education, jobs, inspiration, peace, and justice. Because parks are the creations of a love for the land, its beauty and its in-spirations, a powerful park ethic can be built on these emotional foundations.

For nearly a half-century we have watched the heady growth of science in park management decisions. But in the sterile realm of objective science, park growth has stagnated, park budgets remain embarrassingly inadequate, and park conditions have often plummeted. Even bad science can drive out good emotion. The time has come for the ultimate park partnership to step forward and help reinvent the park movement—the unbeatable team of objective science and subjective emotion.

That parks are massively underappreciated, despite their worldwide popularity, is evident in the limited ways we report their benefits. Preserved acres, open space, and attendance are but small parts of parks' total contribution to life on planet Earth. In explaining the holistic value of parks, it is often instructional to use the metaphor of a student's report card (see Parks for Life Report Card). The grades are admittedly subjective and the benefits are largely immeasurable, but the breadth of potential park contributions to humanity is impressive. You may reasonably question the validity of grading the student on subjects beyond the assignment, but is this really the case? Every one of these "subjects" is subsumed in the mandate: "To preserve and protect for future generations all of the benefits that flow from these lands."

With a barely passing grade in its primary assignment and a failing grade in effort to reach its full potential, our student is on the verge of flunking out. New legislation with a broader mandate is not the answer. Park professionals know that parks must be fully engaged with society. But they remain singularly preoccupied with recreation, and the engagement remains stalled at the flirtation stage. Do we not understand that our parks can be casualties of the widening gap in income, wealth, and power? Until we do, we are unlikely to develop a social justice role for parks. Realizing that feelings of oppression and disenfranchisement can be reduced through corporate underwriting of programs to expose the masses of urban residents to their parks can be a first step. Knowing that parks can provide meaningful employment, retraining, and rehabilitation can be another step. Applying the ecosystem model to social system understanding and community health may be the essential step. Solving the problem of homelessness in the parks could be a convincing step.

If we limit our perspective on parks for peace to memorials for mankind's mistakes and misfortunes, we miss the opportunity to be proactive for peace. International peace parks, border parks, buffer parks, cultural appreciation parks, legacy parks, Nobel peace parks, and an infinite variety of park missions can make a meaningful contribution to understanding, pride, and appreciation of cultural diversity. Parks are a legitimate way to memorialize the past, but they can also be a powerful force for colonizing the future with incentives for peace.

We fail to recognize the fragility of parks as economic engines in the highly competitive tourism economy wherever we ignore the need for limited development zones around parks. The park as a jewel is less likely to be sustainable if its setting is severely compromised. Sustainability of that engine demands a strong and viable partnership between the setting and the jewel. Parks that draw crowds while ignoring the impact of those crowds beyond their borders are not only disengaged, they are irresponsible. Gateway communities are park entrances, and the entrance sets the tone for what goes on inside. The seriousness of park prohibitions regarding feeding wildlife is not enhanced by the carnival approach to wildlife outside many parks. The fortress park mentality can only yield to an ecological park model when there is total acceptance of a shared destiny.

Parks for Life Report Card

Park System: (You Pick One)_____

Subject	Grade	Comments:
Parks as demonstration areas for environmental responsibility	C–	• Alarming deferred maintenance costs • Unknown condition and trend measures • Stewardship mission rarely shared • Parks as stewardship demonstration areas rare to nonexistent
Parks as promoters of peace	D–	• Lacking in program and priority • Largely untapped potential • Parks as "war" zones may outnumber international peace parks
Parks as classrooms	C+	• Some recent progress, but remains a low priority for most parks • At high risk for budget cuts
Parks as catalysts for social justice	F	• Not a performance failure as much as a failure to recognize opportunities • Need and opportunity for expanding budgets and enlarging the constituency rarely recognized
Parks as economic engines	D+	• Notable lack of creative attempts to mesh economy and ecology • Benefits occur through default more than through intent
Parks as inspiration	C+	• Art-in-the-parks and artist-in-residence programs are the exception, not the norm • Inspiration and self-discovery not readily available to society at large
Parks for health	C–	• Continuing failure to participate as major preventive and therapeutic agents in areas of physical, mental, and societal health

One of the earliest arguments for urban parks was that of providing "lungs for the cities." In the same way that trees purify polluted air, vistas can clear clouded minds, and rushing waters can flush poisoned spirits. The challenges of strenuous park hikes can be aerobic for more than the body. Health issues—personal and public, preventive and therapeutic—all have environmental roots and linkages to open space and parks. Stress is a major killer in modern societies, destroying not just its victims but their families and their support systems, thus spreading its tentacles into the community. Parks reduce stress on individuals and communities alike. The unrealized human potential of stress-induced death can be likened to the failure to ever be inspired during life. Parks inspire, provoke, challenge, and tease us to be creative, to be different, to be fulfilled. Parks build diversity as surely as they preserve it.

When science doesn't have the answers, the appeal of a Parks for Life ethic is infectious. Not only does it move parks closer to the center of social issues and toward a broader base of funding, but also it identifies park professionals as valuable problem solvers, networkers, and bridge builders. The major movement toward park partnerships of the past decade seems to herald the emergence of a new park ethic—one of Parks for Life. But partnerships alone reflect an expedient, not an ethic.

With an ethic of Parks for Life, park job descriptions and performance evaluations would include elements of creative problem solving, outspoken advocacy, accountability for intangible assets, constituency building, stewardship sharing, and emotional growth. In an age of Parks for Life, annual reports would subdue the statistics while highlighting the real values of parks, lives changed, communities enhanced, and appreciation gained. With the certain knowledge that parks are for life, scarce research dollars expended on their justification would be redirected toward monitoring park health. With a mission of Parks for Life, people will cherish their parks in greater numbers, for more diverse purposes, and provide more support and visibly less impact. With a worldwide Parks for Life ethic, the World Bank and the United Nations would promote parks for peace, and religions would recognize parks as sacred places for the harmony and understanding they foster. And, in an era of Parks for Life, we will, for the first time, have solid assurance that these assets are forever.

Parks for Life is a radical idea. It moves the test of park success beyond park boundaries. It lifts parks out of their traditional and comfortable niche of recreation and preservation and sets them down squarely in the center of a troubled society. It dares to suggest that all people have a right to live in, not just visit, park-like settings and requires that parks become an essential element of the democratic dream—a barometer of our progress with democracy's grand experiment.

Parks and Peace:
The Need for Parks in a Crowded World

I firmly believe that nature brings solace to all troubles.
— Anne Frank

The fall from the ladder shattered the bones of my right foot. The misdiagnosis for more than two weeks of "severe sprain" shattered my faith in emergency room medicine. Given the relative states of science, social misdiagnoses are probably much more common than medical ones. And, misdiagnoses of social ills can be much more shattering when we learn that we often prefer them to the truth. Nearly a half-century ago when I was starting out in the park management profession, I recall a nationally syndicated article trumpeting the idea that "We are loving our parks to death." So benign and appealing is the misdiagnosis of excessive use by visitors that even now, decades later, it continues to sweep aside the cancerous truths of failing stewardship, underfunding, understaffing, and underconcern for these treasures. The National Park Service admits to a multibillion dollar deferred maintenance backlog—and that's only the infrastructure. Does that sound like we are loving our parks to death?

Unlike Ed Abbey, in his classic *Desert Solitaire*, I take it as a sign of hope that hordes of people are descending on our parklands. What does it matter that they're not quite sure why they are there. So what if they come unprepared, or even if they come overprepared with their air-conditioned, television-equipped motor homes? Something is sending them on a pilgrimage to Terra Pacifica—a place of peace. Our job as park professionals is to help them find it, not to censure them for failing to show up with binoculars and a field guide. Instead, let's give them a field guide for finding peace. Do you happen to know when the highest day of off-season visitation occurred in America's parks? It was a quiet Tuesday in September 2001. Once the initial shock of 9/11 registered and we got tired of the replayed horror, we went to our parks in record numbers—as places of peace and safety in a shockingly unpredictable world.

From time to time, I find myself doing financial consulting for park projects in other countries. It's always shattering to find that the level of park management so seldom rises to the level of park vision. Since the idea was invented at Yellowstone in 1872, all of the major countries of the world have adopted the national park model for preserving a bit of their heritage. That may make it America's most successful export—even ahead of democracy and McDonald's. Visiting Bulgaria's Rila National Park in 1993, I heard some of the results of decades of mining for heavy metals by the Communist regime in the Rila Mountains. Villagers continue to fish downstream from the mine tailings, aware that whole generations of babies suffered deformities from the pollution. In 1997, Croatian national park superintendents told me of how some of their parks had been turned into minefields. The manager of Jamaica's Montego Bay National Marine Park told of how more than 90 percent of the coral reef had been killed by pollution, yet the government still allowed an offshore pipeline to be cut through the reef. At South Africa's Krueger National Park in 1982, the superintendent told of rangers being killed by ivory poachers. In recent years, news reports indicate that National Park Service officers are twelve times more likely to be killed or injured as a result of assault than FBI agents. Parks as battle zones do not quite fit the vision of their founders.

There are some bright lights however. With World Bank support in terms of swapping debt for environmental improvements, numerous Third World countries are able to clean up pollution in and around their parks. Elephant protection in South Africa's Krueger National Park has become much easier with the advent of a border park in neighboring Mozambique. Threats to the world's parks, however, remain largely beyond budgets and beyond ranger capabilities. How did such a great idea become so ill-used? With scores of cultures responding to the idea, what is its universal appeal? I think we need to know so that we can build on it. Was it economics and tourism benefits? No, that's a bonus. Recreation for the masses? No, not all countries consider their parks to be playgrounds. National pride? Unlikely, given the controversy surrounding every new park proposal.

I believe that the reason the park idea has such universal appeal is that it reflects a deep-seated and crosscultural fascination for nature. Parks and nature preserves are the result of a change from centuries of seeing nature as something to be conquered to an ethic of preserving a few special places in their original peaceful state, for themselves of course, but also as models that demonstrate our capacity for doing better. For park management to rise to the level of that vision means seeing parks more holistically than we have in the past. When we begin to truly see parks as necessary for life, for all aspects of life, we begin to see that making peace with the natural world is a prerequisite to peace within and among ourselves.

Despite the much-publicized differences with neighboring ranchers and snowmobile businesses, let me share with you just a few of the things that happen in a typical day in a park like Yellowstone:

- High up in a Ponderosa pine, a hummingbird sits on a nest the size of your eye socket, raising two tiny chicks from eggs no larger than small jelly beans.

- After an absence of 75 years, a reintroduced gray wolf kills one of the park's abundant elk, continuing a predator-prey balance that is older than man, disrupted by three generations of our relentless war on wolves.

- A cow bison gives birth to a healthy bawling calf—one small addition to America's remnant wild buffalo herd, an animal that once roamed coast to coast and was the ecological foundation of the Plains Indians.

- In a mountain meadow so filled with wild flowers that it looks like a painting by Monet, a grizzly bear tears apart a rotten log—peace for bears in one of two remaining pockets of big bear habitat that covered half the country when Lewis and Clark first saw the West.

- At the Old Faithful Inn, a Japanese family takes pictures of Old Faithful to share with friends and family in far off Hiroshima.

- A one-armed Vietnam War veteran finally finds peace sketching the Great Falls of the Yellowstone with the inspired energy of an Albert Bierstadt or a Frederick Remington.

- A lone whooping crane rises like some prehistoric apparition above the early morning fog from a Yellowstone River sand bar.

What has happened to our priorities when there is not enough money to care for these places of peace and healing? Yes, parks are a measure of commitment to peace, enlightenment, and civility. And maybe, just *maybe*, if we had a few more of them to love to death we'd stop killing each other. Maybe the United Nations should promote the creation of parks along international borders as an expression of peace. Maybe the World Bank could expand its concern from protecting the integrity of existing national parks to encouraging the propagation of new parks, "sister park" programs, parks as national investments, and parks for public health. Maybe we could redirect ten percent of our budget for defending the country toward preserving the country. Maybe we should turn all of our parks into classrooms for peace where nature teaches us how to understand and appreciate diversity. Maybe we should start to regard parks as vital tourniquets for a hemorrhaging natural world so that we can eke out a few more generations on planet Earth. The gap between park management and park vision is less a matter of money than it is one of desire.

The connections between parks and peace are as numerous as the parks themselves. I will focus on just two. Originally trained as a natural scientist, I tend to use physical science metaphors to interpret social phenomena. Perhaps my favorite is a paraphrasing of Boyle's law: The more we collide with each other, the greater the resulting heat and pressure. Parks and wilderness areas can be thought of as safety valves in a world where 6.5 billion of us collide with each other. Parks provide us with a bit of cooling-off space. What is the park idea if it is not the essence of peace, calmness, tranquility, silence, harmony, quiet, stillness, and serenity? Continuing the metaphor we might ask where the heat and pressure are most likely to be expressed?

The answer is, of course, at the edges. Just as in a bottle of gas where the collisions are heating up the container when we force more atoms into a confined space, social pressures are going to heat up at our boundaries. If we cushion those borders with buffer zones of parks, we reduce the opportunities for direct collisions.

Peace is not the absence of conflict. Consequently, anyone expecting to find the absence of conflict in nature is bound to be disappointed. Nature is filled with conflict because nature is filled with diversity and competition for space—far greater diversity and competition than we humans can appreciate. What is absent in nature is meaningless conflict and gratuitous violence. Nature, whether at the microscopic level or at the tectonic level, is a most violent place. It is easy to see how humans might misinterpret and misdiagnose that violence. In fact, what is going on in every case is an evolutionary process, a necessary process. Oftentimes, the process is in such slow motion that we miss it altogether. One of the most peaceful scenes we can imagine is that of wildlife at the edge of a meadow. Yet the edges of nature are much like the gas in Boyle's glass bottle in that this is where the action is. Here is where predator finds prey, where the forest tries to crowd out the grass, and vice versa. The stream erodes the land and the land fills in the stream, sometimes a particle of sand at a time, sometimes in spectacular landslides. Fault lines and tidal waves can be catastrophic, but always a new dynamic balance will emerge. That balance in nature may be as close to peace as it gets. We can argue that these events in nature are parallel with those in human affairs but that handily ignores the fact that we have a choice. If by exposing us to nature, parks do no more than to teach us this simple fact, they would be the best peace investment we could ever make.

Another natural law that I find useful is that "nature abhors a vacuum." A vacuum is the absence of diversity. So, just as surely, nature must revel in diversity. Think about all the beautiful landscapes you've seen and what registers is the diversity, the contrast. Now think about the ugly scenes—the war-torn landscapes, wherever diversity has been erased. What did we rebuild in Oklahoma City and what are we building at the site of the World Trade Center? Parks, not just parks as memorials, but parks to restore an element of diversity to the urban landscape. Have you ever noticed that all great cities have parks at their hearts? But is this enough? Maybe every city we carve out of nature carries with it an obligation to designate an equal or greater acreage to parks for the long-term peace of their residents.

What might a field guide to finding peace through parks look like? It might incorporate any of the many existing lists, guides, and tips for communicating with nature, along with suggestions for peaceful uses of nature, such as "Thirteen Ways to Use A Tree Without Benefit of Saw or Axe" (see pp. 38–39). It should build upon the thoughts of American Indian actor, Chief Dan George, in encouraging us "to seek to understand all things because that which we do not understand, we fear. And, that which we fear, we destroy." It should focus less on finding peace and solitude through places in the park and more on attitudes and preparations for finding peace and spreading peace anywhere in the park. Field guides to finding peace through parks need to be as varied as the parks themselves, but running through all of them would be the common themes of encouraging respect for all that we do not or choose not to understand, replacing fear with understanding, and experiencing the sheer fun of looking at the familiar through new perspectives.

If we see our parks and protected lands as places of peace and understanding, it is the worst kind of sacrilege and hypocrisy to allow them to be diminished and to allow them to become combat zones between competing interests. What difference is there between placing land mines in a park and mining a park for its resources? What difference is there in polluting the environment of a park from beyond its borders and allowing a park to deteriorate from within? Parks and wilderness areas, in the words of Wallace Stegner, are part of our "geography of hope." Let's try "loving them to life" as part of that hope for peace and understanding. After 134 years, and adoption by more than a third of the nations of the world, the national park idea still has lots of room to grow. Why not parks for peace? For several millennia we've misdiagnosed war as the way to get to peace. One final analogy from the field of physics: Every action provokes an equal and opposite reaction. If we build parks for peace, we will reduce (by an equal amount) the energies and resources that might have otherwise been focused on conflict. What could it hurt to declare a moratorium on war and use some of those resources to create parks as a way to get to peace? Create parks, fill them with venues for celebrating folk music and cultural art, play games, and listen to old men tell war stories. What's the very worst that could happen?

Make Peace with Nature

If survival is our most powerful instinct,
and if everything we have
and everything we are,
came from nature,
why then are we not driven
to make peace with nature
as a matter of simple survival?

If parks provide peace and sanctuary,
in a threatening world;
and if peace with each other
comes only after peace
with ourselves,
why then do we not make peace
with ourselves
by making parks for each other?

If humankind has suffered
the plague of war long enough;
and wars, particularly against nature,
can never be won,
let us make peace with nature
by making more parks.

Could it be so easy?

Parks for Hope:
Homeless and Hopeless in the Park

And homeless near a thousand homes I stood.
— William Wordsworth

Over the past several decades I have, for very brief intervals, known homelessness, but thankfully hopelessness remains a stranger. Not everyone knows that America's public parks have a long tradition of providing remedies for both. During a recent visit to one of our major urban parks in the Northeast, I found myself obsessing about the role of parks in resolving America's growing numbers of homeless. Issues of sanitation, safety, appropriateness, and park attractiveness swirled around in my head along with the mission and role of parks in our society. I wondered how different is the hermit squatter in a wilderness park from the homeless squatter in an urban park? How different are both of them from the "snowbirds," those modern-day nomads whose mobile homes are their only homes, going from park to park with no permanent address. What about the "camper" who is between jobs and using a park until affordable housing comes along? It seemed to me that the big difference is one of hope. In each of these examples, it is only the urban squatter that is without hope. This is the real American tragedy of the homeless—the absence of hope for so many thousands here in the land and under the government that Thomas Jefferson described as "the world's best hope."

The parks profession can hardly argue that homelessness is not a park problem and still maintain that parks are for people—all people. The homeless dropped the problem in the lap of parks; to now turn away from those without hope would place parks in the untenable position of being detached from the problems of society. This government of Jefferson's "best hope" is the same government that, more than two centuries later, promotes the hopes and dreams of millions of its citizens through public park systems that are the admiration of the rest of the nations of the world. So, I wondered, what might parks do for the homeless besides conveniently look the other way? While I wholeheartedly subscribe to the maxim that "a problem accepted is a problem halfway to its solution," I remained puzzled. How does a park dispense hope?

Of course we can partner with the shelters, the churches, and the social service agencies in the search for solutions. Maybe we can provide meaningful work for tired people restoring tired parks. Perhaps by filling the parks with activities, day and night every day of the year, more people will see the plight of the homeless and get involved, and possibly more of the homeless will find hope in being a bit closer to the society from which they feel alienated. Parks should be able to encourage more government and university-sponsored social research in the parks—problem-solving research on real issues. We should at least be capturing some of their stories. Those stories are every bit as important to include in the park's annual report as are the visits by artists and school children. More use of parks by local schools, including school adoptions of nearby parks, will raise awareness of all park needs. The park profession could give awards—sizeable awards—for creative solutions to the problem of homelessness in parks. Portions of parks can be set aside for vegetable gardens—gardens where at least a few homeless persons might find purpose in nurturing plants. In short, we can try lots of things. Some of them are bound to work some of the time.

But, how does a park renew hope when hope itself is a casualty? It does it by simply doing what is expected of parks—by being vibrant showcases of pride in the past and hope for the future. A park cannot evoke hope in others when it looks hopeless itself—when it is tired, run-down, and worn out. Tired parks can still be a refuge, but only a vibrant park can evoke hope in souls where all hope has flown. Parks are a refuge for all of us—a change of pace, a place to relax from our daily burdens, and a physical and mental space that evokes memories and stirs imaginations. Whenever we hear that the park as refuge has failed and the problems of society have followed us into the park with unspeakable crimes against people, we feel as though a sacred place has been profaned almost beyond restoration, a national treasure slashed and disfigured! So, the park as shelter and sanctuary must be not just a safe place, but also a special place—a true retreat for all levels of burnout, a place where hope is rekindled again and again and again.

Some day soon I will return to that park and to the same cluster of park benches where a homeless family slept beneath cardboard sheets in the rain. They may still be there, perhaps in even greater numbers, but I hope and I believe that the homeless eyes that I look into will not be quite so bereft of any spark of hope. That belief comes partly because I have spent a lifetime among park people, and it comes resoundingly from a sure knowledge that Jefferson's "best hope" still burns bright!

The inscription on the Statue of Liberty by Emma Lazarus is repeated endlessly, if silently, at the entrance to every public park in America: *"Give me your tired, your poor, your huddled masses yearning to breathe free, the wretched refuse of your teeming shore, send these, the homeless, tempest-tossed to me: I lift my lamp beside the golden door."* Who among us has never felt weary, depressed, impoverished in spirit, yearning for simplicity and the free air of nature? Who among us has not found in parks a refuge, a home, a new beginning? Parks can turn their back on the homeless, but at what price? Would we really choose to substitute Emma Lazarus' inspired words for Dante's *"Abandon hope, all ye who enter here"*?

The belief that our parks are a source of hope can easily be a self-fulfilling prophecy with only a rudimentary analysis. Think about it for a minute: Those who created the park hoped that people would treasure it as they did, those who operate the park hope that people will come to visit, people who visit the park are hoping for a memorable experience, and people who support the park hope that it will deliver the benefits they expect of it. However, if we were to ask all of these people about their hopes, we would very likely discover that there was not a lot of doubt in their hopes—most would say that they were confident of the outcomes. In scientific terms, they know that the probability of success is better than 95 percent, which are definitely the kind of odds we all like when it comes to picking a winner! Now then, be honest: What kind of odds do you normally work with on a day-to-day basis? While we may not like to admit it, most of us are not unlike professional gamblers; we like the odds to be in our favor and we work to achieve a favorable spread. Even then, odds that are consistently at the 95 percent level are unheard of, whether we are picking a job, a career, a home, a school for our children, a partner, a special gift, or an investment. Since most of us like to surround ourselves with winners, it might make sense that parks would have an invigorating effect on our hopes, or at least a moderating effect on our fears. Either way, rising hopes result in greater confidence, and greater confidence has a way of opening doors.

How might parks work to elevate hopes and depress fears? Probably it happens in many ways related to our attitudes and our perspectives. The population of lunch-hour joggers in the park is probably motivated at least as much by the need for a change in perspective as in the need for aerobic exercise. The romantic suitor who wants to pop the question on a swan boat in the park is clearly setting the stage away from daily distractions. The writer looking for inspiration, the photographer looking for originality, the pressure-tank investment banker looking for simplicity, and the mother looking for wonder in her child's eyes are all hoping for the 95 percent success level when they go to the park. If our parks are not exactly wellsprings of fulfillment, they certainly are one of the best attitude adjustment retreats we've ever devised.

You see, hope is separated from fulfillment by just a little bit of doubt, a little bit of uncertainty. In much the same way, at the other end of the spectrum, fear and despair are separated by uncertainty. That little bit of uncertainty can be enormously valuable if you are on the edge of despair or on the verge of self-discovery. Scientific thinking seeks to minimize uncertainty, while emotional reasoning maximizes it. There can be no better argument for an emotion-based park ethic. The changeless eternity of the park, like that of the night sky, gives both comfort and challenge.

Parks for Health and Happiness:
An Exercise in Lateral Thinking

It was possibly the only period in human history in which
the happiness of a great people was the sole objective of
government.

—Edward Gibbon

Edward De Bono, the father of lateral thinking, presents the case of the fat Duchess of Devonshire who, after repeated and fruitless consultations with physicians, finally got her obesity under control by eating more often—not less. De Bono's example of lateral thinking, "outside the box," not only keeps hunger under control by reducing the urge to binge through frequent snacking but also makes it possible to substitute other activities for meal time. The reason it worked is that the Duchess, like most obesity sufferers, wanted to change. As America increasingly wants to change its national obesity trend, it could similarly benefit from some lateral thinking.

Depending on your source, as much as one third of the American public may be suffering from obesity. Since the obese image is not one that we aspire to, given the emphasis on slimness, fitness, and health in American marketing and television programming, we can safely assume that obesity correlates strongly with unhappiness. Using De Bono's approach, the cure for obesity is not a diet, but rather happiness. A few will always be willing to settle for whatever limited happiness can come from continued food addiction, but what of the others? What about the social costs of treating obesity? What about obese children with shortened lives and lost opportunities for real happiness? What has happened to a country with a founding ethic of the pursuit of happiness? Could obesity be an indicator of deeper national malaise?

Mr. Jefferson wasn't talking about unhappiness or even about happiness; its pursuit was being put on a par with life and liberty. Actual happiness is a matter of personal choice. I can't make you happy—only you can do that. However, I am willing to wager that I can show you many alternatives to food as an antidote to unhappiness, and since you desire happiness and probably have tried numerous diets in search of happiness, you may be open to creative ways of breaking the cycle of seeking happiness through food and finding only unhappy pounds. Let's explore together what might happen if we were to unleash the creative energies of America's parks and recreation agencies on the problem of obese unhappiness. Of all of the public agencies, at every level of government, only one is totally dedicated to opening the door to the pursuit of happiness—Parks and Recreation.

Of course there's the obvious connection: *parks = recreation = exercise.* No doubt, along with diets, you've tried exercise as a way to lose pounds, but have you tried parks, recreation, and exercise as roads to happiness, self-discovery, and a healthy lifestyle? For the moment, let's forget the last two and just consider parks as providers of happiness. It has been said that there is a slender person inside every obese person struggling to get out. It has also been said that there is a poet, an artist, inside each of us. One of the things that parks do, and do very well, is to help us discover ourselves. Discovery, particularly of the self, can be a lifelong source of happiness. Parks challenge us and dare us to find ourselves within the web of life. They can fill us with music, awe us with majesty, humble us with history, free us with spaciousness, and ennoble us with hopes and dreams. Every public park is the love child of someone's emotional connection to the land. Every public park was set aside to share that emotional connection. And, guess what? You don't have to find it on your own. Most public parks have a wide array of programs designed to make you a part of their reason for existence. Like the Duchess, you might have to try more than one before you find "your" park, a place that opens your eyes to the wonder of discovery, the magic of natural beauty, and the fulfillment of being involved in something that you never considered possible. America's public parks can endlessly feed all who hunger for happiness and fulfillment.

The lateral thinker does not run away from food but rather embraces it in all of its permutations—not just the consumption, but the anticipation, the preparation, the presentation, and the reflection. The lateral approach might take the following sequence of planning a picnic in the park. The picnic would be focused on food quality rather than food quantity, and its theme would reflect the park, the season, and the reason for the event. The preparation would consider the need for keeping things hot and cold, ease of transport since the perfect picnic spot will be some distance from the parking lot, and attractiveness of the setting. The presentation would in every way enhance the theme and prolong the event—not fast food from a bucket, but slow food with good music, good friends, low in calories and high in flavor. Imagine an incomparable setting, no tip, no waiting, no hassling, and no guilt followed by a stroll in the park. A simple life change that is still food-centered, but is close to calorie-neutral simply by laterally changing the meaning of "eating out." Try this a few times and I'll wager that you will soon be going to the park without the picnic basket.

Recreation of any kind as a diversion is well-understood by all of us, right? Wrong! Take a good look at the word, it's re-creation—not amusement. Isn't renewal, revitalization, recovery, rebirth what the Duchess was looking for—what we all expect in some measure from our recreational activities? Take your recreation to the outdoors, to a public park, and you have instantly added value to it. What does a chess game played in a park have over a chess game played indoors? Only sunshine, fresh air, changing scenery, new spectators, and open space. Recreation is to the pursuit of happiness as parks are to the playing field. One of the fastest growing outdoor activities today is the therapeutic use of wilderness. The holistic idea behind it is simple: Expose yourself, even briefly, to the challenges of the wild and the devils of civilization become much less formidable. Obesity is clearly unlikely to yield to simple diversion. Holistically, if recreation is to lead to happiness it must be at least as fulfilling as food. Redefining recreation to focus on happiness is no different than redefining wilderness experiences to make them therapeutic. Volunteering in a park is widely considered "recreation" by many. Volunteering to provide outdoor experiences for school children, to help maintain and restore park features, and to help visitors can all be seen as recreational routes to happiness and fulfillment for anyone, including the obese. Recreation is personal—It belongs to you. It can be as passive or as active as you want it to be. In a park, no one sets the norms for recreation but you. If it re-creates you, it is recreation.

Finally, let's apply some lateral thinking to exercise as a prescription for obesity. Forget about exercise as a calorie burner and concentrate on it as a healthy lifestyle. From literally hundreds of possible examples from parks, I chose the picnic planning sequence because it is so widely available and because a little exercise was included in getting to the picnic site and a little more following the meal. Even more important, the setting was changed from the nearest fast food feedlot with all of its glitz and glamour, designed to reassure us that it's OK to tank up on calories, to a natural setting that appeals to all of our senses and feeds our curiosity rather than our stomachs. That's the key isn't it—breaking existing unhealthy lifestyles? Think about exercise simply as a way of physically getting to new places, places we couldn't get to before, and the calorie burning becomes a bonus. Exercise should not be thought of as the price we pay for eating, but as a way to live life to the fullest! With exercise we get better circulation, and more oxygen to the brain means more and deeper thinking about self-discovery, new challenges, new activities, and new parks to visit.

Obesity is more than likely a pretty solid indicator of a lot of things that are going on in a modern fast-paced society, so it is probably not entirely fair to equate it solely with unhappiness. However, it clearly obstructs the pursuit of almost anything except food as well as being decidedly limiting and restrictive to life and liberty. Therefore, it makes sense to not only address it as a major public health problem but also to declare it a threat to every obese person's independence.

Our public parks offer three important keys to dealing with America's obesity epidemic: the pursuit of happiness, the discovery of self, and a healthy lifestyle. With a hand like that, isn't it time for America to ante up and mandate some creative partnerships between its public health agencies and its parks? Every American will benefit twice: first through reduced health costs, and second because we all can use those three keys in our own pursuit of happiness.

Parks for Meaning:
Senior Volunteers—Working at Their Leisure

A Great Society is a place where the meaning of man's life
matches the marvels of man's labor.
— Lyndon B. Johnson

Many yeas ago while working as a seasonal park ranger, I had the memorable pleasure of meeting a couple of senior hikers. Almost every spring and fall weekend, Ben and Mildred would show up, their backpacks filled with brush clippers, a collapsible saw, a small shovel, a trail axe, even a pulley and ropes. Just as faithfully, before heading off to hike the extensive trail system with its water bars to repair, fallen trees to remove, and the ever-growing trailside brush to clip, they would take a few minutes to visit with the park staff and discuss the trails most needing attention. It was an unspoken secret that their knowledge of trail conditions was superior to ours. The small staff had no time for trails. Maintaining picnic areas and campgrounds, cleaning toilets, collecting fees, and staffing the park store left no time left for trails, which were of course the main reason that people came to Monadnock State Park. As Ben and Mildred headed up the mountain, to our obvious envy, we returned to slapping another coat of stain on picnic tables that should have been replaced years earlier, unplugging toilets, and repairing the ever-failing water system.

Ben, a retired physician, and his wife Mildred were park volunteers before the volunteer idea had fully germinated—before we began to recognize, organize, and coordinate volunteers, and before we began to worry about things like liability. We didn't consider them our extended staff, nor did they see themselves as anything more than ordinary hikers. If it had occurred to us to categorize them, they would have been in a category by themselves— "hikers with a conscience" maybe, but never "volunteers." Ben and Mildred were just being Ben and Mildred, working at their leisure, continuing a valued tradition of public trail stewardship on Mt. Monadnock.

Half a century later, volunteerism in parks is no longer a curiosity—it is a necessity. The Bens and Mildreds number in the hundreds of thousands at uncounted parks all across America. They still work on trails, but they also do campground hosting, endless grass mowing, interpretive programs, visitor center staffing, and help with park planning. I wonder what Ben and Mildred would think about the way volunteerism has evolved, its agreements, insurance, inch-thick volunteer manuals, paid volunteer coordinators, and a growing concern at high levels about sharing power with volunteers. That power, the act of one segment of the public taking back some of the responsibility for their parks, represents a monumental step away from the "let government do it" philosophy of the mid-20th century and a significant step toward a widely shared park stewardship ethic. The wave of park volunteerism was neither professionally inspired or agency ordained. It was often actively discouraged and continues to be quietly resisted in many park systems. It happened as a natural outgrowth of burgeoning demands on parks with relatively static budgets, and seniors were always in the forefront.

At issue today is how the powerful force of volunteerism shall be sustained and encouraged to grow for the benefit of America's public park systems. Volunteerism as recreation has been replaced by volunteerism as an extension of park management. In many parks, you cannot be an unsanctioned volunteer. You must be recognized and registered, and your work must be approved in advance and must often be part of a park plan. Some volunteers get the benefit of insurance and workmen's compensation. Volunteers often get free-use privileges at their park. Volunteer accomplishments show up in the annual report—and rightfully so—but has all this bureaucratization of volunteerism turned away the Bens and Mildreds whose connection to the land never translated to a connection with the bureaucracy?

Coordinating volunteerism is like managing wilderness: both have to be applied in moderation because both have the potential to diminish the experience. The basic attraction of the wild is a feeling of freedom from regulation and regimentation. Wilderness volunteers, because they combine both concepts, are probably our best models for "managing" volunteerism. Having been schooled in the necessity of recreation, we certainly know that senior volunteerism is neither pure altruism nor a second career. What it really is for many is necessary, healthful, recreation. Senior volunteerism is a feeling of being useful—of being valued in a society that places a premium on youth.

For many seniors, who often have the time and luxury to volunteer, the need to "give something back" is tangible and urgent. It is, quite literally, an act of thanksgiving for gifts received. Ben and Mildred had a personal relationship with their mountain and its trails and a need to nurture that relationship. Suppose that one day they had hiked partway up the mountain to work on the Cascade Link trail and then felt an urge to go work on the sunnier Thoreau trail instead? They wouldn't have been where we expected them to be, doing what we expected them to do, but their day would have been better, more rewarding, and more likely to incubate more volunteer days. By following their urge, they would have enjoyed a day of real recreation; to have ignored it would have been a day of volunteer work.

It would be a shame if our management of volunteerism contained the seeds of its own collapse. Might our zeal for documentation, such as a seemingly innocuous daily "volunteer report," be something that some volunteers might find objectionable, leading to unwanted volunteer competition and unnecessary volunteer awards? Would a required report have diminished Ben and Mildred's day, however slightly?

Documentation is important, but we could truly unleash the power of volunteerism if we focused on its rewards rather than just on its accomplishments. Since we are in the business of recreation, shouldn't the annual report include testimonials from casual exit interviews with our volunteers? There are community service kinds of volunteerism in which, hopefully, lives have been changed by the experience. What is more important: changed lives or projects completed? There are corporate adoption workdays in which the employer volunteers the employees for a day. What's more important: the picnic shelter they built or the sense of community it generated? There's the local scout troop whose leader volunteered them for beach clean-up day. What's more important to report: the ton of litter picked up or the youths who became activists for the environment? Even so, there are few groups that can compete with seniors in terms of exchanging a lifetime of skills and experience for the feelings of satisfaction and contribution they bring home from the park. I'd like to think that the miles of trail that Ben and Mildred improved are a distant second to the health and happiness those trails gave them.

There will always be those who choose not to support volunteerism. Their reasons are understandable: It complicates an already complex administrative life; it challenges standard operating procedures; it threatens the existing power structure; it lacks guidelines; and while it may work elsewhere, "things are different here." Like any fear, it is a fear of the unknown and of change. Even a small minority can turn fear into useless power struggles. The answer is to replace that fear with full knowledge of the real benefits of volunteerism—personal, social, and cultural. The organizational and budgetary rewards are very nice "extras." Volunteerism is an exciting new way to manage parks, as people work at their leisure. However, its real power comes not from numbers but from being an incredibly diverse and necessary part of the spectrum of recreation opportunities found in parks. The presence of senior volunteers is a pretty good indicator of a healthy park!

Parks for Discovery:
The Excitement of Learning Knows No Boundaries

Discovery consists of seeing what everybody has seen and thinking what nobody has thought.
— Albert Szent-Gyorgyi

It was the first graduating class, and the statewide interest it had aroused was out of proportion to its modest eleven graduates. The valedictorian had the full attention of his small audience of family members and public officials as he told about the service-learning project that he and his team completed for the state parks and how it had made him feel good about himself for the first time that he could remember. When, with obvious pride, the 20-year-old convicted felon related how he hoped that some day he would show his children, and maybe his grandchildren, the rock retaining walls he had helped to build on Artist's Bluff trail in the White Mountains, no one in the room failed to share the emotion of his dream.

Sitting in that audience and having played a small part in securing the inmate labor services of the state prison's new shock incarceration program for the state park system, I felt a rush of realization that what I had originally seen as much-needed help for parks was really something vastly bigger. The knowledge that parks could play a powerful role in reducing crime, reducing the rate of recidivism in our prisons, reducing the load on our courts, and increasing the sense of self-worth and self-discovery of repetitive youthful offenders was truly a eureka moment! The sudden realization that these are the kinds of accomplishments that should fill every park system's annual reports, pushing the dry attendance statistics into the appendix, was a humbling moment. This is the challenge of contemporary park management, to move parks into the mainstream of helping to solve society's problems, and to demonstrate the incredible power that parks have for changing lives.

That missing section of the annual report, Lives Changed This Year, might well include the artist that I met in Maine who had spent two decades painting surrealistic illustrations for science fiction until the day he discovered the sunrise over Frenchman's Bay from the top of Cadillac mountain. Since then he has focused exclusively on paintings that interpret nature in ways that you and I don't see until he shows us. It should also include the wide-eyed twelve-year-old participating in a tide pool interpretative session who made her lifetime goal one of becoming a marine biologist that day, ten years ago, and fulfilled it last year. An embarrassingly underfunded state historic site, the Robert Frost Farm in southern New Hampshire, has been turning out poets from all over the state for more than two decades in response to its program of encouraging fourth-grade poetry with the inspiring words of Frost: "Nobody told me I could be a poet, I just believed the future in." Someday when one of those youthful poets becomes a poet laureate, it will be a direct result of that program.

Each year's park report might highlight a specific individual, such as the volunteer who followed in his father's footsteps as the official caretaker of New Hampshire's landmark Old Man of the Mountain. Not only did his experiences with his father change his own life, but the two of them also combined to change the lives of countless others who were inspired by the world-famous rock formation to memorialize it in words, in film, with oils, and with watercolors before its inevitable collapse in 2002. Of course, there are the thousands of former teachers, carpenters, masons, and painters who have found meaning in their retirement by donating their skills to the parks and historic sites of America, and in doing so they rediscovered themselves.

When we consider that a state's or a nation's park system is really a collection of the very best of its heritage, it quickly becomes obvious that such a system has enormous potential to supplement the educational system. These are not just outdoor classrooms, but also an encyclopedia of a state's or a nation's natural and cultural landmarks—places where history can come alive for the student, the visitor, and the volunteer. Every park is an historic site offering experiences that can incubate an interest in history, geology, botany, forestry, writing, painting, inventing, sculpting, biology, photography, and exploration. Every park has the potential to enrich the nation by enriching its citizens. Every park has the potential to strengthen the diversity of a nation by celebrating its own diversity, but it can never hope to rise to its potential if its story is never told. Parks are not substitutes for or duplications of the discovery that goes on in classrooms, in museums, or in art galleries; they are sources of enrichment for those programs, offering experiences that cannot be found elsewhere. They are the places where history was made, where pride is born—places that have the ability to change lives.

The power of parks plus the right catalyst is all that it takes to make discovery happen. Sometimes that catalyst can be as simple as an awakening inside each of us. More often it requires an outside force. Commonly, the catalyst comes in the form of someone who adds an element of interpretation to make the park come alive. The proven popularity of art-in-the-parks programs, artists-in-residence, art classes, and art contests suggests that there could be an endless array of potential catalysts for visitors of all ages by simply expanding the concept to include historians, geologists, scientists, writers, poets, musicians, dancers, composers, film makers, and videographers in residence.

Given the relatively low cost of implementing such programs, it is worth considering why so few of them exist among the thousands of parks in America. If there are barriers to discovery in our parks, it is in everyone's interest to see them removed. Have the physical boundaries of our parks conditioned park management to resist reaching outside for help? The logical step of asking local talent to play this role in our parks seems almost too obvious, yet if it were a common practice it is hard to believe that every one of those groups would not have jumped at the opportunity for a park venue. Is it possible that the traditional training of park professionals has been too narrowly focused on managing resources and managing visitors so as to protect resources at the expense of facilitating experiences? Most managers of parks will admit that the boundaries are very real and are reinforced by job descriptions and assignments, but these barriers are crumbling. Most professors will readily admit that traditional training in the science of park management has neglected the art of networking.

There is, however, a third possibility, which lies in the contemporary relevance of the park mandate. Managers may be at least partially aware of the latent potential of parks to change lives, but if their legislative mandate is seen as restricting them to protecting resources and accommodating visitation, activities that already take up much more than a 40-hour work week, it is unlikely that many would take on an additional, nonmandated, uncompensated, and unevaluated chore. Expanding the boundaries of parks and the scope of professional training for 21st century relevance might best be addressed by a legislative revision of park system mandates to do just one thing: Encourage partnerships—Stop trying to do it alone.

Discovery, as a product of management, has become the cachet for bringing success to private parks. It should be even more important to the professional management of public parks where discovery is inherent in the resource. The ethical problem of knowing that our public parks have enormous potential for changing lives and for solving social problems yet not doing anything to tap that potential deserves our foremost attention. Even if the odds are only one in ten that going for a hike or picnic will yield the bonus of discovery, should we ignore it?

> *Although it is true that I never did anything to materially assist the sun to rise, I never doubted for a moment the absolute necessity of my being present for the event.*
>
> —Henry David Thoreau

Parks and Civility:
Gifts of Land and Incubators of a Civil Society?

Civilization exhibits the five qualities of truth, beauty, adventure, art, and peace.

—Alfred North Whitehead

Every true community has one—a gift of land to its people—a place to call our own, in which to play, to relax, to dream, to grow. Robert Frost, in "The Gift Outright," awakens us to the necessity of giving ourselves to the land in order to make it ours. In that spirit, countless individuals have given their land to the rest of us. Each time we visit the parks that they made possible, we also give—outright—to complete their gifts, for it is in using a park that we validate, confirm, and perpetuate it. How different we would be today if these thousands of donors had decided instead to reject the "Road Not Taken" and lock up their land.

Of all the things that we've conjured up to do to the land, creating parks, refuges, and natural areas is by far the most civil. Of course, we may have been doing it for ourselves, but I like to believe that being civil to each other over nature is but a step, albeit a giant one, from being civil to nature itself. Removing dams, revegetating strip mines, avoiding flood plains, and protecting endangered species reflects the same enlightened self-interest, along with a distinct appreciation for the hidden powers of nature. Civility in the face of unknown power is probably a pretty good rule to live by. In setting aside lands for our children, we are also demonstrating a respect for the land's ability to somehow shape the lives of those who are forced to follow us. Public parks may be our single best measure of a civil society.

Imagine a land without parks. An America without public lands and parks? Impossible! An America without places to inspire great music and young minds? without places to smell the smoke of a campfire and take pictures of happy children? without places to build great and small athletes? without places to generate billions in outdoor equipment sales and millions of summer jobs for future leaders, artisans, writers, and fighters for the land? without opportunities for expanding our minds through an expansive landscape? without places that call us, places to identify with, to be stewards of? places to hit a ball, toss a frisbee, and to run free? places to watch an eagle soar and places to catch a fish? places to go to watch the blossoms open and the leaves fall? places to strengthen bonds, build pride, and sharpen identities?

Imagine an America where all is marked *Private Land—DO NOT ENTER!* and the kind of people who would "live" there. Imagine the confinement of their minds—the seething rebellion of the "have-nots," the anxieties of the "haves," and the absence of something we so simply take for granted—community spirit. Imagine the tinderbox of distrust and anarchy that would require constant attention and remediation. Imagine the burden of trespass cases on its court system; the damage to whole sectors of the economy, tourism, camera and film sales, hiking shoes, sporting equipment, magazines and books; and the millions of incomplete lives. Imagine not being able to recount last summer's visit to Acadia or the Grand Tetons or Junior's first homerun at the community park. Imagine the unimaginable costs of public unhealth, and finally, the difficulty of trying to enlist young people to fight for something they have no tangible ownership of. Someone would have to invent a radical idea—public lands! And, just imagine trying to sell that idea to a power structure that owned all the land.

The only reason that we do not have to imagine the impossible is because of the countless gifts of civility by civic-minded individuals; forward-thinking legislatures; and environmentally conscious public, private, and nonprofit organizations. From the town forest to the national park, the idea has been the same—create public lands and the benefits of nature will be assured for all generations. However, civility requires one more step—an invitation. Creating parks has never been enough to assure the benefits of parks to a society, and for a society filled to overflowing with diversions and alternatives, it is totally inadequate. There must be more than just an open gate. Already we are hearing child psychologists speak of the hazards of nature deficit disorder (NDD) and its symptoms which include an unreasonable fear of nature, a decline in sensitivity toward living things, a shrinkage of neighborhood and community, and an inability to form connections to nature and to each other. NDD reverses the age-old rhetorical question of "What kind of world are we leaving for our children?" to one almost too disturbing to contemplate. The thought that the shock waves of untold generations with an obsessive-compulsive need to dominate nature might be followed by generations for whom nature is irrelevant seems like a recipe for disaster for planet Earth.

The natural evolution of the conservation movement has already expanded its focus to include invitations of all kinds to get involved in Earth's future. We all can join the process in exactly the same way as all those past park visionaries did—by imagining what might be possible with a little civility. Imagine the American dream of so many that made public lands a reality. Imagine each of them playing ball with you, hiking with you, and marveling with you at the blending of a land and its people. Imagine the fragility of a democracy in the absence of its parks and public lands. While doing so, just go out and enjoy a park, any park, by extending a civil invitation to a friend or a stranger to join you. Your very presence will be a celebration, a gift outright! Then, just for the mind-stretching sheer joy of it, imagine an even better gift for your great grandchildren—a land where civility caught on as a result of great waves of respect radiating from our public parks. Impossible? No. Necessary? Yes.

Impossible dreams are rarely a waste of time. They are likely to be the stuff of great breakthroughs. "The Impossible," says the bumper sticker, "just takes a little longer." What better place to hope for a resurgence of civility than out of a paradox of gifts being treated disrespectfully. Any number of social commentators in recent years has bemoaned the decline of civility in our society, and our parks are certainly not immune from the blight, but where else do you see anyone doing anything about it on the scale of Carry In–Carry Out litter control programs? In fact, given the rise in park crime over the past several decades, it may be reasonable to conclude that decreasing civility may be a harbinger of a rise in crime and that parks have a special responsibility to promote civility.

The blooming of incivilities across our social landscape has taken on agribusiness proportions. In just a few short years, we've seen the fines for roadside littering double and redouble again to no avail (in our national parks, the penalty should probably be expulsion and banishment!). We've seen traffic impatience escalate to a near epidemic of road rage. And, as the costs of solid waste disposal have reached unbelievable levels, we've also seen our public lands become the repositories of stoves, refrigerators, used tires, abandoned automobiles, industrial wastes, toxic chemicals, and the all the ugly residues from beautifying the home grounds. Finally, the hidden costs of vandalized park property, sometimes replaced but often not despite their obscene and hateful messages, invade and diminish every park visitor's experience.

We label the gross incivilities as crimes and dismiss them as acts of the minority, but the cumulative effects of all the smaller acts probably take a larger toll on our vital need for feelings of community. The smoker who empties the car ashtray in the vista parking lot, the harried young mother who buries her baby's disposable diaper in the beach sands, the dog owners who unleash their pets right in front of the "Pets On Leash" sign, the hosts and hostesses who can only say "How many?," the servers who ignore you while holding their private conversations, the cashier who never says thank you and never makes eye contact, the students who leave soft drink cans and news-papers on classroom floors for the custodian to dispose of, the officemate who keeps a half-eaten chicken sandwich in the refrigerator for two weeks, the driver who refuses to use directional signals or dim the headlights for oncoming traffic, the parking lot bullies who dent and scratch your car, the police officer wearing one-way sunglasses while talking to you under a visor cap, the neighbors who blow their leaves onto your yard, the primal music buff whose bass overwhelms a moving city block, the shooters who use roadside signs for target practice, the gum chewers who leave their deposits on the undersurfaces of chairs and tables, the hunters who hang their prize in the front yard for all to see, the line jumpers in the cafeteria, the urban dog walkers who leave messes for your child to step in, and the gawkers, starers, tasteless joke tellers, privacy invaders, horn honkers, defacers of library books, misusers of handicapped facilities are all the cumulative toll of an oxymoronic "me first" culture. A woman glared at me the other day, with suspicion and mistrust, for holding the door to the public library for her. Many of the once meaningful gender civilities seem to have become casualties of equality of the sexes, but have we reached the stage where civility is viewed with suspicion?

What, you rightfully ask, have our public parks to do with all of this incivility? Well, first and most obviously, a visit to the park is not a visit to the supermarket. Park visits are expected to be stress relievers, not stress inducers. Parks have a self-preservation role in dealing with such behaviors, as evidenced in their attempts to instill ethics such as Leave No Trace and Carry In–Carry Out visitor behaviors. Happily, the acceptance of such programs has been overwhelmingly positive, with many visitors offering such encouragements as, "Why haven't you done this before?"

This leads to the second role of parks being proactive on a much wider front in the war for civility—that of advocacy and activism in the promotion of park benefits. It is an act of civility to pay the fees necessary to support our public parks; and it is an act of civility for parks to clearly tell their patrons where the money goes. It is an act of civility to volunteer and donate time and energy in the cause of our public parks; and it is an act of civility, indeed an act of professionalism, to ask for help. It is an act of civility for visitors to ask how they can help; and it is equally professional for parks to have a list of needs and opportunities. It is an act of civility to write letters to the editor, testify at hearings, and otherwise vocally support the sustained flow of benefits from our public parks.

Among the many possibilities for improving the civility of park use is the enlisting of park visitors in the cause. One who does not litter is a good park visitor, one who picks up the litter of others is a great park visitor, and one who encourages others not to litter is a good citizen! Feeding park wildlife, taking home a bouquet of park wild flowers, impatiently honking the horn in the lines at the park gate, and playing loud music in the campground at night may all seem like minor transgressions, but each erodes the idea that we are all part of a community of nature—the community that the park exists to protect. The costs of ignoring our connections to the land are for the most part unknown to us because they are paid by others. Those that we do know about tend to be enormous and avoidable.

The first responsibility of park management is to send the message, "This is a Special Place!" In special places we adopt different norms of behavior. In libraries, we are quiet. In cathedrals, museums, and graveyards we are respectful. In schools we are attentive. In the homes of others we are deferential. At ball fields, playgrounds, and stadiums we may be wildly exuberant, but hopefully within the realm of good taste and sportsmanship. And in public parks we may exhibit all of these behaviors, but overriding all must be the ethic of sharing — sharing with nature, with other visitors, and with future visitors. Those behaviors that tend to reduce the opportunities for sharing are simply uncivil and inappropriate in parks — and in communities.

Thirteen Very Civil Ways to Use a Tree—
Without Benefit of Axe or Saw

Climb it. John Muir did it well into his eighties. Robert Frost wrote a great poem about swinging from birches. The air is better, the view is clearer, and it gets you very close to nature. Climb higher and feel your absolute dependency on nature.

Add it to your library. A tree is a book. A library is a treasure house. They belong together. A tree is a compendium of stories—stories about what it has "seen," what it produces, and how it survives. Open the book and treat yourself to a good read!

Visit it. You might be surprised what a regular visit to a tree can do for you in different seasons of the year, different times of the day, and in "bad weather" as well as good. Your visit will become its own reward.

Add it to your list of friends. Why not count a tree among your friends? It's always there. It has a network and connections. It has charm and character; maybe a little will rub off on you. Like any good friend, it will shelter, listen, and never judge.

Talk with it. A tree listens beautifully. When talking to it you are giving it the carbon dioxide it needs. A small gift, but it will respond. Learn to listen in new ways. Hear it murmur at the breeze and groan at the storm.

Learn from it. Listen closely. Learn to speak tree. Don't just study its scientific nomenclature and its place in the ecosystem. Learn its lessons of commitment to one place, to community, to sinking roots and branching out, to reaching for the stars, and capturing the sun's energy. See it bend and recover, break and start anew.

Grow with it. A tree can be a remarkable companion to grow with. Let it challenge you, comfort you, awaken you, shade you from the storms, and revitalize your sense of wonder. Good things happen through nature.

>>

Thirteen Very Civil Ways to Use a Tree—
Without Benefit of Axe or Saw (continued)

Hug it. Getting close to nature is what this all about. Putting a face on nature begins with you. Recognize it as an individual, know its texture, its scars, and the smell of its bark, borrow from its inner strength. Let it imprint you—physically and spiritually.

Celebrate it. Try to capture its meaning with your words, your song, your sketches, photographs, and art. Decorate it, just for itself—not as a cut holiday specimen. Photograph it in all its moods. Dance around it. Write its biography or its epitaph.

Champion it. Defend a tree. Sit in it, chain yourself to it, buy it, claim it for your own in the face of a threat. Defending the defenseless is humanity's highest calling. Champion Trees aren't always the biggest or the tallest or the oldest.

Adopt it. Even when it isn't threatened, especially when it isn't threatened, adopt it. If you can truly care for a tree, you are a responsible citizen. It's a fairly simple formula. Make a commitment. Use your adoption as an excuse, if necessary, to get away from the meaningless chaos of life on a regular therapeutic basis.

Become one with it. If you practice thinking like a tree, you will gain many useful hints on surviving and coping. A tree builds compression wood on its stressed sides to keep from tearing itself apart. A tree seeks to wall off infection by insects and disease. A tree knows when and how to rest. Remember, not all trees compete successfully. Pick a good role model, one that fits your life—Are you an oak? a willow? an apple? a sequoia?

Share it. Teach with it. A tree is an unbeatable visual aid. Introduce it to someone you care about—not with a carved heart and two sets of initials, but with genuine affection for all that it means to you. Build a tree house for a child. Share an overnight beneath its branches. Start a support group—for when you're gone. Your story will be added to its leaves.

Parks and the Economy:
The Essential Environmental Partnership

We've binged on our ecological currency, and a depletion of
our ecological wealth should not be mistaken for income.
— W. Victor Rozek

For more than a century we have been setting aside the very best of our natural and cultural heritage sites as parks and protected areas, and our reasons for doing so required no economic justification. We were preserving nature, building cultural pride, providing for future generations, and enhancing the quality of American life. Concurrently, tourism became the world's leading and most competitive industry, and parks emerged as the keystone to our successful position in that economy. What we had been managing as cultural resources have now taken on the heavy mantle of vital economic assets.

This very natural but nonmandated role for parks raises serious questions about park management's capabilities as providers of a sustained flow of economic benefits. Given the intensely competitive nature of all tourism markets, can we really afford to allow these economic engines to be shut down by continuing budget resolutions, risking closures and cutbacks and condoning deteriorated resources to the tune of billions of dollars in deferred maintenance? Can we continue to afford the charade of long-range planning implemented, if at all, by short-range budgets? What is the relevance of a management philosophy that treats these places as "islands of permanence in a sea of change" when we haven't been able to afford to inventory and monitor the condition and trend of the assets on these islands? Should we blindly accept an accountability system that assumes everything is all right because we have "professional" stewardship when we haven't adopted, or even agreed upon, the best management practices for these assets? Can we really be comfortable with quantitative indicators of park performance, such as visits, when we know that the real benefits of parks are subjective, emotional, and often only identifiable long after the visit?

Twice in the last half-century we have seen national blue ribbon commissions appointed to examine the adequacy and the maintenance of our public parks and outdoor recreation areas. Both initiatives, in the early 1960s and again in the mid 1980s, failed to aggressively underscore the underlying causes of park malaise—the absence of a set of best management practices agreed upon by park professionals and the holders of the purse strings. So, we go on deferring monstrous bills for maintenance to our children, placing the park preservation mandate at risk, and now jeopardizing the sustained vitality of our tourism economy and the millions of diverse jobs it provides.

The prospect for yet another high-level review seems very real, and very necessary, until we can correct the cyclical nature of addressing park needs. While the attention may be welcome, it should be realistically viewed as another indictment of our collective failure to discharge the preservation mandate. This leads me to suggest the need for a preemptive professional strike—a commitment to known and proven "best management practices" and a park-by-park certification program for parks having demonstrated a commitment to those practices. The prescription for aggressively addressing the pervasive park malaise of deferred maintenance is clearly a broad-spectrum antidote, but it should certainly include, at a minimum, elements of each of the following eight practices.

First is a commitment to a partnership approach to management. Just as "it takes a community to raise a child," it takes a community of partnerships to protect a park. Partnerships with industry, commerce, the public, schools and universities, and with other organizations are proven ways of stretching the budget and building an expanded constituency. To paraphrase an old maxim about war, parks are too important to leave to the professionals. Most park professionals know this, but few of them are actively encouraged or trained to develop partnerships. Park partnerships have grown enormously over the past decade but are still far from being the norm in park management.

Second is a commitment to heritage appreciation: a program for the public, delivered by every park employee and cooperator. The single best way to ensure park values is to know those values and to use them to build pride among an army of protective eyes, ears, and hands that could not be purchased at any price. Visitor centers, nature centers, websites, outreach programs, education programs, speakers' bureaus, artists-in-residence, scientists-in-residence, writers-in-residence, and school visits are some of the ways that a few parks have successfully implemented heritage appreciation programs. However, these things are still widely perceived to be extras, frills, and something we'd like to do someday, but expendable whenever the budget axe falls. Both Freeman Tilden and Aldo Leopold said that "the most important duty of management is to improve the quality of public use." Heritage appreciation does this while reducing the cost of management.

Third is a commitment to an active friends group for the park. Friends of the parks are more than partners; they are advocates, associates, and activists. A park without friends cannot survive, but active friends groups are still in the minority at our thousands of public parks, natural areas, and historic sites. Friendship is one of the highest values of human endeavor, so why not encourage friends for parks—one of humans' most lasting achievements—and not just in the bad times but in the good times as well. Friends are a special kind of partnership for parks because they constitute the first line of defense when park values are threatened.

Fourth is a commitment to an accountability system that is meaningful, available, and a candid expression of park needs, conditions, trends, and performance. It is not enough to simply account for the dollars and the equipment. While a surprising number of parks cannot even do this effectively, equipment and even the infrastructure are the minor assets of any park. It is not enough to track visitation and programs. What the public deserves to know is whether the trust remains in place. Are their assets secure from internal and external threats to park integrity? A critical element of any accountability commitment is the continuous education and training of a park's human resources. Many of our park assets are entrusted to the care of people with no training, or no recent training, in the skills and tools of park protection. Would we tolerate this in education, in public health and safety, or in any other public program?

Fifth is a commitment to asset inventory and a monitoring program to make accountability meaningful. This is admittedly an overwhelming job. It is long overdue but is possible with the help of partners and friends. Biodiversity inventory and monitoring is at the very heart of discharging the park preservation mandate, and it will never be accomplished in any other way. The loss of cultural artifacts from our public parks is an equally serious issue that only inventory, monitoring, and reporting can effectively control.

Sixth is a commitment to being a good neighbor. Just as parks need a community, the community needs a park that is not constrained by real and imaginary boundaries. Park professionals know that a real land ethic has no boundaries. The reservation mentality may have been appropriate in the very early years of park protection, but it ceased being relevant decades ago. Being a good environmental neighbor means a commitment to no litter and to minimization of park-generated air, water, and noise pollution. It also means a heightened level of sensitivity to all of the park's impacts on the community and responsiveness to all of the community's needs for assistance.

Seventh is a commitment to advocacy and activism in support of park values. Confusion in loyalties has clearly contributed to past park failures in maintenance, inventory, monitoring, pollution, and heritage awareness. Agency loyalty can be a poor surrogate for loyalty to the land. Today's park professionals are trained in the subculture of objective science and are steeped in the subculture of a neutral bureaucracy. However, parks are subjective and emotional resources. It is not possible to be a neutral and objective park professional. Park professionals are expected to be activists for their parks, not pacifists in response to the norms of their other subcultures. It took emotion and passion to create these public places and to make them the economic assets they are today. Surely those same qualities have a place in their management and preservation.

The eighth best management practice is planning. Without a master plan for every park, none of the other seven can effectively achieve their potential. Without a plan to sustain the resources, the tourist economy that depends on those resources is in jeopardy. Without a plan to work with economic interests, educational interests, community, social, cultural, and historic interests, the park resources are in jeopardy. The model for park planning cannot be limited to seeing the park as something to be developed; that model has to be built on the same ecological model of connectedness that the park exists to preserve. The most important kinds of park planning occur outside of the current domain of the planners.

It is interesting to realize that while all of these practices are professionally recognized and proven effective, very few parks have a meaningful commitment to more than one or two. A selective commitment to a few of the best management practices does not work. Remove any one, and the fabric of the commitment falls apart. A commitment to heritage appreciation without a commitment to inventorying park assets is no commitment at all. A widely endorsed set of best management practices is not available to students and has not been adopted by park management professionals, and yet, other resource professionals see this as a continuing responsibility. As a prescription for the sicknesses of park apathy and decline, it is the one measure that can yield immediate results in restoring park vigor, morale, and credibility.

It should be of interest to park naturalists and cultural interpreters that every one of these practices requires a deep appreciation of the principles of interpretation. As Tim Merriman, Executive Director of the National Association for Interpretation, says, "Interpretation is not a tool of management, it *is* management." Given this fact and the inescapable fact that park interpreters ultimately have to explain park decline to visitors, the national association clearly has as large a stake in promoting best management practices as do the park management professions. While agreeing on the principles and implementing a program of certification based on them would be a complex task, it would still be vastly easier than having to interpret the multibillion-dollar tab for neglect of public resources and the consequently diminishing role of parks in a vital sector of our economy.

Parks as tourism, parks as partnerships, and parks as economic engines all reflect the widespread blurring of traditional distinctions between the public and private sectors. The merging of the sectors within parks is both a healthy and an inevitable trend that is new to parks only in terms of their potential for seriously damaging local economies. Some park managers may not like the idea of being driven by economic interests, but most will be quick to see this as the effective preservation tool that they have been lacking for decades. They probably realize that one more blue-ribbon commission, along with the inevitable management by legislation, can only further diminish their professional and administrative discretion. Managing parks for their sustained economic benefits can be totally consistent and supportive of the mandate for the preservation of nature, heritage, and recreational opportunities. However, none of these benefits can be achieved in the absence of a continuing commitment to some set of proven best management practices.

Parks and Pride:
The Land Defines Its People

Land of the Pilgrim's pride

—Samuel Francis Smith

All across America's landscape we find reminders of our evolution as a people: stone walls, cellar holes, abandoned mines and mill sites, long-forgotten cemeteries, ghost towns, and worn-out farms, the rapidly fading traces of the almost forgotten places that wrote our history. Once idle curiosities of another day, these artifacts are now increasingly protected as part of our cultural legacy. Less fragile and less in need of protection are the indelible marks of the land on us, permeating every aspect of our national expression. Words and phrases like "The West," "The Frontier," "The Appalachians," and "The Rockies" evoke instant images for most of us, yet we seldom realize just how sweeping the land has been in defining us and in shaping our American culture.

Our national music, literature, art, and speech are liberally seasoned with references to the land and the outdoors. Classics like *Grand Canyon Suite* and *Appalachian Spring*, pop tunes like "Rocky Mountain High," and songs of patriotism like "America the Beautiful" celebrate the land in all its awe-inspiring spaciousness and abundance. Similarly, the artistry of Remington, Cole, Moran, Bierstadt, Adams, Jackson, O'Keefe and countless other sculptors, painters, and photographers reveals our unmistakable connection to the land. The classic writings of each generation's great writers, the Whitmans, Muirs, Frosts, Kilmers, Leopolds, Dickinsons, Cathers, and Abbeys, reveals not only a love of the land but also a plea for preservation.

With just a little reflection it is easy to arrive at the sweeping conclusion that much of the intangible American spirit flows directly from the American landscape as captured by the giants of our cultural expression. Consequently, the American outdoors must be seen as an undeniable source of our national identity and a wellspring of our national vigor and vitality. If not the first to link our national character with the nation's landscape, Walt Whitman was certainly the most outspoken in charging the American people with the need to rise to the level of a perfect match with our scenery, anything less being obscene. Indeed, could human pettiness flourish in view of the Grand Canyon, or greed on an endless fertile prairie, or despair on a mountaintop? It could, and it has, but only when we have failed to see ourselves in the land and to preserve its inspiration as one of our great natural assets. To fail to see the land as a reliable barometer of our national health would indeed be obscene. Whitman's challenge is as resoundingly fresh and relevant as it was when he wrote his preface to *Leaves of Grass*.

In so easily taking for granted the images of our artists, composers, and writers, we must surely be oblivious to the many influences of the outdoors on our everyday culture—the vernacular of our regional expressions, humor, cooking, advertising, place names, coins, stamps, folk art, and folk tales. Descriptions of American people, places, things, and ideas would indeed be poverty stricken without that endless reservoir of outdoor metaphors and images. Just as purpled mountains trumpet majesty, the people we admire may be "strong as an oak," "wise as an owl," "busy as a beaver," "refreshing as a waterfall," "pure as the driven snow," and as "generous as all outdoors." Those that we don't like may be condemned as "lower than a snake," "ornery as a polecat," "sly as a fox," "mean as a grizzly," "bloodthirsty as a pack of wolves," or as "slippery as an eel."

We all know that the outsiders who don't come from "our neck of the woods" are incapable of "seeing the forest for the trees," and oftentimes "blind as a bat," making it as easy to recognize them as "falling off a log." The greedy tend to be those who "clear-cut and burn," the skinflints are "tighter than the bark on a tree," and a benevolent spirit is as giving as a "gentle rain."

Perhaps the love-hate relationship that we have with our politicians has something to do with the fact that they are often seen to be "at loggerheads," engaged in "log rolling," "running ridges," and "straddling fences," while bragging about their "watershed legislation," their "prairie fires of support," and their "avalanches of mail." Some claim to have come from "log cabins," and may even be accused of having a "backwoods mentality" as they engage in "summits" and go "on the stump," but rarely "out on a limb." Their orations may be "clear as a mountain stream" or as "muddy as the Old Miss," but then, we all have "new ground to break," "floods to contain," "seeds to plant," "fish stories to tell," and "mountains of work" to catch up on.

Consider the places that call to us: the "Lone Trees," "Echo Lakes," "Crystal Springs," "Mountain Views," "Hermit Islands," "River Bends," "Lookout Points," and "Snug Harbors." There are also, of course, the places we call home, even in sterile subdivisions like "Forest Park," "Cedar Ridge," "Eastern Shore," "Summit View," "Spring Creek," "Falling Waters," "Elk Park," and countless others that evoke a pristine era that today exists only in the name.

For most Americans, our national treasures are not locked up in a London Tower or a Fort Knox; they are the Yellowstones, the Sequoias, Yosemites, Grand Canyons, Hot Springs, Rockies, Sierras, Niagaras, and every jewel in that vast Smithsonian of the outdoors—our national and state park systems.

Let's not forget all the things that make our lives complete, like outdoor toys in every imaginable price range for every age. Outdoor themes dominate our gift stores with simulated plastic effigies of bear, geese, loon, and raccoon. Outdoor clothing and equipment from L.L. Bean, Coleman, Cabellas, and Orvis have joined the high-end of catalog sales. Our automobiles and our sports teams, America's two great passions, proudly bear the names of Panthers, Cougars, Wildcats, Rams, and Rangers. It has become fashionable, and pricey, to dine on the very foods that were once the fare of country folk: fiddleheads and mushrooms, venison and clams, trout and duck, maple syrup and pickled herring. Euell Gibbons, an outdoorsman and proponent of natural diets, and a few score imitators have taken us way beyond foraging for fun. Outdoor cooking equipment and cookbooks are major industries. Just look at what the backyard barbecue/smoker has done for the once lowly mesquite!

The color of the outdoors in our language is probably at its peak when we are looking for images and symbols to describe complex ideas. If we had a science of iconics to explain the sources and power of images, the outdoors would comprise a major section. "Counting the rings" means determining age; a few rings identifies a "babe in the woods," while lots of rings describes someone who is as "gnarly as old oak tree." Images of trees are found in nearly every poet's notebook. Pines are always "noble," aspens are "musical," oaks are "strong," while "agelessness and the ability to endure hardship" describes the Sequoia.

Wildlife, always an endless source of metaphors, has become a gold mine of marketing images and sales similes. Consider the eagle, the swallow, the snail, the beaver, the hawk, the robin, Smokey and Bambi. "Happy as a clam at high tide," "surefooted as a mountain goat," "crow's nest," and "eagle's nest" are word pictures totally lacking in ambiguity. Can you imagine a better metaphor for the irresponsible loss of a resource and human greed than the passenger pigeon or the American bison? It isn't just poets that capitalize on outdoor images; tired humorists tell jokes that are "older than the hills" while Heckle and Jeckle, the Goofy Gophers, Chip 'n Dale, Woody Woodpecker, Bugs Bunny, and the Roadrunner still evoke a smile.

All of this is not simply to belabor the ubiquity of the outdoors in American lives, but is rather a preamble to two questions posed on Walt Whitman's behalf. First, if America's outdoors is so integral to our character as a people and to our national spirit, are we doing all that we should be doing to protect and preserve it? Second, if the outdoors so readily evokes emotional responses, why are we using the logic of science instead of the endless reservoir of pride and emotion to protect and preserve it? For generations we have been training land managers in the sciences. Think about what that means: The park manager looks at nature and sees scientific questions, while the park visitor looks at nature and sees beauty, challenge, identity, and a whole bundle of emotional answers. Do they communicate or just tolerate one another?

Rachel Carson's *Silent Spring* provides a classic model of presenting science in a way that evokes popular, emotional support. Science may tell us what the threats are to our parks and natural resources, but science alone cannot dispose of them. To meet that challenge, our professionally trained land managers must have a balanced kit of tools; they must be humanists as well as scientists. They need to be literate in both logical and emotional thought and persuasion. Perhaps until we achieve that level of management, we are in a very weak position to ask the first question: Are we doing all that we should be doing to preserve and protect this fundamental source of American character and spirit? However, speculating with a few what-if questions may not be a complete waste of time.

What if we were to stop looking at parks and public lands as "natural resources" and instead consider them in the same category as libraries, museums, schools, and other cultural assets? The difference between the two is a real one; resources get used while assets get protected. Is a park truly a renewable resource, once it has been overused, worn out, and had its inspiration damaged through overdevelopment? Granted, we aren't exactly overgenerous with our public budgets for schools and libraries, but they do tend to attract a lot of private-sector attention. As part of our public natural resource estate, park assets seem to always be at the very bottom of the list in comparison with resources like timber and minerals that have clear market values. What if we started to regard parks as irreplaceable assets, as investments in the future like schools and treasure houses of the past like museums?

What if we started looking at threats to parks and threats to nature as threats to America instead of just bad decisions and inadequate budgets? What if the parks and open spaces that inspire great music, art, and literature were valued as highly as the American spirit that they help to create? The land is the source of a nation's wealth. The inspirational landscape is the source of a nation's pride. I can't put a value on pride, but I know that without it wealth is meaningless. What if we were to honor the land with the same reverence that we honor the flag—the symbol of the land? What if we were to honor the people who have died for the land with something more than a misdemeanor penalty for those who deliberately defile that sacred land with their litter and trash? What if, tomorrow, we started honoring America's landscapes by ensuring their preservation for future generations of landscape artists? Yes, the marks that the land has made on us are impressive, but have we been as generous to that landscape as it has been to us? Or, as Whitman feared, has our mark on the land been an obscene comparison? The Whitman standard may sound emotionally extreme to some, but it can easily be converted to hard economics with one simple question: Have we been spending our children's inspirational capital? If so, that indeed would be an obscenity.

The literary and artistic explosion of American themes in the latter half of the 1800s has been referred to as the rediscovery of America. The convergence of improved highways, economical transportation, and access to public lands in the latter half of the 20th century is seen as the second rediscovery of America. It was through this second rediscovery that masses of Americans had their first opportunity to see their country firsthand. It seems impossible that in those hundreds of millions of experiences, the seeds of an enduring pride in the land would not be sown and that the fertile soil to blossom into something resembling Whitman's 150-year-old vision of a special people to match a special land would not find its place on the nation's agenda.

We were the land's before it became ours.

—Robert Frost

Parks and Wonder:
Environmental Interpretation and Eureka Moments

I can remember the very spot in the road, whilst in my carriage, when to my joy the solution occurred to me.
—Charles Darwin

The recurring adjective in those oversized coffee-table books about the national parks is "wonder." The really great landscape photographers and painters seem to be able to actually capture their own sense of wonder in their creations and pass it along to the viewer. It is difficult to look at an Ansel Adams's Yosemite or an Albert Bierstadt's Yellowstone without feeling a little bit of the artist's wonder. So prevalent as to be almost cliché, it is easy to conclude that our parks are places where we can go to get our Sense of Wonder batteries recharged. It is an accepted fact that the works of these and other equally talented artists set in motion the forces that helped to save many of our greatest American landscapes. That fact requires us to address the question of what the parks' role might be in preserving not just the majestic scenery but also the wonder, the epiphany, the "a-ha" that such a scene evokes? If all parks are indeed capable of fostering some small moment of wonder and humility toward nature, then isn't their national value somewhat larger than that of mere pleasuring grounds and nature preserves? If such power exists in the scenery, how might park interpreters help us to understand its message?

There is a well-documented event that is associated with human creativity that is defined as taking place in an instant. What has come to be known as the *eureka moment*—a flash of insight, a new light on an old view, when everything finally comes together—is in fact just one step of a mental process in which we all engage. Whether seemingly instantaneous or the result of prolonged and intense study, these moments can move mountains. Biographies of famous scientists are filled with such well-known eureka moments as Newton's theory of gravity, Einstein's equally revolutionary theory of relativity, Darwin's theory of evolution, and Jenner's world-changing theory of immunization. Artists have reported similar eureka moments when struggling to capture the essence of a scene, an experience, or a special moment in nature.

While reports of eureka moments suggest they occur as flashes, they are but one step in a mental process. That process begins with an imprinting, an initial impression, and then proceeds through periods of reflection and saturation to illumination (i.e., eureka) before concluding with validation. The realization that a process exists makes it clear that eureka moments are not the exclusive domain of so-called creative people. The process is available to anyone, and it has potentially powerful applications in the field of environmental and cultural interpretation. We have all used the process many times in our lives, perhaps not with the speed of an Einstein, and probably without ever recognizing it as the way we gain understanding of complex relationships, discover ourselves, develop a sense of place, fall in love, complete a puzzle, find our life's work, and give our lives meaning. While the process is orderly and sequential, it is often not recognized as such because, unlike most human processes that we are familiar with, it is totally free from time constraints.

Getting to Eureka

Chance favors those who court her.

—Charles Nicolle

By characterizing eureka moments as chance, intuition, imagination or serendipity, we discount the importance of the logical sequence that sets the stage. In support of the pure chance argument, there is sometimes a catalyst present in eureka moments. However, the evidence against chance discovery and in favor of a prepared mind is overwhelming. In short, it is possible to increase our odds of having such moments by knowing and using the process. The inventor and the problem solver know that problems are not solved until they are recognized. Recognition goes beyond simple acknowledgement to include dismantling, analysis, and reconstruction. For an artist, the first impression of a scene or an idea that needs to be captured provides that same initial stage of recognition or imprinting.

Impression is the moment that plants the seed, starts the process and imprints the idea. Impression suggests that there is something more here—something that cries out to be explained, interpreted, developed and understood. It is the beginning of a process that can be turned off with such simple dismissals as "I don't have the time," and "I'm not a creative person," or it can be an open door to extending that process with a commitment to look deeper and make a claim of ownership that says, "This is mine. I must find the answer. I must complete the picture!"

If the first imprinting is successful, it will lead inevitably to the next steps of reflection or germination and saturation or immersion and even obsession. These steps can take moments or years before illumination and final validation. For Edward Jenner, the time from his first impression that cowpox exposure safeguarded certain people from contracting the more deadly small pox to proof and testing was 30 years of obsession. During the reflection or germination period, the first impression gets "worried" by its owner. For the artist, reflection may mean wondering what that scene would look like at first light or what those ocean waves might sound like on the piano. Reflection places the problem in different settings so that we can see if it's still a problem. Germination embellishes the problem by adding elements: first light, plus fall color, plus a storm, plus a wild creature, or the notes of a piano, the sound of a violin, a full orchestra. For the park visitor who is seeking a simpler life, germination is the time for answering the questions of "How do I get there?"

As the problem fails to yield and the opportunities expand, reflection gives way to saturation and even obsession with finding the solution. The pressure and the focus at this stage can become intense. The saturation stage may involve experimentation, physically manipulating the elements, even rearranging one's life to have more time to devote to the problem. Creative writers often immerse themselves in their subject—actually living the life— before trying to write about it. Nevada Barr, a well-known writer of national park mysteries, actually lives the life of a seasonal park ranger, then retires to write in the off-season. This intensely focused energy primes us for eureka moments by making us more acutely aware of the reality of finding solutions in unlikely places, which suggests the possibility of planned serendipity. That focused energy can serve as an accelerant, speeding up the process to a level where it is no longer recognizable as a process. The composer who hears musical notes in the landscape, the artist who sees colors on a gray day, the scientist who sees relationships as formulas, and the park visitor who is in a rut looking for a new career are all primed for a eureka moment.

Enjoying the Moment

Those who have not known the torment of the unknown cannot know the joy of discovery.

—Claude Bernard

Almost by definition a eureka moment is a new interpretation, often more elegant in its simplicity and insight than previous interpretations. If the process has been long and arduous, the elegance is probably overshadowed by the sheer joy of a problem solved. Also, since the moment is both a tiny fragment of the process as well as a powerful impetus to immediately seek validation, we are unlikely to savor and analyze the moment. The emotional stimulus of discovery combined with the release of frustrations that accompany an unresolved problem probably combine to create something akin to an adrenaline rush.

Considering the enormous significance of eureka moments to the advancement of science and art, it is unfortunate that there appears to be so little documentation of their accompanying mental states, stimuli, and feelings at the time. From what limited observations exist in the field of science, there does seem to be a commonly reported feeling of freedom and relaxation attendant to many eureka moments. Problem solved!

Einstein reportedly had many of his revelations while shaving and had to be careful not to cut himself while simultaneously reacting to the event. In fact, many such moments are reported to come from dreams. The very fact that we have dreams tells us that our creative minds never sleep. If we can assume that alternating periods of intensity and relaxation are conducive to the process, there is an interesting corroboration of the old maxim about all work and no play.

> *Clarity, insight, and understanding are only possible when thought is in abeyance, when the mind is still.*
>
> —J. Krishnamurti

Just as there is an orderly process leading up to it, "The Moment" probably contains a lightning-like sequence of its own steps; however, the moment itself should probably just be enjoyed for what it is—a beautiful breakthrough in human understanding. Albert Einstein recorded one of his breakthroughs as the happiest moment of his life! Could it be any happier than the park visitor who has found simplicity, tranquility, and peace?

Beyond Eureka

> *A healthy ego requires its creations to be both communicated and accepted.*
>
> —George F. Kneller

Given the saturation that preceded it, the "why didn't I think of that before?" moment can be an anticlimax. More commonly however, as Kneller suggests, validation is ego-driven. If enlightenment provides a new interpretation for an existing dilemma, it also contains the provocation to seek validation—to test the idea, to prove the breakthrough.

The park interpreter wears the somewhat uncomfortable cloak of a facilitator of eureka moments. The purpose of interpretation is to build appreciation for our cultural and environmental heritage. That appreciation, in economic terms, is value-added to the visit to the museum or to the park. If we have taken those assets for granted, appreciation becomes a new way of looking at them—an understanding that the assets are collectively "ours" and that we are collectively reflected in them. That simple enlightenment may be a mini-eureka, a reawakening for some. For others, it can be a life-changing experience, leading to validation in the form of career changes, volunteerism, advocacy, activism, and artistic expression. The power of interpretation to create change in the ways that we look at things is clearly beyond measure. At a minimum, the interpreter is in a critical position to initiate the process by providing countless first impressions for others.

The principles of interpretation provide a relevant way to look at the eureka process. Each of its six principles—relevance, information, story, provocation, holism, and specialized focus—can be directly linked to this process. When relevance is lacking, the probability of any interpretive message "sticking" and providing that essential first impression is extremely low. By providing information sources along with relevance, the interpreter opens the door to the second stage of reflection and germination. By combining new information and relevant examples into a captivating and memorable story, the interpreter increases relevance and provokes listeners to do a little relevance testing on their own.

Most interpretive provocation encourages further study, reflection, and involvement, which is the second step of the eureka process. Some provocation comes in the form of a challenge, to get involved and become immersed in the issues, which is precisely the third step of the eureka process. By presenting the interpretive message holistically in order to link it to the larger web of life, we set the stage for countless eureka moments. Once in a great while, the validation of those moments may actually come back to the interpreter in interesting and circuitous ways.

Putting the Principle to Work

The paradox is the source of the thinker's passion... the thinker without a paradox is like a lover without a feeling.
—Soren Kierkegaard

Although all eureka moments are interpretations, it would be unreasonable to expect that more than a very few interpretations are eureka moments. Nevertheless, interpretation is a facilitator of eureka moments and the eureka process is a tool available to the interpreter. It is a process that embodies and validates the principles of interpretation. As interpreters look at their many potential audiences, they might want to consider giving greater attention to those that are most likely to be searching for solutions—those who already have the focus and the intensity that is the precursor of a eureka moment. One of those audiences is the administrators and policymakers of our parks, museums, historic sites, and natural areas whose main charge from Aldo Leopold is "to improve the quality of public use." If there is a better way of promoting an improved quality of public use than interpretation, what might it be?

Other highly receptive audiences are the potential benefactors, volunteers, and prospective partners in the endeavor, all of whom are highly focused on finding life-fulfilling and rewarding relationships with their land. People who have been deeply moved by their exposure to nature, its art, and its mysteries are often only lacking an interpretation—an emotional and an intellectual connection—to illuminate the possibilities and find their own destinies.

Other eureka-ready audiences for interpreters include the scientists and artists whose needs for truth and beauty can be provoked by new interpretations of the cultural artifacts and natural history of the land. Interpretation can open whole new vistas to the artist and the scientist—perspectives that can satisfy their own interests while potentially yielding important new insights for the interpreter and the administrator. If we approach the traditional interpretive audiences—visitors and school children—with the knowledge that we can move them towards eureka moments that are life-focusing, we might find a few more eureka moments of our own.

The preservation of our culture and our environment is filled with paradoxes that are fertile territory for new interpretations: Why are the things that we value so highly so often taken for granted? Why do we often fail to follow an act of preservation with an act of appropriation? Why do we persist in seeking economic values for things that are beyond price? And, why has the elegant harmony of nature that inspired the designation of our public parklands failed to foster a complimentary administrative ethic?

On a humbling note, nature's ability to imprint us, along with its record as an unlimited storehouse of eureka moments, would make the interpreters' task unnecessary were it not for the fact that we have distanced ourselves from our natural heritage. The same is true of our cultural legacy. However, the key to unlocking countless problems through new interpretations is just a eureka moment away.

> *There are certain times when, as on the whispers of wind, there comes the clear and quiet realization that there is indeed a presence in the world.*
>
> —Ansel Adams

Parks and Sanity:
Parks and the American Nature on the Day After

If you can keep your head while all about you are losing theirs...

—Rudyard Kipling

The day after the unrelenting repeated televised horror of September 11th, many parks across America recorded unseasonably high visitation, often setting new records for a post-season weekday. In the urgent need for peace, normalcy, sanity and reassurance, thoughts of the peaceful places we knew sent many of us to our public parks. We were clearly looking for peace, not picnics. Many park professionals were surprised by the numbers, and outdoor writers sought to explain the phenomenon in numerous articles. Perhaps the years of getting beat up in the budget process had managed to convince some of us that parks really are "not essential." Those budget impasses that said "only essential employees need report to work" had made it clear that we were not the people who saved lives or kept the economic engines running.

The provision of a sense of normalcy in troubled times is emphatically essential! The exodus to parks on the day after our nation was stunned by terrorism carries with it four profoundly important lessons. First, parks are not and never were nonessential to the people who need them. Second, people visit parks every day with needs that go far beyond traditional recreational activities but ones that parks obviously need to address. Third, the bundle of benefits available from parks and the bundle of human needs of park visitors will remain an imperfect match until we are willing to radically change our existing park management model. And fourth, parks are a vital thread in the fabric of our community.

Lesson One: Parks Are Not Optional

The notion that "parks are nonessential government services" is worse than an outdated way of thinking; it is a dangerous way of thinking for the budgeters and policymakers who have not changed along with the dynamic society they serve. While the idea of benefits-based park management has been with us for two decades, it is fair to say that the vast majority of parks systems are still using activity-based and satisfaction-based management models. If we will only use it, September 12th could provide a powerful kick-start to the more contemporary view of promoting parks for their limitless values and benefits rather than for limited activities. The plague of underfunding parks might become simply an embarrassing footnote of park history.

Try this small example. Suppose parks were promoted with the theme: *"It's a walk in the park,"* and suppose that signature theme was preceded by a question superimposed on a powerful visual image that forces people to make a connection between their lives and their parks. The theme then becomes a recurring answer to questions, such as *"Seeking peace? — Feeling stressed? — Want to slim down? — Need a lift? — Batteries weak? — Lost your sense of wonder? — Had a eureka moment lately? — Want the simple life? — Searching for your music?"* The answer to them all is, *"It's a walk in the park,"* or *"Think outside."* For trail systems, *"Take a hike"* could do the same thing. Now, imagine that same imagery adorning mass transit systems and, yes, even billboards. The connections and the ideas are endless and so are the possibilities for funding such messages through partnerships.

However, for such a program to be effective, it would require an honest dialogue with those park professionals who believe that our parks are overused already and that more visitation will just aggravate the already out-of-control problems of overuse and underfunding. Increased use could be just the kind of lateral thinking that has been missing to resolve both of these problems. The park profession has been bemoaning overuse of "its" parks for half a century, yet have we ever asked why "they" keep coming? Is it because our concept of carrying capacity is based on dated and idealized experiences while theirs is more a matter of contemporary reality and perceived benefits?

Since parks are already stretched to the breaking point just by providing for recreation and preservation needs, how can we insist that they also address roles in public health, mental health, physical health, community health, economic health, peace at our borders, social justice, pride of place, educational needs, heritage preservation, and the pursuit of happiness? How can we not? Healthy park systems are indicators of healthy societies, making them truly not optional. If the slogan "Parks are for People" means anything, it has to mean that parks are for life—all of life. When parks close, life rushes on by them and their relevancy is eroded.

Lesson Two: They're Not Visitors—
They're People and They're the Owners

Those who came to their parks on September 12, 2001, didn't fit management's available taxonomy; they were not "tourists," "day visitors," "repeaters," "seasonals," "recreationists," or "campers." They were seekers perhaps, but whole people first. The second lesson of September 12th is a powerful reminder that our shorthand labeling of park visitors is of limited value in meeting their needs—needs that are not necessarily congruent with our seasons, science, budgets, and biases. Ranger Abbey's great line in Desert Solitaire, *"Our itch for naming things is almost as bad as our itch for owning things,"* recognizes exactly why we create taxonomies of people—to "own" them. Abbey concedes that through naming comes knowing. Perhaps this is true, but naming also leads to dismissal, pigeonholing, labeling, and reducing. By casually dismissing the rest of the bundle that makes a "visitor" a person, we start down the road to callous objectification, along with hastening our own burnout and job dissatisfaction.

Just as parks contain bundles of benefits, the people who come to them have bundles of needs and wants. Any one of those needs might be the dominant trigger for a visit, but the rest of the bundle is never far behind. To the extent that the label becomes the perception, it is less than science and less than modern management. At a time when most other service professions are embracing an expansionist view of their clientele in order to better serve them (and admittedly, to reduce the litigation potential), the park profession persists in a reductionist, activity-based labeling of people and visitor services.

The antidote of holistic park management seems simple, but it requires a major shift in the way we manage parks. The very tools that best promote the human equation in parks are the ones that we have prioritized last and cut first from the budget. The activity-based management model forces us to accept a reactionary role in response to industry-sponsored changes in recreation activities and equipment—a role often characterized by conflict—that continually marginalizes the nonactivity oriented park visitor. The pursuit of happiness devotee who isn't locked into an activity in the search for peace, inspiration, discovery, understanding, and identity and the visitor who can't identify with the only two choices at the park entrance—"Campers bear right, Day Users bear left"—take neither and turn away, never to return.

The shift to a proactive and holistic park model requires a major commitment to an extension/outreach program at the highest levels. Going far beyond personnel exchanges with other parks, speakers' bureaus, partnership building, in-school programs and traveling exhibits, the outreach office serves as liaison as well as broker for placing park specialists on the staffs of other agencies, corporations, legislative offices, nonprofits, and dozens of other settings. When parks are discussed as solutions in the conference rooms of public health agencies, correctional institutions, tourism and trade organizations, corporations, educational institutions, arts commissions, senior centers, and conservation groups, park budgets will grow.

Lesson Three: Was Anybody Listening?

The question that plagued the aftermath of September 11th is also relevant to September 12th: Where was our intelligence? That even one park professional was surprised by the September 12th phenomenon is astonishing. The real surprise is that more people didn't come to the parks. In retrospect the gaps in our intelligence—our knowledge—can be seen as widespread. Was anybody listening on September 12th to the silence? Was anybody listening before that day to what park visitors were seeking? Was anybody listening fifteen years earlier when the President's Commission on Americans Outdoors held hearings all across America and reported testimony from hundreds of people about why our nation needs parks? Was anybody listening when extensive research on managing parks for their benefits, rather than their activities, was published over the last two decades?

When the bundle of available park benefits is seen to match the range of human needs, no park will be left behind in the nonessential category. The image of parks will shift along a scale from exclusive and specialized to inclusive and holistic. The meaning of *park* can be glimpsed in the inspired eyes of a youngster learning about life in the forest from a ranger. The pride that flows from a park, like mountain spring water, can be felt in the new life of a retired senior volunteer greeting arrivals at the visitor center. The restorative value of a park can be overwhelming when listening to the testimony of a group of adults with developmental challenges around a campfire on their last night in the wild. These are the kinds of accomplishments that dominate the annual report in a holistic park management model, forcing the mundane attendance figures into the appendix.

That so many of our nation's parks can trace their origins to the inspiration of artists and their creative works should suggest that the re-creational benefits of parks must at least equal their recreational value to the nation. If the wonder of a landscape can set in motion the creation of a park, what else might it inspire? stewardship of that park? heightened national spirit and pride? From inspirational landscapes to inspired art to land protection, why should it stop there? If an artist has a eureka moment looking at a landscape, perhaps for others that same mind-clearing setting can lead to creative problem solving leading to new inventions or to stronger and healthier societies, peace initiatives, social and environmental justice, and stronger economies. Numerous and equally unscientific accounts are readily available to suggest the efficacy of park experiences in reducing crime, accelerated recovery after surgery, promoting exercise, reducing obesity and heart attacks, and improved learning.

For decades we have assumed that the nonrecreational benefits of parks will just happen as an automatic by-product of managing for recreation. We have similarly assumed that others were aware of those "extra" benefits. Neither assumption has any place in a holistic park model. All the benefits need to be documented, and all the benefits need to be told. How else can we be sure that our management efforts for recreation are not counterproductive to the equally important needs for re-creation? At the simplest level of implementation of this paradigm, we could begin programs of experimental funding for parks that choose to pilot such initiatives by actively partnering with others for shared re-creational goals. At the advanced level, we need to take another look at supplemental, zero-based, budgeting that encourages pulling down the artificial boundaries around parks and allowing a refocusing on solving problems. Yes, the parks' plate is already full of unmet needs, but parks have the respect of the people—it's one place that they go for answers.

Lesson Four: Needed—A New Park Ethic

The final lesson of September 12th is that our parks say who we are as a people and as a nation in profound ways. Subsumed in that lesson is a challenge to the profession—a challenge to do a relevancy check on the business of parks in a new era of social and personal needs. As part of that relevancy check, we might begin with the following three questions:

1. *Why do we not have a park ethic reflecting their holistic role?*
   The absence of such an ethic may help explain the perennial underfunding and massive deferred maintenance backlog in our parks. Leopold's land ethic, while still largely ignored, offers guidance in assessing our respect for natural communities: *"A thing is good if it tends to preserve the integrity, stability, and beauty of its community."* In like fashion, a park ethic ought to reflect our commitment to the integrity, stability, and beauty of the human community that our parks celebrate. Along with libraries and museums, our parks are society's treasure houses, and in a much greater sense, a park is also society's reflecting pool in which we can see our vigor as

well as our blemishes. The park that is damaged, closed, and nonessential reflects a similarly afflicted society.

2. *If our parks are wellsprings of renewal and pride for community, state and nation, why are they not permeated with in-residence programs for artists, scientists, writers, and humanists?* With parks as a natural blending of science and spirit, nature and society, past and future, why have we limited our stewardship and accountability to the narrow focus of recreation and preservation? The professional park steward is expected to interpret the legislative mandate as broadly as necessary to do the job. Administrative discretion is a rubber band: It works better and lives longer when flexed regularly. If the park "machine" is only producing at 50 percent of its capacity, doesn't that belong in the accountability report? If the "re-creation accomplishments" section of the annual report is blank or missing, perhaps now is the time to at least start listing the potentials.

3. *If parks are as symbolic and nonpartisan as our flag and our national anthem, why the politicization of parks?* With park administrations pursuing partnerships today like the Holy Grail of modern management, how come the first partnership is not with the city council, the state legislature, and the Congress? Why should parks be a budgetary whipping boy when they are bigger than life and smaller than any other item in the budget? If we don't have any presidential and congressional candidates talking about parks as national identity, any governors and university presidents arguing for parks as economic engines, or any educators and researchers fighting for the book of knowledge represented in every park, whose fault is that?

Our many and diverse American public park systems have a common denominator of service to their communities. We can consciously choose to limit that service to a strict interpretation of the authorizing legislation, as further limited by the budget, or we can adopt an ethic that parks are a vital part of the fabric of any community. The integrity, stability, and beauty of that fabric are strongest when it incorporates the threads of parks, nature, streams, forests, and wildlife.

Parks and the Purpose of Life:
The Mountain as Metaphor

*The mountains are fountains of men as well as of rivers, of
glaciers, of fertile soil—able men whose thoughts and deeds
have moved the world and have come down from the mountain.*
                                                    —John Muir

Life is a trail through a forest of awakening senses. We begin life in a profoundly sensory way, fascinated by the smells, the touches, sights, sounds,
and tastes of this new place. Very soon, we begin to develop slightly more
advanced senses of wonder, humor, and intuition. Somewhat later, a sense of
justice and a sense of place begin the shaping of who we are. At some point,
a sense of purpose of life's meaning begins to be a nagging fellow traveler on
the trail. All too often, the urgency of life itself begins to push aside our sense
of purpose as we sublimate it to the needs of family and the job. However, if
we manage to live through the pressure-cooker years, the sense of purpose
may come back in a crescendo just in time for—you guessed it—retirement!
Numerous writers have challenged the winding down or the golden years
approach to retirement, encouraging an aggressive return to the trail of life to
discover the indisputable logic that makes our sense of purpose the last of the
eleven senses to fully awaken.

Our parklands are extremely sensory places, overflowing with the sights,
sounds, smells, tastes, and touch of nature. They are literally fountains of
wonder, insight, and a sense of place. Public parks exude the good cheer of
recreation and subtly celebrate the social justice of just being there. But it is
through the sense of purpose—ours as well as theirs—that parks achieve
their destiny. Why do we grieve at the cutting short of young life? Is it not
because life exists to complete a cycle? Isn't the real meaning of life—any
life—to fulfill its genetic potential and to achieve completeness? The purpose
of setting aside great parks and wildernesses is to allow them to achieve their
natural potential unfettered by human constraints. In much the same way, our
own potentials are unlikely to be fulfilled by being a slave to the constraints
of obligations, career, and the job, however rewarding. It seems perfectly
natural to begin to give serious thought to our purpose once the family has
moved on and the job no longer needs us. It also seems perfectly natural to
look at the park as a metaphor for the maturation of our sense of purpose.

My earliest introduction to public parks was as a seasonal ranger at a small state park in southwestern New Hampshire. My duties allowed me to spend timeless hours on the summit of Mt. Monadnock visiting with countless hikers and meeting their endless needs for information, refreshment, occasional assistance, and sometimes protecting the mountain from them. The greater part of my time for several summers was spent observing and absorbing. For young hikers, the mountain seemed to be little more than a challenge of racing up and then racing down, beating their own time or someone else's. Younger climbers, exclusively, were the ones exhibiting a need for marking the summit by carving initials in the fortress-like fire lookout cabin and most egregiously bringing along a can of spray paint for the rocks. Thoreau visited this summit 100 years earlier and commented on the incessant banging of hammer and chisel recording names and dates of conquests, some as early as 1801. Only the tools have changed. I rarely saw an older hiker show any interest in such marking, and I suspect Thoreau never saw one on any of his four trips. Even slightly more mature hikers didn't rush, though they clearly could have. They were much more likely to ask questions, absorb the answers, and engage in discussion. Their visits seemed less like challenges and more like fulfillment. To them, the panoramic view in all its vast detail was as intriguing as were the tiny alpine plants. It was like witnessing a return of their sense of wonder. Often they were reticent to leave even in the face of a storm, whereas racing the impending storm might be just another challenge for younger climbers. I found that mountains can be good teachers. They endure a lot, and they keep on teaching. Maybe it is that they slow us down just enough so that fulfillment can become something more than rushing to the top to make our mark.

The idea of physically losing ourselves in the wilderness as a way of mentally finding ourselves is, of course, at least as old as the Old Testament. It is the basis of much of our outdoor discovery, vision quest, and mental health philosophy and exercises. For the overwhelming majority of us, the option of *"going into the woods to live deliberately"* no longer exists. Yet, it doesn't take a desert or a wilderness—Any park can be the facilitator if the desire for discovery is present. The idea is to break the pattern of life, clean out some of the mental clutter, and simply observe and absorb.

Nature helps to make it happen by awakening the senses in endless ways—a starry sky, a cougar's cry in the night, the call of an owl, the yipping of a coyote pack, the smell of pine bark in the heat of the day, the feel of a smooth rock beneath softly flowing waters, the taste of blueberries on an exposed ridge, our intuitions about who may have walked this trail before, the wonder of a soaring eagle, the humor of a scolding squirrel, the simple justice of sunrise spreading softly across the land. At first blush, the idea of a sense of purpose seems somewhat out of place in the midst of nature's sensory banquet, yet it is the essential first step in clearing away the clutter, a sense that you are connected to something larger. That sense of connectedness is the critical awakening of human ecology, where every thing and every one has purpose.

Purpose exists through connectedness. Therefore, if parks and nature heighten our awareness of our connections, the obvious conclusion is that experiencing nature through parks might help to awaken a sense of purpose in our lives. At some dim point in our evolution, those connections to nature were undoubtedly far more powerful. In fact, our purpose of survival required that we keep the connections in good working order. There is some evidence that when we lose one of our sensory abilities others become keener, perhaps reflecting this ancient survival capability. Some years ago, I had an opportunity to witness the strength of our latent connections to the wild when a terminally ill child was given her final wish. Before losing most of her sensory abilities to a ravaging nervous disorder, she had been fascinated by wolves and had "adopted" one of the wolves at the wolf center in northern Idaho that I directed. Upon arrival at the center she was able to communicate only with her eyes, yet the hypnotic power of the locked gaze between her and her adopted wolf defied any interpretation other than that of some primal level of connecting. During several meetings over a period of three days, their silent connections were respected by the rest of the eleven-member pack, which kept its distance. When there were no more meetings, her wolf howled and walked the perimeter of the enclosure for hours.

What communication, if any, was taking place at those meetings between a dying girl and a wolf despaired of freedom can be at best only conjecture, but they were clearly connected on a level that none of the rest of us understood. I like to think that connections are important and what we witnessed was the fierce desire to be connected, however briefly, even through the strands of a hurricane fence. Perhaps it was just another manifestation of that same fierce desire that we have to be connected to other objects in space, with our pets, and with the past.

I still climb mountains to reestablish connections. Like all of us, over the course of a lifetime I've lost a lot of connections, and I feel the loss. We have a way of disconnecting those circuits that no longer work for us, but they remain in the memory and later on we usually find out that they had a purpose. I do know that one of the first rules of problem solving through brainstorming is that anything goes. The problem will eventually yield by plugging into connections that we might never have thought of. Finding purpose can be that kind of brainstorming. Whatever your purpose, it's going to require connections.

Moving from connections to purpose and problem solving is such an obvious association that it has opened the door to using our public parklands for all sorts of formal and informal, facilitated and unassisted, free and pricey retreats and awakenings. The best way for most of us is still to just do it. Go climb the mountain and see if you do not come down a slightly different, more focused person. If you are young, try letting the mountain make its mark on you. If parks existed for no other reason, their simple reminder that we are all part of nature would be justification enough because in that realization lies the seeds of our survival as a species—a single species in a world where, by some estimates, 200 species a day are ceasing to exist. As Daniel Quinn of The Ishmael Community says, "The most dangerous idea in existence is that humans belong to an order of being that is separate from the rest of the living community." Quinn's observation screams for answers. Parks for *all* Life can be one small step toward putting things back together.

Conversation with a Mountain

I would like to learn from you,
The student said to the mountuain at first light.
I would not presume to teach, came the soft reply.
And the spruce trees bowed almost imperceptibly.

I only wish to see the world as you do.
But, you are the one with eyes!
Perhaps your focus is not where it should be.
And the ceiling of mist lifted slightly from the summit.

Like you, I wish to be blind to time.
I have my clock—you have yours.
Have you considered exchanging yours for another?
And the sun began to peek though the mist.

That's great! I wish I could think like you do.
Ah, but I do not think; therefore I am —
And therefore, I must continue to be what I am.
The red squirrel chattered its scold from high in the spruce.

You are a great puzzle to me, said the student.
You are even a greater puzzle to me —
So small, so soft, and so destructively powerful!
A chill breeze stirred the leaves; the student shivered and persisted.

I am told that I must temper my knowledge with your wisdom.
Do you so easily let your advisors abdicate the future?
To dispense only knowledge with a cautionary label?
In the quiet, a nearby stream chuckled softly.

But doesn't wisdom only come with age and experience?
That's one way—If you want to wait as long as I have.
Why not try tempering facts with feelings?
The doe looked up, searching, and went back to its feeding.

It's just that I want to be a better steward —to think like a mountain.
Would a beaver be a better logger if it thought like a tree?
Would the tree be a better survivor if it thought like me?
The raven's raucous call punctuated the stillness.

How do I know that the beaver and the tree don't share their thoughts?
That's a good beginning! Maybe there's hope for both of us.
The morning sun dissolved the overcast,
And a warm glow spread across the face of the mountain.

Parks for Beauty in Our Lives:
Wilderness and Cultural Identity

I like to walk amidst the beautiful things that adorn the world.
—George Santayana

There exists by common belief something more to America than land and people. It is that indefinable national attitude and outlook on life that is distinctly ours—the American spirit. It finds expression in many ways and is the patriotic glue that binds the many ideologies and idiosyncrasies that are America together. One of the most powerful sources of this country's essential cultural fiber is clearly the land. The roots of this new nation and its people became entwined with the forests and the rivers, the deserts and the mountains, and the challenges and the inspirations they presented—not the ruins of ancient civilizations that most other nations look to as their ancestral identity.

Our profound influence on the land is unmistakable, particularly when flying over it. The indelible print that we have made on nature's landscape should leave little doubt that it also molded us. Even from 30,000 feet the visual impressions of abundance, opportunity, transportation, community, and recreation can be read by a child. To the trained eye our dependence on the land is obvious, as is the realization that no aspect of our history, culture, work, play, energy, reverence or creative expression could have escaped the influence of such a diverse and wonder-filled geography.

If culture mirrors national spirit and if the American spirit evolved from and is nourished by the land, the linkages should be obvious in our literature, our song, and our art. If that is so, the entire paradigm for managing our public lands might well shift in the direction of sustaining the American spirit. The preamble to the 1987 report by President's Commission on Americans Outdoors alluded to these vital connections, suggesting that no mere accident of history matched a national character of independence, generosity, and ingenuity with a land of vast abundance and opportunity. Some might argue that only the bold immigrated to America, but are we sure that Americans' resourcefulness and creativity are not at least in part a product of the endless challenges and inspiration of the land? A pervasive theme throughout the report is that we have traditionally taken our outdoors for granted until faced with a crisis.

The outdoors' very characteristics of vastness and unlimited abundance encourage such complacency, as does our expansive networks of public lands
and the common belief that they are preserved and protected for all time.

By periodically responding to the current "outdoor crisis" with typical
American generosity of spirit, we have created more and more public lands
while also providing a one-time shot of funding to repair and replace infrastructure in existing parks. The President's Commission strongly suggests that
this kind of periodic response fails to address the root problems such as multi-
million dollar bills for annual litter and trash pick up on public lands and
multibillion dollar bills for deferred maintenance in these special places we
call parks. The Commission's conclusion is that these are indicators of a much
larger problem—the lack of an outdoor ethic, a national belief in the essen-
tiality of parks as economic engines and as cultural incubators of pride, creativity, health, and community spirit. The Commission's recommendations are
aimed at creating that national outdoor ethic, through a prairie fire of support
across the land, for inserting the outdoors in all elements of the primary and
secondary curricula, developing a national system of greenways, massive
expansion of partnerships for the outdoors, and a new look at how we fund
our outdoor recreation lands. We cannot hope to retain our cultural vitality if
we have to send our future artists, sculptors, writers, and composers to the
remnants of wildlands or to museum wildlife dioramas for inspiration.

A convincing storehouse of testimony to our outdoor connections already
exists buried in the biographies of creative Americans from all walks of life
and in the published and unpublished analyses of American music and other
forms of creative expression. At the turn of the 19th century, Frederick Jackson
Turner expressed his grave doubts about our national future once the challenge
of the frontier was gone. The thought that *"in taming the wilderness, we also
tamed ourselves"* is still a very sobering one. The frontier may be gone but
we remain surrounded by challenges, not the least of which is to understand
who and what we are. As Roderick Nash put it, *"The challenge now is not to
conquer the land, but to restrain ourselves from destroying it."*

The Land as Literature

Given the closeness of nature to the lives of Americans, it cannot be surprising
that the earliest art form to celebrate the nation's landscape was our literature.
Van Wyck Brooks' *History of American Life as Seen Through the Library
Window* was intended to document the fullness of our literary heritage, but
even a casual reading reveals the powerful influence the outdoors had on
America's most celebrated writers of the 19th and 20th centuries. William

Cullen Bryant, botanist, poet and father of American song, daily escaped the city to seek refuge among the groves of the quiet Hudson. At the age of seventeen, his poetry indicated that he had already discovered his country and *"freed it from the faded fancies of an older world."*

Solitary communing with nature and the simple life, or "living deliberately," became popular themes in the writings of other literary giants like Thoreau, Emerson, and Whitman. Edna St. Vincent Millay's poetry of the salt smell of the ocean and the natural outdoors of New England; Willa Cather's sights and sounds of the plains, the wind in winter, and the drumming of the quail; Washington Irving's romantic and inviting Hudson River; and Mark Twain's exciting and adventurous Mississippi speak to a national character as much as they do to the land. The solitary Emily Dickinson found a poetry in nature that few have matched. Sarah Orne Jewett wrote mostly about people but found her source of inspiration on the coast of Maine and its land of pointed firs and wisps of sea fog. Helen Hunt Jackson's concern for the American Indian was focused on their dependence, reverence for, and interaction with, the land.

To single out any one literary figure as exemplifying the creative inspiration of the land would be to miss the point of the land's remarkable diversity of inspiration. However, Walt Whitman provided us with a detailed self-analysis of poetic inspiration when he saw the summer grass as a symbol of democracy:

> The Americans of all nations at any time upon the Earth have probably the fullest poetical nature. The United States themselves are essentially the greatest poem in the history of the earth. The largeness of nature and the nation were monstrous without a corresponding generosity of the spirit of the citizen. Here the theme is creative and has vista, the land and sea, mountains, and rivers are not small themes. All is an old and varied sign of the unfailing perception of the poetic in an outdoor people.

New England's impenetrable forest, the frontier's religious fervor, the Southwest's simplicity and mystery of the land, California's expansiveness, Alaska's challenge, the earthiness of the South gave theme to America's most respected authors for over 200 years. Sandburg, London, MacLiesh, Faulkner, O'Neil, Snyder, Nicholes, and McPhee are only a hint of the authors who tried to share their awe of the land.

Of all the inspirational sources—war, urban life, society, social injustice, reform, love, innocence, the workplace, crime, mystery, adventure, and the American dream—none seems to have the universal popularity of the outdoors and its elements of nature, wilderness, wildlife, Indians, and the frontier. Even in losing some of those inspirations, a new breed of contemporary literary giants has emerged including Edward Abbey, Barry Lopez, Rene Dubois, David Brower, Rachel Carson, Roderick Nash, Mary Oliver, and Terry Tempest Williams.

The Land as Scenery

In 1840, N. P. Willis of Portland, Maine, published a massive treatise on *American Scenery*. Profusely illustrated with steel plate engravings, Willis introduces his text with these words:

> There is a field for the artist in this country which surpasses every other in richness of picturesque. The great difficulty is where to choose. How [to] draw the vanishing lines which mark the greener belts through wilderness, which betray the wandering watercourses, or the airy wheel of the eagle?

One hundred and thirty six years later in commemoration of the bicentennial of the American Revolution, Joshua Taylor's *America as Art* was introduced with the idea that even in the mid-20th century it comes as a surprise to many that the nation's art has played a role in America's identity. Taylor, then director of the Smithsonian's National Collection of Fine Arts, not only devotes nearly one-half of his book to themes of the land and its symbols but also includes a major essay updating Turner's frontier thesis.

The "second discovery of America," as Taylor describes it, was perhaps more exciting than the first. It was the realization that not only was America a continent of fresh new ideas and imagery but it was also a cultural revolution every bit as powerful as a political revolution. Politicians at this time were extolling the economic and exploitive opportunities for America; artists, writers, and musicians were drawing from its natural inspiration.

American artists weren't so much rejecting European rigidity in artistic style as they were seeking to capture America's newness, its freshness in style, its vitality, and its grandeur. In doing so, they not only liberated their art with new images of reality but also provided the visual companion to what was happening in American literature and helped set in motion a powerful wave of international interest that would become what we would eventually call "tourism." By the 19th century, portfolios of American landscapes became popular and landscape painting emerged as a livelihood independent of portraiture. Once discovered, the business of landscape imagery grew with dazzling speed and variety. By the time the westward movement had become a national fever, it was an established industry fueled by the sketches and written descriptions of lands beyond the imagination of all but people like

Lewis and Clark, Zebulon Pike, Jedediah Smith, William Ashley, and so many others that had experienced the phenomenon.

In 1825, the Hudson River School had firmly established the American landscape tradition, and William Cullen Bryant's friend Thomas Cole had achieved pre-eminence in capturing the American wild on canvas. John James Audubon was already drawing birds in Kentucky, and Samuel Seymour and Titian Peale had painted the Rockies as part of the 1819–1820 expedition. In rapid succession, the American landscape produced the timeless art of George Catlin, Thomas Moran, George Bingham, John Mix Stanley, James Alden, Rudolph Kurz, Paul Wimar, William Ranney, Albert Bierstadt, Frederick Remington, Charles Russell, and a list that will continue to grow as long as there are wild places where the beauty of nature captures the imagination of artists like Georgia O'Keefe, sculptors like James Earle Fraser, composers like Ferde Grofe, and songsters like John Denver.

By the 1870s landscape photography was in vogue, and stereopticon images made it possible for Americans everywhere to become armchairs travelers across their country. Photographers like E. O. Beaman, James Fennemore, and Jack Hillers were officially recording the geological studies of the few last places to be visited such as John Wesley Powell's explorations of the Grand Canyon, and the captivating call of wild Alaska. Frontier photographers like L. A. Huffman produced pictorial documentaries of the last of the Indian wars and the decimation of the buffalo herds, while others like Silas Melander and William H. Jackson captured the breathtaking scenery of Yosemite, the Sequoias, and the intimate detail of life on the prairie, in the logging camps, on the cattle drives, and on the railroads. In the midst of the frontier photography boom, Ansel Adams was born, a man who was destined to bring to landscape photography a new way of looking at nature and to America the most powerful tool imaginable for the preservation of the wild. Originally trained as a musician, Adams photography sang of the wilderness; and the Adams tradition is carried on today by hundreds of photographers and the environmental organizations that are fueled by their images.

Nature on canvas, on photographic plates, carved in wood, sculpted in stone, or cast in bronze is never so much a theme as it is a statement, a statement of the virtues of a wild, rugged, and enduring nature. These virtues of the land, translated into attributes of its people, made it easy to sermonize and moralize that the salvation of western nature resided in America. The linkage of the land and a people to match that land was as much a part of the person and popularity of Theodore Roosevelt as it is in explaining the enormous popularity of western cinema as expressions of a national vitality and spirit. Clearly America's love affair with the outdoors continues today, whether expressed as art or as obsession with outdoor equipment and clothing. We are not only products of the land, we wish to be seen as embodying the character of that land.

The Land as Song

There can be little doubt that in music America has found its most pervasive celebration of the land. The perennial popularity of classical, patriotic, and folk songs dedicated to the people of the land, the rivers, and the mountains suggest that their composers have tapped a depth of feeling in the nation's consciousness that other art forms cannot approach. Obviously, music like "This Land is Your Land," "American the Beautiful," and "Rocky Mountain High," conjure mental images of pride, grandeur, but they do something else — they pull at the heart, they call us to see the land and to protect it. They embody the idea of national patriotism just as jazz and country and western music speak to regional pride.

Though much slower to develop its own distinctive flavor, America's music eventually became the world's music, drawing from the land and pulling us to the land. Gilbert Chase's authoritative analysis points out that America's music had to wait much longer for the equivalent of a Melville or a Whitman. As late as the 1850s, the New York philharmonic was criticized for never having played an American composition, although it had once. And, that once, was the music of George Frederick Bristow, a champion of American music who was inspired by the land. His final work was a symphony titled *Niagara*. William Henry Fry, the man who protested the Philharmonic's European bias, was a composer and lecturer on American music who called for an American Declaration of Independence in Art, guided only by nature and inspiration.

In just a few short years, Edward MacDowell was acclaimed as "America's Greatest Composer" and the one name in music that could be paired with that of Whitman in poetry. The fact that MacDowell was profoundly influenced by nature is evident not only in his subjects but also in his inspirational retreats to the New England woods where an art colony in his name continues to flourish today. In rejecting the Germanic tradition of a purely national music, MacDowell called for music as youthful and as filled with the optimistic vitality and undaunted tenacity of spirit that characterizes Americans themselves.

American fascination for European musical styles lingered on despite the countless European composers who upon visiting America encouraged us to experiment and create an American music inspired by our national scenery. Antonin Dvorak, one of the most outspoken of these visitors, lived for a while in Iowa where he wrote a cantata to the American flag and a symphony titled *From the New World*. Charles Ives, one of America's most prolific composers, often drew his inspiration from the outdoors and from the literary heroes therein. His *Concord Sonata* celebrates Thoreau, Emerson, Hawthorne, and the Alcotts a half-century after their passing in an impressionistic attempt to capture their sense of wilderness, melody, and strength of nature.

Drawing from its regional songs and jazz, American music by the 1930s and 40s featured big bands, symphony orchestras, and names like Aaron Copland, George Gershwin, and Roy Harris; it was finally 100 percent American. The inspiration of the outdoors was also still present in cowboy songs, folk ballads, and spirituals. Today's American music persists in reflecting the rich complexity and diversity of the land and people, and the land's influence continues to be subtly expressed in its themes. Often, the subtlety takes a backseat to concerns for nature, such as in *Orca's Greatest Hits* and Joni Mitchell's "Big Yellow Taxi," with the words ... *they paved Paradise and put up a parking lot* in an attempt to get everyone dancing with the environment instead of trying to dominate it.

The possible diminution of national spirit and cultural vitality with the loss of wild places and wild creatures has profound implications for our future. One has only to look at those nations that have lost their natural diversity and agricultural vitality to know that we are defined by the land. Change the land, and change the people. Drain the energy from the land, and drain it from its people. The primary fault for such losses is a lack of connection with the land. The major connections to the land for millions of Americans today are its public parks.

Parks for Food and Flavor:
A Taste of Biodiversity for the World's Pantry

We find in the fields of nature no place that is barren, every spot on land and sea is covered with harvests always ripe and ready to be gathered.

—John Muir

While riding a train the length of Scotland, I was intrigued by the clusters of garden plots in community parks along the way and decided I had to get off the train for a visit with some of the gardeners. The tending of a garden is one of life's most satisfying diversions and these Scots villagers had taken it to a new level of quiet (sometimes not so quiet!) competition. Their assigned plots, averaging 4 by 30 meters and reminiscent of World War II victory gardens, seemed like extensions of both their homes and their personalities. Often the plots included a small tool shed and a composting area, making them the embodiment of a "small is beautiful" philosophy. The gardening appeared to be almost exclusively a male activity, perhaps accounting for the competitiveness of the gardeners, but the sense of ownership engendered was hard to miss, sort of like grazing allotments in the West. The crops were impressive, the plots tidy and almost military in their orderliness, and there was obviously something growing here alongside the cabbages and beets. The sense of fellowship and meaning, of pride and achievement, was obvious even before talking with the gardeners. The explanation of staying in touch with the land might be an emotional stretch, but I think not. Perhaps you had to be there to sense how much the land means to these Scots, and to hear the stories, their histories of the soil that produces both greatness and food.

While not common, garden plots in public parks in America can be found in many communities, and even large farms continue to operate on many state and federal lands under permit arrangements after the government has purchased the land. Such arrangements provide a way of maintaining open space and preserving the fabric of an attractive landscape. In fact, the attractiveness of some of these public-private park landscapes raises the obvious question of why we felt that we had to buy the land in the first place. If preservation of the heritage of a working landscape was our goal, wouldn't it have been a lot less expensive to come up with a zoning plan that would retain present uses and present sizes of ownership within a designated cultural heritage area? Wouldn't ownership in title result in a higher level of stewardship than a leaseback arrangement? One need only to travel through any number of zoned parks in Britain to realize that it works. We might have to foster a stronger ethic of respect for private lands and gates, but it could work.

While garden plots, farms, and zoned agricultural areas within parks offer some interesting food for thought for park planners, very likely the most important food-related value of our public parks lies in their potential as biodiversity reserves for the future. As America relentlessly embraces the monolithic, monoculture, agribusiness model of food production, our large tracts of preserved biodiversity on public lands take on a special value as potential sources of seed for the future. With millions of acres of America's best crop-producing lands that are chemically controlled for weeds, chemically sanitized for bugs, and planted with engineered and patented high-yield seed, we might want to consider a social insurance policy of dedicating more land to diversity. In fact, given the impact of large-scale agribusiness practices on the diversity of the public's wildlife, it seems only logical to expect the producers of our food to bear some of the cost of such an expansion in our biodiversity reserves.

The precedent of a "no net loss" policy for wetlands might have some value in this discussion. Why not a no net loss policy for biodiversity? Obviously we cannot hope to reverse the alarming global loss of species that occurs each day, but we can and should accept some responsibility for the largely unknown consequences that productive land practices have on bio-diversity. As a very limited start down this road, we could do some careful biological monitoring of those parks and reserved lands that lie adjacent to, near, and downwind from intensively treated crop-producing lands.

No net loss policies reflect a need to put the brakes on developments that compromise biodiversity and to provide a long-overdue recognition of ecosystem connectedness, the idea of equal and opposite reactions and our role in them. If Parks for Life is ever to become a reality of our thinking, the single biggest hurdle the parks community faces is to completely free itself from its self-imposed leisure services paradigm. For the vast majority of park professionals, I suspect that Parks for Food is about as alien a concept as parks for mining and oil production. Had we been watching all these years, we might have noticed that the vast majority of park visitors bring food with them or buy food in the park. Ninety-nine percent of the trash in a park is food wrappers and drink containers. Food is an integral part of the park experience. The planners of one of America's earliest private camping resorts recognized the role of food in camping and chose not to have fireplaces but did offer meals-on-wheels delivered right to the campsite, along with their own charge card services. The delivery of meals not only made money for the developer, it freed the campers from cooking and cleaning, giving them more time for recreation. Food is a necessity, but in a park setting it is often also ceremonial as an integral part of family reunions, barbecues, weddings, and ethnic and cultural festivities of all sorts. Parks and food go together like baseball and hot dogs. Given this immutable connection, it's an easy step to embracing the idea of Parks for Food and to the potential benefits to parks from stepping up to the plate.

Many parks around the world, recognizing the incredible feast for the eyes that their settings provide, have creatively added highly popular fine-dining concessions to their offerings, which have resulted in new park experiences and new sources of park revenue. Many more parks add to the diet and save on the food bill by serving up sustainable supplies of edibles such as nuts, mushrooms, herbs, berries, fish, meat, and medicinal plants. As biodiversity reserves and biodiversity interpretation and training centers, parks can rightfully take a place in the community of scientists concerned about the ability of our planet to sustain unlimited growth. The two critical needs for that future are food and water, and while well-recognized, the role of parks in assuring clean water supplies has certainly not taken on the importance that it deserves in setting aside park land. If parks and food are natural partners, parks and clean water are even more so.

The opportunities for parks to get into the business of food are bountiful. One obvious place to begin might be to certify all food products sold in the park as being eco-friendly and sustainable. Another might be to host a weekly farmer's market in the park. Yet another might be to make space available in the visitor center for local farm-produced products and exhibits. Surely America's pride in the land's ability to produce greatness alongside sustenance is no less than that of the Scots gardener.

Parks for Inspiration:
Artists, Tourists, and the Search for the Elusive Sublime

You will find something far greater in the woods than you will find in books.

—*St. Bernard*

The Artist as Tourist, Interpreter, and Promoter of Tourism

Artists have played a major role in promoting and interpreting wildlands to tourists for more than a century-and-a-half. But, there is much more to the artist-tourist connection than artistic products and their seemingly infinite ability to persuade us to preserve public lands and to visit them for recreation. The little-understood process of creative inspiration, beginning with the artists' need to experience nature and ending with their need to share that experience, reflects parallel needs of tourists. The major landscape painters of the late 19th and early 20th centuries often spoke of being in search of "the sublime," meaning that elusive but perfect manifestation of man in nature—or "Heaven on Earth." Reflecting this artistic quest, the traveling centennial celebration of Frederick Edwin Church's paintings bears the subtitle: "In Search of the Promised Land." Many of the idyllic scenes of nature by Church, Cole, Bierstadt, and Remington strikingly convey the artists' reverence for landscapes that are almost transcendental in their context. Ironically, they and scores of others of their era became tourism's early promoters, often helping to propel the very heavens they had found toward a state of the sub-sublime!

Pamela J. Belanger's *Inventing Acadia: Artists and Tourists at Mount Desert* matter-of-factly begins with the assertion that "Mount Desert Island owes its nineteenth century distinction to the painters from New York who discovered the island." Belanger goes on to point out that "in less than half a century the Island, first regarded as merely a rocky, barren, and largely inhospitable wilderness… became a scenic destination for thousands, especially the nation's wealthy elite."

The artistic celebration of the outdoors of the 19th century was not limited to the visual arts, and works such as Caroline Gilman's *The Poetry of Traveling in the United States* appeared as early as 1838. Similarly, singing groups such as The Hutchinsons traveled around the country praising the wonders of New Hampshire's White Mountains.

The artists of today who find their inspiration in America's natural landscapes seem no less in awe of their subject. In an ongoing series of interviews with photographers, painters, composers, performing artists, and writers whose creations celebrate Acadia National Park and Baxter State Park in Maine, the emotional connections to the landscape are equally evident. Their creative interpretations clearly continue to influence travel to these two parks.

The interpretive successes of nature-oriented artists have over the last 150-plus years catapulted tourism promotion into a multibillion-dollar business and have not infrequently taken us from the sublime to the ridiculous. Some of today's promotions have been so successful that the very numbers of visitors they produce often threaten the attraction, the tourist market, and even the resource itself. Increasingly, we see reports of local concern being voiced in ways that polarize the visitor and the host community: "Welcome to Our State—Now Go Home!" or "Fishing and Bathing for Residents Only!" A recent *National Geographic* article about one of Maine's premier tourist magnets reflects the growing antipathy toward tourists in its title "Welcome to Monhegan Island, Maine—Now Please Go Away," while paradoxically increasing tourism itself with images that capture Monhegan's allure as only *National Geographic* photography can.

The search for the promised land clearly resonates with tourists. There can be little doubt that tourists in general, and ecotourists in particular, are looking for something not unlike that which drove the landscape painters of the last two centuries deeper into the wilderness. One difference between a Frederick Church interpretation and that of a 21st century marketing firm can probably be characterized as a "truth in advertising" issue. The early nature artists were often accused of exaggeration but the more recent depictions of serenity and solitude, sans transmission lines and development, can probably not be found anywhere today except perhaps in the airbrush studio. With today's mass tourism to hundreds of thousands of traditional outdoor venues, perhaps we all should view that elusive perfect trip as a "work of art."

A second difference between Church's era and today is that we no longer have to work at finding heaven; it can be as simple as following the directions in the advertisement! Despite the increasing number of tourism "advertorials," it is the rare tourism ad that attempts to provide the visitor an in-depth understanding of the destination and what to expect. After all, advertising success is based on numbers responding and we know that any attempt at interpretation can have the effect of reducing the numbers. "Bring foul weather gear" might be interpreted as "Expect foul weather" (and besides, we sell foul weather gear here!). Similarly, "Return to an earlier time when life was simpler" might be interpreted as "Share a bath—and enjoy our limited menu."

Traditionally, at least in our culture, interpreters and advertisers do not share offices and job descriptions; both have a discrete piece of the communication job. Promotion gets the visitors to the site, and interpretation then has the job of satisfying them. Of course, the more unrealistic the promotion, the more challenging the interpreter's job will be. In the field of tourism where the one universal axiom could be "Satisfied customers are the best advertising," this organizational flaw seems to be potentially fatal, and yet it is the American norm. Meanwhile, in other places like Scotland we find this dichotomy starting to break down, with stunning interpretive books such as *The Love of Scotland* being published with the assistance of the Scottish Tourism Board and *Interpret Scotland* being distributed to tourism promotion offices.

Finding Flow

In seeking to prevent tourist heavens from becoming tourist hells, we need to consider expanding the roles of interpreters of our cultural and environmental heritage. As one approach to a rethinking of traditional roles, we might look at the problem as one of replacing the flaw with flow. Mihaly Csikszentmihalyi has advanced the concept of "optimal experiences" through his extensive research on how we engage in the pursuit of happiness. Summarized in a word, a concept and a book, *flow* convincingly portrays the search for and the achievement of happiness as occurring in a channel that lies between the states of boredom and anxiety. One of the primary characteristics of flow is a feeling of control, or of being in charge of one's own life and more. For artists and tourists alike, flow begins with information and planning. Some artists report periods of anxiety related to park rules and crowds at scenic vistas and periods of "boredom" waiting for the right conditions of light, absence of crowds and so forth, but every artist mentioned something akin to the idea of flow when all of the human and natural conditions converged in just the right way: "The music just came to me"—"When the sun came out from behind the clouds at just the right moment it brought tears to my eyes"—"The scene almost seemed to paint itself." Many of the artists interviewed during this research seemed to also see a common element of time flow, seasonal and even geologic, in their interpretations of nature.

If we were to examine our own tourist travel using this model by charting our flow through the various stages of a vacation trip, it would quickly become evident that most of us bounce between the fields of anxiety and boredom, spending less time feeling in control than we'd prefer. If each of those instances of boredom and anxiety is cumulative rather than compensating, the result is likely to be severe trip dissatisfaction and an eagerness for home.

If trip planners, travel agents, service providers, hosts, information providers, and interpreters see their role as one of maintaining flow, tourists will be more likely to have satisfying experiences. For example, the feeling of being in control is at its highest when planning the trip. Once we start to make decisions and commitments, control starts to ebb away. Anxiety increases and we hope that we have made the "right" choices. We all know that travel is supposed to be an adventure of discovery with no surprises, or at least no negative surprises. If upon arrival we confirm that we seem to have made a right choice, our anxiety diminishes and we return to a state of near-flow. It is unlikely to be perfect flow as yet because there are many other decisions awaiting confirmation, such as where to eat, what activities to engage in, and what side trips to take. Hopefully our need for control has not been so overpowering as to take away the chance for pleasant surprises. Otherwise boredom may be just around the corner.

For the traveler exploring a new destination, flow can be more like a tightrope than a channel! Good tourist hosts know this intuitively and respond with planned serendipity—pleasant surprises. Interpretation in all of its many forms is an important if not critical element in maintaining the visitors' flow and avoiding boredom! Interpretation can replace the flaw in most tourism communication with *flow!* It can do so by providing flow among all parts of tourism experience: planning, travel, destination, and recollection. Good interpretation, by focusing on holism, relevance, and provocation can turn a paint-by-numbers trip into a work of art for the traveler. The field of ecotourism is already doing this by encouraging in-depth and continuing involvement by the tourist. Committed ecotourists do not emerge upon arrival at the site. The flow from thoughtful planning, environmentally sensitive travel, minimal impact visits to an "ending" with a long-term commitment to sites and issues is quintessential holism—travel for life! The seamless trip that blends with life at the edges rather than one that is an abrupt departure from our everyday lives probably provides a higher level of satisfaction for most of us.

There is a challenge for the interpretive profession at each stage of the experience. Thoughtful trip planning clearly requires more than simple information. Good ecotourism operators know this and introduce their visitors to cultural and environmental interpretation. This contact not only opens the door to making decisions that are environmentally and culturally sensitive but also it can also begin a dialogue for the future by exploring questions such as "How can I best make a difference in the long run?" Personalized, relevant, and provocative interpretation builds on that dialogue.

Flow and the Art of Interpretation

The twin needs for "the experience" and to creatively respond to that experience were clearly paramount for all artists interviewed. However, contingent needs to share the experience and to preserve the opportunity were always present. Ansel Adams made a similar observation about his photography: *"All life and art are justified by communication and are to be shared not hoarded"* (Nyerges, 1999). Like artists, tourists have a need to share the experience, which they demonstrate by taking pictures, sending postcards, purchasing gifts, and telling their friends about their trip. With the exception of ecotourism, we rarely make it easy for tourists to demonstrate what must be an equally profound concern for resource preservation. When given the opportunity to contribute, park and historic site managers are often amazed at tourists' responsiveness. They may even see the contributions as some kind of affirmation for their good work when in fact it may simply be an expression of the tourist's need for greater personal relevance which they achieve by making the experience a larger part of their lives, even if in a token way.

In terms of fitting experiences to life, holism is good art, good interpretation, and good tourism. It may be that ecotourism is the fastest growing segment of the tourist market simply because it is the smallest segment, but more likely it enjoys this distinction because it focuses on creating experiences that are complete and flow with life. In that way it fills a vital need in today's increasingly compartmentalized society.

Whatever the connections may be, it seems clear that environmental and cultural interpretation can play a vital and significant role in making tourism markets more vibrant and more sustainable. In doing so, the interpreter's role becomes more personally fulfilling from a user of art to an artist of experiences.

Flow and the Larger Picture

Robert Cahn argues that *"Conditions in the national parks can provide an early warning signal that can alert the nation to what may be happening to the natural environments as a whole"* (Huth, 1990). Just as parks can serve as indicators of the broader environment, artists can provide the "canary in the coalmine" for what is happening inside the parks. In the last few decades, popular art has frequently lampooned the conditions in our public parks and the landscape artist has often retreated into the less crowded areas and times, inevitably beginning anew the submission of the sublime to the crush of the crowd.

Just as we need to be able to interpret parks as early warning signals of what may be happening in our environment, interpreters on the tourist scene must be cognizant of what may be happening to tourism markets as a result of unmet tourist expectations. Parks are valuable sources of human inspiration and local economic benefit. The artistic connection between these two should not be taken for granted or ignored in the scramble for economic justification of parks.

Precisely because artists provide an enhanced opportunity to better understand and appreciate how these priceless lands release our creative energies and make us who we are as individuals and as a culture, we need to vastly expand our arts-in-the-parks programs. Every park inspires, thus every park can benefit from an artist-in-residence. Since that inspiration may not always be artistic, why not have a scientist-in-residence—someone who monitors both the natural and social changes over time at that park—as well? And while we are painting the picture of the perfect holistic park, what park is complete if it is not in some way a classroom? a laboratory? an observatory? a museum? a gallery? a provocateur? a reservoir of ideas, opportunities, and cultural pride?

If culture mirrors national spirit and America's spirit evolved from and is nourished by the land, the linkages might be expected to be demonstrable. If this is so, terms such as *the limits of acceptable change* and *carrying capacity* that guide our thinking about park management take on a new meaning. The notion that overuse of our parklands might effectively diminish national spirit and individual creativity places parks at the very top of our national agenda— a position taken by the President's Commission on Americans Outdoors in the preface to their report which states, in part, *"We find that the outdoors is a wellspring of the American spirit, vital to our belief in ourselves as individuals and as a nation... We believe that the outdoors is a statement of the American condition."*

Searching for the sublime in the 21st century need not be the impossible dream; it simply requires a 21st century model in which the sublime is defined by flow and sustainability rather than a singular conception of the idyllic. Today's artists and today's tourists are still looking for personal fulfillment and meaningful experiences, but they are searching in a world vastly more populated with other searchers, many of whom are becoming weary of the trip and cynical of the destination. Unless the seemingly inevitable restrictions that go along with growth can be countered by an expansion of the opportunities for more fulfilling experiences, nature as sublime will become an illusion. A focus on whole people living whole lives must include a universal canon of interpreters and all of those who work to sustain a tourist economy based on nature. Art and nature are an essential element of that holism and life flow. Ansel Adams asks us "What is more natural than Man?" when we have spent millennia trying to distance the civilized world from the wild. All too often we have achieved that distance by being uncivil to the wild. Today's economies and tomorrow's generations may measure our civility by the ways we find to embrace wildness, to praise the picturesque, and to celebrate the search for the sublime.

Parks for Creativity:
Conversations with Creative People

Without this playing with fantasy no creative work has ever come to birth.

—Carl Jung

The idea that nature speaks to us on some conscious or subconscious level seems to be a surprisingly comfortable view for most of us despite the absence of any scientific validation. Nature's messages of beauty, grandeur, danger, and mystery often communicate as well or better than the scenic vista signs we erect to say the same things.

People commonly say that a certain scene "speaks to them," meaning that it resonates in some way with their sense of place, their memory banks, their curiosity, or their concepts of appropriateness and beauty. Some individuals are convinced that they actually receive sensory messages from wild creatures, plants, landscapes, seascapes, and inanimate objects in nature—and perhaps they do! Such messages may very well explain the unmistakable "something" that we see in their art, hear in their music, and celebrate in their poetry.

The inspirational powers of nature seem to be inarguable. How we process and act upon that inspiration is probably as diverse as our individual skills and abilities. A painting, a photograph, a poem, a donation of time or money, a musical composition, and a performance might all result from a single inspirational moment or scene. Inspired works vary not only in their style of expression but also in their emotional intensity. A single snapshot may suffice to *capture* the mountain's power for one photographer while for another *appreciating* the mountain may mean a collection or even a life's work. Perhaps in the same way one mountain climber is content to *conquer* it with a single ascent while for another *knowing* the mountain may not happen with a hundred visits.

The range of creative responses to nature's inspiration seems so incomprehensible that we have to content ourselves with occasional insights—bits and pieces of nature creatively interpreted and possibly even creatively experienced. Some of the following insights were provided by people who have been inspired by public parks and some are from artist-in-residence journals.

The relationships between nature and creative people might provide us with an added insight into the inspirational role of public lands that transcends justifications of recreation, open space, and economics. Just as their creative works in music, the visual arts, performing arts, and literature seem to capture the shouts and whispers of nature, the artist's insights seem to reflect and magnify those special feelings that many of us experience in the outdoors. Their interpretations of what moves them share many characteristics: a strong sense of exhilaration, an almost physical need for the experience, the importance of extending the moment, conflicting feelings of humility and pride, and sharing the experience versus concern for its loss through too much sharing.

It's not a major leap to make a connection between the American spirit and America's landscape. Many writers have done so. The distinctive American culture, like its spirit, is widely recognized to be a product of the land and its opportunities and inspirations, like "wilderness." We seldom think about the sources as we enjoy popular music or symphonic pieces, admire classic art, or appreciate powerful photography. We recognize interpretive genius while taking for granted the inspirational event that must have been associated with the work. To assume that the potential for inspiring events will always be there just because the land is "protected" seems a little naïve.

While writing an article in the 1980s for the journal *Parks and Recreation* on wilderness and culture, I received a handwritten copy of a talk about the national parks as personal inspiration from the composer Richard Adler. His insights profoundly influenced my thinking and he subsequently agreed to be interviewed. Adler, composer of *The Wilderness Suite* and *The Yellowstone Overture*, along with such Broadway hits as *Damn Yankees* and *Pajama Game*, recalled the moment when he first saw the Grand Canyon of the Yellowstone:

> As an artist, as a composer, I remember what happened when I walked onto the rim of the Grand Canyon of the Yellowstone for the first time. I remember the colors, the vermilions, the yellows, the blues, the burnt sienna, the lavenders. But I remember them differently, I guess, than most people. I *heard* the colors. I heard them as distinct notes, even with the gradations of sharps and flats, and as the whole visit of the Grand Canyon of the Yellowstone appeared before me, the beginnings of the principle theme of my *Yellowstone Overture* began to take shape.

My own interpretation of Adler's insight is that "creative" people see landscapes in ways that match their own expressiveness and with an intensity that allows them to connect to that landscape, resulting in a creative work. To further explore this idea, I visited with a number of creative people whose inspiration comes from Acadia National Park and Baxter State Park in Maine.

One of these artists, Maine composer Barbara Smith, comments about the moment of her inspiration in discussing *A Sense of Acadia*, her twelve-part piano composition:

> I didn't really have to sit there and wait for the music to come.
> By loving the outdoors and feeling very serene and peaceful
> and appreciative of being there, it just all came together. One of
> the tunes I wrote while sitting at Somes Sound. It was one of
> those beautiful blue sky late September days and the sun was
> like diamonds on the water and this tune just came to me just
> very bright and lively.

Smith's description of the moment echoes that of Thomas Paquette, an artist from Portland, Maine, whose work focuses on similar settings giving voice to nature:

> I definitely see whispers—it's landscapes that call out to be
> painted... I have to turn and look, and I think what was that?
> What is that?... and then I try to recreate those whispers...
> sometimes I want to shout the whispers, and whisper the
> shouts... it's the experience of whatever nature is that I'm after.
> I once tried to paint from somebody's photos and it was a
> disaster because I didn't have the experience. The photo wasn't
> the mountain, and I didn't know the mountain... to try to paint
> the mountain from those photos was presumptuous."

Finally, compare this with the words of Michael Lewis, whose Acadia painting was inspired by the same setting as Barbara Smith's piano composition and the range of emotions he feels as he begins to paint:

> Gradually I don't feel like I'm an observer, I'm a part of it.
> The dissolving of that distinction is invited by the landscape
> and it lets impressions just come in. Sometimes I'm not even
> aware of what it is that I'm going to focus on when I start
> painting. I feel like I need it the way I need to breathe, the
> way I need to take in food.

Each new insight provokes deeper wonder about the connections between nature and creative expression. We need to better understand these connections if we wish to truly preserve all of the values that these protected public lands have to offer. Creative works, along with the mental renewal and inspirational transfer that they represent, tend not to show up in the park's annual reports of numbers served, revenue generated, programs offered and acres protected, and yet are they not reflective of the real output of our protected lands? Isn't there a direct connection between these inspirational resources and the positive attitude, the feelings of pride, challenge, opportunity, and sense of wonder that epitomizes the American spirit? Isn't there a direct connection between these experiences and the visions of the donors of these lands? Along with their science training, isn't it this very same sense of wonder and unending passion for nature that defines a park professional?

Some observations about creative people flow from these interviews and mingle to form a number of common streams. Irrespective of the artists' specialty, they all seem to experience many similar emotions.

Emotional High

John Denver captures the essence of what many artists report in describing their feelings of the inspirational moment in his song "Rocky Mountain High." John Muir's almost rhapsodic descriptions of "the range of light" that he found in the Sierras reflects this same intensity of emotions as does Walt Whitman's poetry and Ansel Adams' photography. It is both a range of emotions—awe and humility, ownership and belonging, sharing and protecting—as well as an intensity of emotions that can block out other concerns and perhaps even sound judgment (almost like the descriptions of "rapture of the deep" experienced by divers). Michael Lewis says, "The range of emotions is amazing… It isn't just visual—It takes you away from the human context—It's like being a kid again—It's so sensorial, there's nothing like it."

Humility, or perhaps more descriptively awe, is a recurring response to inspirational moments. In one way or another, all of these artists expressed feelings of being overwhelmed by natural landscapes and doubts as to their technical adequacy in the face of oftentimes awesome natural challenges, such as reducing Mt. Katahdin to a 20-by-18–inch canvas or an 8-by-10 print. As Richard Adler said, "What more can this man, this composer, this human wish for… to have the privilege of feeling, hearing, seeing, smelling, even tasting, these joys in these magnificent special remnants of the wilderness."

For other composers the connection, while more illusive, is just as real as a comment from the Acadia artist-in-residence journal reveals: "I wish I could explain how I make a musical correlation to something visual or from the smell of low tide."

Terrell S. Lester, landscape photographer, describes a moment of awe at Baxter State Park:

> I'd hiked up to the pond before daybreak and had everything
> set to capture a Katahdin sunrise… and as it started getting

lighter, I happened to notice a moose down the shoreline watching the expanding rim of light with me... It was one of those special moments when everything stops and you don't even realize you're breathing. I always feel that nature is overwhelming—but in a good way. The idea that I am such a small part of it is a wonderful feeling... to be in awe.

However, humility can hardly be considered a universal characteristic of creative people, as an excerpt from an early 20th century landscape painter's correspondence with a colleague reveals in speaking about Mt. Katahdin: "I shall immortalize that mountain as no one else has or likely will, as it is my mountain and I the official portraitist of it."

Not surprisingly, creativity and competitiveness appear to be strongly linked. Frederick E. Church was obviously enchanted by both Katahdin and Mount Desert (Acadia) country, returning to it several times, bringing relatives and friends, and painting spectacular scenes of both from 1852 to 1865. Sometimes referred to as the dean of landscape painters of his period, Church's Acadian and Katahdin paintings are classics of the search for the sublime in nature.

Signature, identity, individuality, and distinctiveness of style are closely related to the artistic response and to sharing that response. It is both a way of identifying with the source of the inspiration as well as a vehicle for feedback from sharing. It is consistent with the complexity of emotions and the apparent contradictions expressed throughout these interviews. Volunteers often see their work as unique, as a representation of themselves, and even view trimming the brush alongside a trail, engaging in rock work to stabilize a mountain trail, building a water bar on a trail, or building a trail-marking cairn above tree line as a signature of their particular style. Don Curley, a very creative Acadia trail volunteer observes, *"If you can't write or paint, it's a way of expressing yourself."*

> *I believe that we are capable of creating a remarkable future for mankind.*
>
> —Paul Hawken

Part Two
CHANGING THE RULES

If parks have faltered in recent years in their quest to "preserve and protect for future generations," the failures certainly haven't been a result of flagging dedication. In fact dedication to park ideals is probably higher today than ever in response to the real source hobbling the parks—the continued failure to change the rules of the game to reflect new conditions. Our park assets are too essential to the nation's well-being to be handicapped by general fund restrictions, continuing budget resolution stalemates, cutbacks and closures as "nonessential services," and an antiquated view of the role of parks in society. Often buried in a natural resources bureaucracy, parks get viewed as "just another resource." Is it any wonder that their assets above and below ground are coveted for their cash value rather than being esteemed as cultural treasures? For parks to be able to discharge their mandates of public service for today and tomorrow, they need the freedom to experiment not just with fees but also with alternative ways of managing and protecting resources, contributions that are not countered by budget reductions, and partnerships of all kinds—all under a new system of accountability to match their freedoms and commensurate with the value of park assets. Rules that make park employees second-class citizens by constraining them from speaking out for their parks bespeak a level of fear that is unseemly in a democracy and inappropriate to the goal of parks and community. If parks are truly forever, they need to find ways around life's little annoyances—like the annual budget—and resist the constant pressures to reduce parks to an exercise in bean counting.

Paradox: If our public parks are truly a wellspring of creative energy, would we expect to ever find them:

- neglected?
- closed and empty?
- underfunded?
- short staffed?
- littered and dirty?
- cold and uninviting?
- vandalized?
- fenced and restricted?
- damaged?
- empty?
- old and outdated?

- unloved and forlorn?
- boring and bland?
- worn and tired?
- unresponsive?
- unfriendly?
- eroded and polluted?
- excessively regulated?
- poorly maintained?
- unimaginatively developed?
- irrelevant and uninteresting?
- taken for granted?

The Art of Park Management
Creative Management for Creative Settings

The chess board is the world... the rules of the game are
what we call the laws of Nature.

—Thomas Henry Huxley

Even in the intentionally colorless world of the bureaucracy, sparks of activism and creativity can flare up briefly, only to be damped down by the cautious and content. "Creative budgeting," for example, carries undertones of some secretive, self-serving act rather than a search for ways to stretch tax dollars. Small amounts of creative tinkering with the system are capable of unleashing disproportionate avalanches of resistance and ridicule. So, rashly proposing to discard the dominant paradigm by which we manage our parks is predictably open to brandings of *idealistic, utopian,* and *patently impractical.* But, it is already well under way. The rules and the rule makers are already changing!

Our public parks have long been managed under the same transactional paradigm used for selling shoes, sausages, and cell phones. The park's role in the transaction is reduced to that of an inanimate commodity being bargained over, complete with an implicit contract, agreed-upon rules and considerations received by both parties. The roles of management and visitor are simply to complete the transaction—abide by the rules and enjoy the park. Such a transactional paradigm, along with its attendant focus on buyers and sellers of services, results in park employees who see themselves as having only an incidental stake in the outcome of visits, and a vague feeling of having pimped the resource. Simultaneously, the transaction generates visitors having little or no stake in the long-term health of the park, but a sure belief in their having got the best bargain. All we ever really know for sure is that a transaction and a visit have occurred—a statistical success! From time to time we have attempted to generate qualitative measures of success, such as the proportion of "highly satisfied" visits, but, even here, the focus is invariably on the delivery of services.

What would happen if we were to shift the dominant paradigm away from service-centered transactions and toward relationships that are transformational? (see *Transactional and Transformational Parks*, p. 101). Wouldn't we expect to see changes in the focus, roles, and outcomes as we start transforming the way parks are viewed and experienced? When park managers become advocates for visits that are memorable, not merely satisfying; visits that connect to the land, not just use the land; visits that have the potential for changing lives, isn't management becoming vested in visitor experiences? And, isn't the park visitor becoming a stakeholder in the park's future? The magnitude of change is bound to be greatest in the outcomes, as we move from visits having a beginning and an end, to deeper understandings and continuing relationships—partnerships benefiting the park. While it may seem obvious that parks cannot function, cannot even survive, in the absence of visitors, the transactional approach clumsily gives a first impression of indifference to the uniqueness of the visitor. Dramatic changes in the public's concept of being in control of their leisure have evolved over the past two decades, but our parks have largely failed to evolve into something larger than just places to visit and add to the album. For park evolution to catch up, the impetus must come from managers who eagerly welcome visitors as allies to their cause, as vital to their own growth, and as fellow seekers in the search for fulfillment.

In examining the inspiration received from nature by artists, composers, writers, and photographers, much more is revealed than feelings about park landscapes and the importance of sharing their inspirational experiences. Artists often express their feelings about managing parks for inspirational benefits. Each of the six essential elements that all artists to some extent seem to share has a direct connection to how the park is being managed.

Capturing the Moment

"It's the moment, not the mountain" is a common theme. For the landscape photographer the moment—the perfect morning or evening light, shadows, wildlife activity, reflections, clouds, and other ephemeral visual components of the scene—provide an obvious *moment*. It is a fleeting experience mentioned by painters as well. Some of the highly creative park volunteers who have been interviewed also seem to seek to capture or relive the moments that inspired their volunteerism. For either artists or volunteers, if management restricts the hours that they can be "present for the event," they feel marginalized and their inspiration and creativity may suffer.

Beyond the Moment— It's the Experience

Dianne Eno, a creative dancer and artist in residence at Acadia National Park, described a moment in her troupe's performance on the summit of Mt. Monadnock in southwestern New Hampshire:

Transactional and Transformational Parks

Paradigm	Focus	Roles	Outcomes
Transactional	Providing public services	Visitor as buyer Manager as broker Park as object	Recreational experiences in parks
Transformational	Creating public benefits	Visitor as partner Manager as advocate Park as subject	Emotional connections to parks Appreciation for visitor diversity Park conditions no longer ignored Park benefits widely expanded.

A Few Indicators of Transformational Parks

- an experimental approach to park management
- community-sponsored programs in the park
- park-sponsored programs in the community
- varied and exciting learning opportunities throughout the park
- access and a sense of welcome to all levels of park administration
- an annual report in which statistics are secondary to the influence of visits
- a vibrant artist-in-residence program
- budding programs for scientists, writers, and musicians in-residence
- bilingual (at least) receptionists, greeters, and hosts
- minimal reliance on systems; maximum confidence in people
- a sister park in a Third World country
- high incidence of return visitation
- absence of employee burnout at the close of "the season"
- a "season" that never ends
- visits predominantly longer than planned
- the absence of deferred maintenance
- strategically placed visitor centers
- several roving nature guides for each one assigned to visitor centers
- numerous park friends, activists, cooperators, and partners
- a seamless approach to park boundaries and employee job descriptions
- park administrators and staff that get out of the office on a regular basis
- the absence of litter, litter baskets, iron rangers, and automatic gates
- gate handouts, about the park and about its friends, changing daily
- exciting opportunities for becoming involved in park goals and operations
- easy access to all park program venues
- broad involvement in neighboring communities by park employees
- at least a 1-to-1 ratio of volunteer hours to park employee hours
- a volunteer-generated park newsletter that is regularly disseminated
- state-of-the-art environmental management

At that one particular moment the sun broke through, and the dancers burst into tears, and the audience responded the same way. That was one of the most spellbinding moments that I can remember. Definitely a "ten."

And then there was this observation from Terrell S. Lester, landscape photographer, at Katahdin: *"Sometimes I just put away the tools, so that I can simply enjoy the experience myself with no thought of having to share it."* Artists expressed concern that park management seems to focus almost exclusively on the recreational visitors and their own interpretations of what those visitors want, with little understanding of the artistic and esthetic elements of a visit.

Beyond the Experience—It's the Spirit

Consider this observation from a landscape photographer writing in the Acadia artist-in-residence journal:

The sound of breakers rushing back to sea with what was once a wave creating a symphony of sea and land that captures the essence of timelessness. Witness that which has occurred for thousands of years and one can find themselves stepping back to a place of belonging.

Similarly, the following expression of an almost transcendental nature comes from an interview with one of Acadia's many landscape painters:

And then there are times when the experience evaporates into a profound sense of the landscape and its history, the first people to sail into Frenchman's Bay at Acadia, or even beyond that into the prehistory of geologic time.

Artists express concern that such experiences are likely to become increasingly rare with the park's growing popularity at all hours of the day and during all seasons.

Sharing the Moment

Sharing the moment, or at least sharing the opportunity for similar moments, was common to all of the artists interviewed. There would be little point to the capture of moments if sharing were not the expected outcome, but the sharing seems to be vastly more than "show and tell." It is also the validation of effort. From the sale of images and the publication of recordings and books to the recognition of volunteer efforts and teaching excellence, the sharing seems to provide a source of approbation and feedback that may be vital for the creative process. What the artists seek is the recognition that their products are as vital to the park and its goals of stewardship and preservation as recreational visits, if not more so.

Caring and Concern

Not surprisingly, concern for the park landscape is a repeated theme in every interview with creative people. It would be easy (and erroneous) to assume that volunteer creativity reflects a more caring attitude than does commercial photography. While income may be an overriding concern for many struggling artists, it is revealing and satisfying to discover how many artists also volunteer their time to supplement park staff and freely donate their works in support of park causes. Caring is also a powerful motive for many of the volunteers who continue to do strenuous tasks well into their retirement. Caring is often the identifying characteristic of park employees. It's a natural partnership—one that needs to be nurtured—stewarded by park management.

Essential Conflict

Every artist and every creative volunteer alluded to a degree of conflict they experienced, expected, and somehow enjoyed in the process of their creative expression. Perhaps "creative tension" is a more appropriate description for wanting to keep the moment private and yet share the experience. Feelings of wanting to experience the moment for one's self while having to capture it for others can be opposing forces. Consider the tensions contained in the following:

> ...finding your own artistic identity within the landscape, yet having another identity uniquely your own; sharing the moment, yet needing to protect the site from too many others visiting it and perhaps spoiling it; reveling in the freedom of the moment, yet needing to capture it; being humbled by the scene, yet hoping to become identified with it.

Volunteers frequently express a deep-seated conflict with park visitors who are uncaring about their environment as well as a sense of conflict with the bureaucracy that administers the parks. And yet they continue to volunteer. Park management deals with conflict in many ways every day. Most managers would probably admit that while difficult, conflict resolution is a necessary and even rewarding part of the job.

Some Implications for Park Management

The language of inspiration, as shared by artists, volunteers and teachers, should resonate strongly with the park professionals who have devoted their careers and their lives to caring for these places. The very language creative people use resonates with the reasons for choosing park management as a profession. They mirror the expectations that park managers have of their visitors, and they vividly articulate why parks exist. Creative management should feel challenged to find an expanded role for creative people to play on the park stage.

Creative People as Park Visitors

Because of their intensity, creative people provide an opportunity for an in-depth look at a common phenomenon—inspiration—and to learn from it. If you are a geneticist, you probably prefer to study something that reproduces intensely, once every 20 hours, rather than once every 20 years. If you are a seismologist, you want to work where the earthquake activity is most intense. If you want to understand activism, you prefer to study the crusader rather than the dilettante. In the same way, if you are interested in emotional connections to the land, you can probably learn a lot about everyone's needs for re-creation by studying those who feel these connections most intensely and are best able to articulate and act on those feelings.

Creative People as Park "Staff"

Dianne Eno feels that park administrators need to have a chance

> to see everything in their park anew, through the artist's eyes…
> that's what's rich about having artists in the park. It allows you
> to have completely new perspectives, and sometimes remedies
> for problems come through from that new perspective.

Perhaps we should not just be looking at these people as volunteer cheerleaders for parks but also invite them into our staff meetings and planning sessions.

Painters, composers, writers, volunteers, and teachers would bring much more than their art to staff discussions. Would not the presence of creative people increase staff creativity and enhance their satisfaction with their jobs? Wouldn't interacting with artists help increase staff sensitivity to the public as individuals rather than as masses? Yet, how are parks treating this extended staff? Do they welcome them and their insights, or do they see them as simply commercial artists who should probably be required to have a permit? While the distinction between commercial art and "the arts" is admittedly vague, I doubt that composers, writers, and poets would be expected to have a permit even though they too sell their products.

Creative People as Research Subjects

How does primary inspiration from nature to the artist, teacher, or volunteer differ from secondary inspiration from their creative works to the broader public? What are some creative outcomes of this "secondary inspiration?" Do primary and secondary inspiration breed creativity among people who do not consider themselves "creative?" How does the inspiration to share directly through volunteerism and teaching differ from the inspiration to share indirectly through art? How does the inspiration to preserve nature differ from the inspiration to develop nature? How can we build an ethical foundation to protect the inspirational resource and still be able to compete with the development ethic? Doesn't park management need to understand its creative clientele better before developing resources in ways that might diminish the inspirational potential? Are public hearings enough to insure a full range of concerns?

Creative People as Indicators of Park Health and Vigor

While creative people are seemingly unique, their inspirations may not be. You only need listen to the clicking of three-dozen cameras and indrawn breaths when the vans unload at the top of Cadillac Mountain in Maine, or Mt. Evans in Colorado, or Mt. Washington in New Hampshire to realize that we are all inspired by the spectacular in nature. What is different is the ways that creative people see nature, their responses to it, and their styles of sharing the experience. To the extent that we compromise the experience for them, we compromise it for all. Like the miner's canary, creative people can be management's indicators of a healthy park environment, but only if management has a relationship with them.

If we overmanage, bureaucratize, and overdevelop the outdoors, creative people will be the first to know and to react. When looking for public reaction to our development plans, the concerns of creative people may very well be a threshold to which we need to be alert. When do pressures for increased development compromise creativity? If we can accept deferred maintenance as a park norm, why not accept deferred development until we can be sure that we are not making a mistake?

Many artists comment on the productive settings that they find in parks. How can we avoid damaging those settings? Aren't these same productive settings just as important for the stockbroker, the teacher, and the sales clerk? What is the connection between productive settings, life changing experiences, and management's actions? When do visitor numbers begin to reduce the quality of individual visits, and how is it most likely to first become evident? How can we avoid overmanaging creative people? Volunteerism is a form of creative expression. Are we sometimes overmanaging to the point of destroying the experience and turning away our most creative and valued volunteers?

Creativity as a Product of Parks

Many creative people have alluded to park experiences as being turning points in their careers. To what extent do we see parks as life-fulfilling potentials— or parks as catalysts for change? Parks for *re-creation* may need to be managed quite differently than parks for *recreation*.

Many parks close their gates without exception (well, maybe they open them for VIPs) at certain times of the year. Perhaps these are the times that are best-suited for many creative people to visit—when the distractions are minimal and the range of light is greatest? Do we try to make exceptions for the very people who can best help us to achieve our goals? Do we honor that special vision of the donors and founders of our parklands through the quality of experiences or through numbers of visitors?

Should we, perhaps, consider a revised annual report format focused on quality of experience, of life, of lives changed, of the resource itself? If quantities of visits, programs, income, and protected acres must take center stage, we should at least consider appending one or two narrative testimonials of quality experiences. Should park management ground its philosophies of the *limits of acceptable change* in terms that reflect inspiration and develop some inspirational indices? As one well-known artist said

> Emotions cannot be calibrated, cannot be measured, cannot be computerized. To me, the wilderness that I have seen, provided me with an ingredient that I hadn't experienced before, a very special kind of inspiration.

I cannot help but believe that very same inspiration, available every day to park managers, could not fail to provide the creative management that is the key to sustainable park benefits. Perhaps the creative act could be as simple as bringing the unbending legislative budget committee out to experience the inspiration. I wonder, has anyone ever thought of creating a park's friends group made up solely of budget committee members' spouses?

This I Believe about Parks
The Belief-to-Action Connection

*A thing is good if it tends to preserve the integrity, stability, and
beauty of the biotic community and wrong if it tends otherwise.*
— Aldo Leopold

More than a half-century in print and still required reading for all who consider
themselves conservationists or environmentalists, Aldo Leopold's simple
definition of a *land ethic* is anything but simple in practice. It is memorable
not solely for its simplicity, but also for its *believability*. It simply makes sense.
If we closely examine the implicit beliefs of the park profession we would
find that they too simply make sense, and yet we are no closer to adopting a
national ethic for parks than we are to embracing Leopold's sensible land ethic.
In fact, it might be argued that the adoption of a land ethic presupposes the
existence of at least a few component ethics for parks, wildlife, water, soils,
and forests.

Why have we made so little progress on good sense? The answer may
lie in relying too heavily on the fact that parks (like a land ethic) do in fact
make good sense, while they fail to widely share their underlying foundations.
Just maybe, in a world dominated by science, we have been a little reluctant
to present our beliefs without the buttress of scientific proof.

What are the fundamental beliefs about parks — those truisms that bind
us together as a profession? To promote them requires that we state them and
not just believe them. The fact that most if not all of our beliefs about parks
can be scientifically tested for their validity is probably irrelevant, the power
of science notwithstanding. What becomes impossible to ignore in any examination of park beliefs is their cumulative power and their overwhelming good
sense.

A few common beliefs about the benefits of parks are that

- People need parks.

- Parks contribute to personal well-being and to public health.

- Parks are essential reservoirs of biodiversity.

- Parks have economic benefits for a community and a nation.

- Parks are important sources of inspiration and creativity.

- Parks contribute beauty to our lives.

- Parks strengthen a nation by preserving its heritage.

- Parks are a part of the intangible American spirit.

- Parks help purify polluted air and water.

- Parks are places of peace and understanding.

- Parks add quality to our lives—even if we never visit them.

A few common beliefs about park management are that

- Management seeks to reflect exemplary environmental ethics.

- Management is concerned with visitor satisfaction and safety.

- Management minimizes today's impacts to better meet tomorrow's demands.

- Management seeks to improve the quality of public use.

- Management values partnerships with communities, visitors, and supporters.

- Management is highly committed to preserving park resources.

- Management has environmental concerns extending beyond park borders.

A few common beliefs about park visitors are that

- Park visitors will use a park respectfully if they know the norms.

- Park visitors will financially support their parks given the opportunity.

- Park visitors have at least a vague sense of their ownership of public parks.

- Park visitors highly value their parks and their park experiences.

- Park visitors expect and believe their parks to be well-managed.

- Park visitors will respond to threats to the integrity of their parks.

- Park visitors are "loving their parks to death."

Such an impressive list of beliefs makes understandable how easily we have come to take parks and land for granted. With so many beliefs converging in one place (e.g., the park, the park agency, the park profession), the normal assumption might be that parks are too important to be neglected and unprotected. Complacency is a very logical outcome of such a pervasive belief system and may even provide an element of resistance toward changes in park system operations. However, unless the beliefs are periodically aired and reviewed, complacency may and often does result in significant slippage between beliefs and reality. For example, pick any one of the above two-dozen beliefs and ask what is being done in support of that belief. If parks are important sources of inspiration and creativity, why do we have so few park programs in support of the arts, the sciences, and the humanities? If management cherishes its partnerships, why are there not more affiliations with groups that could expand the role of parks and their constituency? And if parks promote peace and understanding, why do we not have major programs of building border parks and peace parks as billboards for our desire for world peace?

The Belief-Action Connection

The slippage between beliefs and reality deserves as much professional attention as is given to research on the believed benefits of parks, simply because those beliefs already guide park practice. The potential for professional action is clearly evident in the above list of beliefs. Demonstrating beliefs is a matter of self-interest for any profession. The medical profession displays its creed of "First do no harm" in every physician's office. The dental profession takes a public stand on fluoridation to avoid cavities. The legal profession requires pro bono involvement in support of "equal justice for all." The park profession promotes park visits because it believes in the benefits of those visits.

The connection between beliefs and action is commonly expressed as policy. We have broad public policies in support of parkland acquisition, maintenance, and programs because we believe that parks are necessary in a functioning society, and because the profession overseeing those park programs has strong beliefs about how parks can best serve society, a secondary level of policy emerges. Traditionally, that level of policy is expressed in terms of a budget. Despite decades of short budgets, those professional beliefs remain strong and have led to myriad extra-budget policies encouraging volunteerism, partnerships, cooperation, corporate underwriting of programs, adoption of park facilities and entire parks in a seemingly endless array of combinations. It is important to realize that the power of our beliefs successfully assaults budgetary limitations and not the power of tools such as partnerships.

Putting our beliefs to work for parks can be viewed less as a battle of the budget if it is viewed as a campaign for constituency in which public support is critical. The belief that our "parks are being loved to death" by the public misrepresents that public. In fact, our parks are being used exactly as their founders meant them to be. What those founders did not expect was management that fails to address park needs with the same fervor and passion that they brought to creating the parks. Why is it so hard to believe that those hordes of visitors are the park profession's strongest ally? Could it be possible that as the role of park science has expanded, the role of park beliefs has diminished? Perhaps in a world dominated by science, in the field of natural resources where science has been so powerful, and in the pursuit of defensible public policy we have been overly cautious in not pointing out that our beliefs really do not need scientific corroboration. If so, that would be unfortunate since the belief system that gave us public parks was never intended to be justified by the weight of scientific evidence. It was expected to be defended, however, because it *just makes sense*.

> *The best time to do something for a child is 100 years before it is born.*
>
> —ancient Chinese proverb

Ethics and the Health of Public Park Systems

*All ethics rest upon a single premise: that the individual is a
member of a community of interdependent parts.*

—Aldo Leopold

It would be a mistake to assume that our dedicated public parks are somehow immune from the post-Enron tide of skepticism that is so destructive to public trust in our institutions. Investment brokers and accounting firms deal only with financial assets. Our park systems are entrusted with something vastly more precious—the very symbols of our heritage. The push for increased public-private partnerships, combined with every park system's "chronic wasting disease," could easily spotlight a broad array of stewardship lapses, maintenance deferrals, and accountability oversights.

Park administrators are much less likely to get caught up in what has been popularly referred to as our "National Ethics Crisis" if they are sensitive to the distinction between ethical and legal guidelines. In arenas of high public trust where financial accounting is not sufficient, the public expects a higher standard than simple compliance with the law. The public has every right to expect that its park assets are being managed in an "extra-legal" manner. As owners, they might logically assume that their parks, historic sites, and natural areas are being managed at the cutting edge of science for the benefit of future generations. If not exactly at the cutting edge, the public at least would like to believe that its parks are not contributing to the very environmental degradation that they were created to protect.

A concerned public also likes to think that the health of its parks is being monitored and that candid assessments of park conditions are being generated to support essential budget increases. Monitoring and reporting of park conditions are two fundamental best management practices that help to define professionalism in park stewardship while lending assurance that parks are being managed a notch or two above the bare minimum of the statutory requirements.

If a park system does no research or monitoring of its assets, operates in the absence of professional stewardship standards, subscribes to no generally accepted best management practices and fails to provide meaningful accountability reports on a timely basis, is that system ethically bankrupt? The answer to that question may depend upon whether these are the profession's norms. Is that same park system perhaps ethically naïve and likely to be challenged by a concerned public? Of course it is. The assumption that healthy sustainable parks are simply a matter of complying with the letter of the law is no more valid than assuming that healthy communities will emerge by simply observing zoning laws.

Paradox is the nature of public service in parks. Mandates are routinely underfunded and sometimes not funded at all. Protectors of priceless park assets have become the bottom feeders in the public budget tank. Mission and goal statements invariably set the bar at levels that park professionals aspire to, but in doing so they open the door to criticisms, accusations, and condemnations when they fail. Restraints on employee activism on behalf of the mission are more real than imagined, contributing to the pressure-cooker atmosphere where whistle-blowing is schizophrenically condemned internally and welcomed from outside the organization. Like any corporation, public park systems survive as much on public trust as on performance. As a result of today's increased scrutiny and skepticism, park systems cannot tell their stockholders to simply "trust us." That trust must be earned, which happens by being candid about park conditions, ethical guidelines, values, and issues of park management. That demonstration requires the same level of candor that any good physician uses in interpreting a patient's condition and prognosis.

Ethics are band-aids that we apply in the absence of an overarching ethic. If a broadly based outdoor ethic existed, there would be little need for such stopgap ethics as Leave No Trace, Carry In–Carry Out, Tread Lightly, or any of a dozen other remedial surrogates for generations of poor outdoor training. Building a comprehensive outdoor ethic—one that is as widely understood as an education ethic or a savings ethic—should be the major concern of every parks-related profession and the powerful recreation equipment industry whose products need public lands. It is doubtful that an overarching ethic could happen without their support. Credibility is the linkage between the ethics of park visitors and those of park administrators. Visitors cannot be expected to embrace any greater level of stewardship than that demonstrated by the park itself. They may not know the name of the disease, but they know when their park looks starved and tired. They also may not be able to prescribe the right medicine, but they can sense when their park's health is declining, and they should stop having to bear the burden of blame for "loving their parks to death." There needs to be an assumed contract between visitors, land managers, and equipment suppliers. That contract is a shared outdoor ethic— the foundation for a meaningful partnership.

We can have an outdoor ethic. It can happen in some remote future by taking the form of a legislative mandate provoked by a crisis in park conditions, or enlightened self-interest on the part of the stakeholders in our public lands can produce it now. It can grow over a generation or two by focusing exclusively on education, or it can emerge "full-grown" as an implied "visitor contract" subscribed to by all who use our public lands as a condition of that use. Such an agreement might address responsibilities for stewardship, avoidance and acceptance of risk, subsidized use, equity of access, resource accountability, participation in planning and management, limits and restrictions on use, and responsiveness to changing public demands. While a reversal of the tragedy of the commons is implicit in such an agreement, its goal is a much more modest redefinition of "stewardship"—one that links rights and responsibilities to the use of public lands.

The natural resource management professions are the logical places to encourage such an ethic. Corrine Gilb, in *Hidden Hierarchies: The Professions and Government,* describes the professionals in agencies as persons wielding considerable though often inconspicuous power. It seems reasonable that the park management professions must take the lead in developing ethical guidelines and in helping to resolve ethical dilemmas in park management. These are the people most likely to experience the challenges and to have the strongest needs. Professions can serve as clearinghouses for the discussion of ethical dilemmas, questions, cases, and formulation of guidelines. The professions are logical sponsors of surveys to determine their members' shared ethical values, allegiances, and concerns.

So universal as to be almost invisible, ethical values cling like shadows to every aspect of park administration. Ethics provide an unseen guide to the development of partnerships; the setting of fees; the enforcement of rules; the priorities of the budget; the implementation of plans; the role of volunteers; the level of reporting candor, closures, contracting, maintenance scheduling, information services, publicity, interpretation, and every kind of personnel action. Given this pervasiveness, it is remarkable that formal ethical training is largely absent in most park systems and ethical guidelines are reduced to periodic, routine, form-letter reminders. Have we simply presumed the existence of shared values in order to avoid conflicts over ethical positions that are likely to be lose-lose battles?

The assumption of shared values seems cavalier when public assets are at issue. For illustrative purposes only, consider the range (and potential conflicts) among ethical values that can impinge on a "simple" park-planning decision about appropriate levels of development. The democratic ethic insists that the public's preference, or at least the majority, should prevail. The professional ethic calls for colleague consensus. The scientific ethic demands an impact analysis, or at least a call to err on the conservative side. The service ethic may encourage a decision that errs on the liberal side. The architectural ethic will seek beauty over capacity. The engineering ethic sees it as a design-reinforcement question. The organizational ethic will push for advancing the agency agenda. The land ethic will want to make sure it does not damage the integrity of the biotic community. The advancement ethic will seek the boss's position. We haven't even considered economies of scale, shifting markets, and sacred sites.

Remarkably, this potential for chaos works itself out. It works in this example because the different disciplines with their different ethics are focused. There is a mandate and there will be a development plan. There may even be an Adam Smith–like "invisible hand" at work to find common ground. Now, lift this mix out of the planning room and move it to the boardroom. Replace the mandate with a "desirable"—a policy change to improve public involvement or a more equitable distribution of a diminishing budget. The setting has changed, the mandate is less clear, and the invisible hand seems to have been left on the other side of the door. The stakes are higher, the cost of error is much higher and much more personal, and power emerges. It happens subtly, but it is there.

The process of finding common ground in the schoolyard between competing ethics of team and individual, fairness and winning, learning and doing are not particularly elegant. All of the ethics are legitimate. We may not always like the solution, but a sometimes shaky common ground emerges in the form of a respectful hierarchy of ethical values. The weaker players get to play once the outcome is no longer in doubt. We tend to support the policies and practices that reinforce several ethical positions. For example, we like individual volunteerism because it is both conservative and progressive, cost-effective, democratic, personalized, and adaptable. Yet we are wary of corporate volunteerism even though it has the same values because it might compromise the overriding ethics of control and identity. However, since we really admire a science ethic, a hierarchical solution emerges by making the corporate relationship "experimental." We manage to resolve major dilemmas of stewardship dollars for the future versus public service dollars for today through an overriding ethical value called *compromise*.

Compromise is an ethic. What's different today is that the old paradigms, not only the operational models and compromises but also the very foundations of public park philosophy, are being challenged. What is a "park" for today's needs? What do we expect from our parks? If parks help to define who we are as individuals and as a people, then they must be more than pleasuring grounds and preserves. Is a park still a park when visible deterioration makes a lie of the stated park mission? Even more to the point, can the problems created by the existing park paradigm ever be resolved within that paradigm? Clearly the search for common ground among competing ethics has been working, if not always perfectly. It is just as clear that if we continue to ignore the need for discussing ethics then it will be at the real cost of park health and future benefits. Will past processes continue to be appropriate in a future that is increasingly skeptical and critical of values that compromise a park's integrity? Is there perhaps a better, more transparent way to deal with the hidden hierarchy of ethics? Perhaps we must wait for an overarching outdoor ethic. In the meantime we can at least implement a set of best management practices so that our ethical dilemmas can rally around the common ground of healthy parks and the sustained flow of benefits from healthy park systems.

The powerful ethic of sharing is what created parks. It's why most of us visit parks and why we interpret parks. It is the basis for professional association. Why not allow sharing to be the operational ethic for keeping parks healthy? It is through sharing our best management practices with each other, sharing our stewardship responsibilities with the visiting public, sharing the facts about park conditions with their owners, and sharing the broad range of park successes with every possible source of support that the "healthy park" ethic can become a reality.

A Question of Ethics?

- Do parks have an ethical responsibility to be environmental leaders?

- Do parks have an "attractive nuisance" responsibility for the blight outside their borders in response to the park's mass appeal?

- When is the failure to preserve and protect park assets simply an "ethical lapse," an abdication of responsibility, or malfeasance?

- Do (Should) the park-related ethical values of prospective employees play a role in park employment practices?

- What competing ethical concerns lead to setting the level of park fees, and is the mix shifting?

- Are there issues where compromise is not as appropriate as the determining ethical position? What are they?

- What are the ethical constraints, in terms of shared responsibilities, on creating partnerships?

- Is accountability being ethically short-circuited by policies for controlling the content and timing of reports?

- The good neighbor ethic requires employee involvement in community problems, but can that ethically be required of all employees?

- What are the ethical limits on managing wilderness? When are wilderness areas no longer wild because of management intervention?

- Are park closures an ethical response to budget cuts?

- How do we resolve the ethical dilemma between numbers of visitors and the quality of visits?

- Is there an ethical distinction between employee advocacy and employee activism for parks?

The Carry-Out, Leave-No-Trace, Tread Lightly, Litter-Free World of Parks

A long habit of not thinking a thing is wrong gives it a super-ficial appearance of being right.

—Thomas Paine

In the beginning when Man, in awe of the wonders of Nature, created the first park, he made a fire ring to cook his meals, a picnic table upon which to eat them, a place to park his vehicle, a conveniently located facility, and oh yes, a barrel in which to place his trash. All of this was done to consecrate the site and to make it more comfortable to enjoy the wonders.

The people came, and came, and came, and the barrel filled to overflowing. Crows and seagulls visited the barrel, looking for gifts, and lightened its load. Skunks and raccoons, sensing fine treats in the barrel, knocked it over and further lightened its load. The now-battered barrel did not smell nice, so people lit fires in it. Someone rolled the barrel down the hill into the creek where it emptied its load and stayed.

Now people left their trash in the fire ring, as a courtesy for the next visitors to more easily start their fire; and nature's creatures visited the fire ring and spread the trash in search of the food they had learned was there. Even-tually a new barrel, one made with wire mesh for better air circulation, was installed and chained to a tree so that it couldn't migrate to the creek. The holes in the wire mesh made it easier for the chipmunks, squirrels, and little birds to get in and out of the barrel. The people continued to come, and well you get the picture! Litter in the park is there because it is encouraged by the countless, conveniently spaced, sometimes quaintly painted barrels. It is hard to appreciate the wonders of Nature when Nature has been adorned with the discards of thousands of earlier pilgrimages. What began as a consecration became the first step in a desecration of nature.

In recent years, parks have initiated major campaigns to remove the trash barrels, eliminate the litter, and change the ways in which visitors use their parks. The new ethics of *Carry In–Carry Out, Leave No Trace,* and *Tread Lightly* have been largely embraced by an appreciative public as long overdue. And while we are still in a period of transition between a "service" ethic and a "responsibility" ethic in our public parks, it is probably safe to declare the experiment a success. It would also be nice to conclude that the experiment was initiated by ideals nobler than simply reducing the enormous solid waste disposal bills that parks assumed over the past several generations—ideals such as appropriateness, avoidance of damage to wildlife, and building responsibility among visitors. However, there is scant evidence to support such an assumption in the form of acknowledging the mistake and examining other park management norms for similar practices that lead to a diminishing of, rather than a strengthening of, park values and personal responsibility.

Because the litter mistake is a powerful and expensive lesson for park management, it would be a shame not to use it to the fullest extent as a continued self-examination of how well our practices match our policies, our ideals, and our goals. It might be equally instructive to examine other "services," such as lifeguards and park police, in places where encouraging personal responsibility may be the more appropriate practice. It seems difficult to unquestioningly accept the idea that parks are committed to public service when the almost universal norm of deferring maintenance will inevitably lead to future costs that are a huge disservice to future generations, dwarfing the relatively modest savings that flow from litter-free parks.

Prior to the advent of Leave No Trace, parks commonly advocated an ethic of "Take Only Pictures—Leave Only Footprints," an evocative message for how to care for your park. In fact, there is a world of anecdotal evidence and even some observational studies showing that permanent damage to fragile trailside vegetation results from the footprints of photographers searching for just the right angle for a shot of the children in the foreground of a spectacular view, not to mention the litter from discarded film wrappers. "Leave Only Footprints" for the person with a camera seems to be almost a license to ignore the much more important message of "Stay on the Trail." Given the fact that relatively few visitors take anything from a park, such a message seems to suggest that theft is a major problem while condoning footprints at a level that today's Leave No Trace ethic would find unacceptable. Again the behavioral norms are in a state of transition, but success here is a little more difficult to predict. Digital cameras will certainly reduce film-related litter, but the powerful persuasive force of taking even more pictures to get it "just right" could mean even more damage by photographers who are unmindful of where they are stepping.

If Tread Lightly is a good maxim for park visitors, it is an even better one for park planners and administrators. Damage done by park visitors can often be mitigated by imposing limits on visitation, but the damage done as a result of misguided planning and management is likely to be irreversible or at least enormously expensive to correct. Park managers, like all of us, have a tendency to look at problems in terms of finding vertical solutions. It is difficult to believe that what we are doing could be wrong, particularly if it might have been right in an earlier and simpler era. We tend to seek solutions via the "get a bigger hammer" approach: Put out more trash barrels, chain the barrels, make the barrels attractive and fun, increase the fines for littering and vandalism, and increase the police presence. Not only do we often create our own problems, we just as often end up aggravating them.

At a seacoast park in New Hampshire that had once been a coastal defense site riddled with underground bunkers and tunnels, management had problems with vandals and troublemakers living in the old fortifications and surprising park visitors. Muggings and attacks were feared, so bulldozers were brought in to close up all the known entrances. It was a relatively simple matter for the same miscreants to tunnel back into their old haunts and continue their objectionable activities. More heavy equipment returned to place huge boulders over the bulldozed entrances, and once again, tunneling around the boulders proved to be no more a challenge. Finally, management seized on the idea of spraying a liquid cement coating a few inches thick over the entire mess, which of course also failed. The cement could easily be broken up and moved. The continued vertical search for solutions, already in the tens of thousands of dollars, might have led to spreading grease on the cement or maybe flood-lighting the ugliness that had been created. Fortunately a change in management resulted in a little creative, horizontal thinking and solved the problem. The relatively simple solution, now made much more expensive, was to open the fortifications up, clean them up, and interpret them to all visitors. In short, turning the park's negative into a positive attraction—filling the park with good visitors to drive out the bad was successful. How we look at problems clearly makes a difference in how we solve them, and the first step in that process is an assessment of whose problem it is. In this case it was a problem of management's limited park vision.

Instances of park administrations not treading lightly are well-known in most park systems, usually in the form of overdevelopment of sites, inappropriate facilities, overzealous attempts to assure total visitor safety, and mismanagement of park wildlife. With today's requirements for greater public involvement in park planning, such errors are far less likely to happen. However, the guideline of erring on the side of conservatism still seems to offer an excellent fail-safe for any agency charged with the sometimes conflicting missions of long-term stewardship of public assets and service to today's visitors.

The concept of providing layers of protection, such as multiple designations, for our protected lands and heritage sites suggests that additional safeguards might well be an appropriate way of assuring that park administration, which is so often subject to political pressures, will make decisions consistent with long-term stewardship. For example, the planning requirements for public involvement and environmental impact analysis could be expanded to include other administrative functions such as budgeting, staffing, and policymaking. To the extent that the stewardship of a park's assets is strikingly similar to the stewardship of a museum's treasures, it might make contemporary sense to move park agencies out of their historic homes in natural resource departments where decisions are pressured by in-park interests and give them the kinds of protection that characterize cultural resource management. After all, the entire park is a cultural resource, not just its historic elements.

While it may still seem visionary to some, the carry in–carry out, leave no trace, tread lightly, litter-free world of parks is a logical evolutionary step in America's public park movement. Its lack of universality today in no way diminishes its reality for tomorrow. We need only to look at the evolution of fees, interpretive services, and development standards to know that the way the public views and uses its public lands is changing. All of this collectively means that our public lands ethic is growing, and it is growing in a positive direction of greater public interest and responsibility for these priceless assets. Such growth, warmly welcomed by the park management profession, must also be matched by new approaches to its leadership role for parks. The adoption of a set of best management practices would be one such new approach— but, that's another subject!

I believe that a friend of mine had it right when he said that one of our principle jobs in life is to leave the campsite cleaner than when we found it.

—Sam Daley-Harris

Parks and Simplicity
The Shrinking Outdoor Recreation Opportunity Spectrum

Our life is frittered away by details: simplify, simplify, simplify.
—Henry David Thoreau

To what extent should our public parks promote simple living rather than catering to every changing mood and trend in society? It seems axiomatic that parks exist to provide refuge from the noise and the clamor for attention that typifies modern society, yet we seem to find that gradually those same social "ills" inevitably show up in the park. Public campgrounds now provide electricity at many campsites, allowing us to have our televisions and our toasters in the "wild" along with our Internet connections, water connections, and sewer connections. Rather than struggle with the hardships of the great outdoors, modern camping has truly become a home away from home, complete with the very same computer games, microwaves, hair dryers, and espresso machines that we might once have hoped to escape. Cell phones have invaded the wilderness, and the roar of off-road vehicles shatters many pristine settings that were once a refuge where humans could get reacquainted with their public lands and its wild residents.

From the vantage of hindsight, it is obvious that the ideals of simplicity and knowing the land became victims to the much more powerful forces of marketing and convenience. The joys of sitting around an eye-watering campfire and scouring blackened pots and pans just couldn't compete. Slapping mosquitoes and slogging along rain-soaked trails are easy to "edit out" of a virtual outdoor experience sandwiched in between eighty-seven other choices on our laptops in the air-conditioned motor home. But what else may have gotten lost along the way? the discovery of our own abilities? the chance to see a real live eagle catching a fish? the satisfaction of total physical exhaustion after a daylong hike? the ability to know a bit of geography personally, if only for a while, and to know that it is yours? However, if we fail to provide the comforts and conveniences, many people might never bother to have even a watered-down experience with the outdoors, and lacking that experience, they might never come to its defense when it is threatened by neglect.

To a large extent we have rationalized our role to one of providing an array of outdoor experiences that are, in the words of park professionals, a "spectrum of recreation opportunities." That spectrum, which ranges from urban parks to remote wilderness area is a good idea in theory but has never been given the sanction of mandated policy. Without that clear mandate, the gradual creep that converts a roadless experience to one with road access can only continue. Without the force of the approved policy of a legislated mandate, the spectrum can only shrink toward standardization in response to the seemingly endless demands of marketing and convenience.

Over the past several years, I have been involved in a number of litigations from Maine to Alaska where someone was injured during a recreational outing on public lands. Invariably, the plaintiff's lawyer introduces an expert witness from the urban end of the spectrum in an attempt to suggest that those common practices should extend to all public lands and be accepted as the professional norm with the failure to do so being deemed negligence. The common practice of having lifeguards at urban pools and beaches, for example, is much less universal at designated swimming areas in state and national outdoor recreation areas and is almost nonexistent at backcountry sites on public land. Were we to have a single court-imposed standard of common practice, the spectrum of recreation opportunities in America would suffer a severe blow.

Resource managers recognize seven distinct categories of recreational settings in the spectrum: primitive, semi-primitive nonmotorized, semi-primitive motorized, natural without roads, natural with roads, rural, and urban. Textbook descriptions of each of these leave little doubt that the management prescriptions for any one of these categories must necessarily be quite different from all the others, and the elimination of any single category would drastically reduce the number and types of opportunities available to the public. Probably no other concept gets to the heart of what outdoor recreation resource management is all about as well as the opportunity spectrum because it blends the needs of visitors with the needs of sustaining the resource's ability to satisfy those visitors.

Preservation of a range of choices for visitors—a spectrum of outdoor recreation opportunities—should not become a matter of default based on the location or jurisdiction of recreational resources. Urban park and recreation administrations ought to be able to offer a spectrum of opportunities to their clientele, but this can only happen through the park profession's endorsement of the public having choices. In short, if the de facto range of choices were to be legislatively protected in the same way that the resources themselves have been protected, much confusion would disappear. In making the opportunity spectrum a matter of policy, not only is the agency better able to defend its practices but also the number of court cases would probably decline as people become aware that their choices have personal consequences.

Without such protection, the recreation administrator might lose a small amount of administrative discretion, but the recreating public could be faced with a significant loss of choice. It would therefore seem to be an ethical responsibility as well as matter of self-interest for the recreation profession to monitor and report threats to that spectrum. The obvious question then is: "Where are those threats most likely to arise?" While the possibility of adverse court decisions requiring a change in practice might seem to be a major threat, the outdoor recreation management profession itself is probably the biggest single source of spectrum decline through both inappropriate development and the failure to defend the spectrum in the face of litigation.

There is probably no recreation management concept that is more subject to challenge, and rightfully so, than that of "appropriateness." In the early decades of park system management, the policy of appropriate development was the major buttress against pressures to develop public parks in ways that were patently inconsistent with the park designation, such as placing water slides in a natural park in an attempt to boost attendance revenues and, ultimately, appropriations. As park management moved into the late twentieth century, requirements for public involvement in park planning meant appropriateness could no longer go undefined. Decisions on appropriate kinds and levels of development are no longer to be made in the mind of the administrator—and rightfully so if we hope to avoid the changing definitions that invariably accompany changing administrations.

The park and recreation profession has ethical responsibilities for preserving choices and for interpreting the consequences of those choices for participants. However, interpreting the consequences of choices is hardly the same as assuming full responsibility for visitor safety. Park management is committed to rewarding and satisfying visits; unsafe behaviors can diminish the chances of such visits. Making known the hazards of visitation and participation is a generally accepted role of park management, but parks' role in eliminating hazards to make a safer environment is not that easy to define. Natural hazards are part of a park's attraction. Manmade hazards might conceivably fall into that same category if the attraction is an abandoned coastal fort or an abandoned mine. Visitor awareness of the hazards of old forts and abandoned mines might be equivalent to that of park management's, but visitor knowledge and appreciation of those hazards could be significantly less.

Both the appropriateness of different levels of resource development and the appropriateness of different levels of visitor services are directly linked to the continued availability of a broad spectrum of outdoor recreation opportunities for the public. In both instances, the ethical concerns of management deserve the support of a legislated mandate to preserve those opportunities.

The Language of Public Finance
A True Parks Confession

*Change is the most powerful law of Nature. You can never
plan the future by the past.*

               —Edmund Burke

Much of my first year as a guardian of the public's parks was spent in learning
the language of the guardians of the public's treasury.

It was a rough year.

Languages were never my strong suit and this was to be a crash course
in code words. *Appropriations* are not really appropriated, budgets are not
really operating plans, and increases are often smoke and mirrors. *You're just
going to have to learn to do more with less* is not meant as an encouragement
to be creative. It is an emphatic slamming of the power door, dismissive of
reconsideration, which leaves no room to respectfully point out that parks had
pioneered the concept of doing more with less decades ago. But blunt and
honest code words may actually be kinder than the empty euphemisms, such
as *Next year will be better, Just be patient,* and *Everybody's taking a hit,* all of
which were untrue but at least were cordial. The bald-faced, arrogant untruths,
which are meant to be off-putting, actually display a remarkable flair for
inventiveness: *We just gave parks a big increase a few years ago,* or *It isn't
your turn,* and worst of all, *I know that there's still some fat in your budget*
were clearly intended to make one wonder what "they" knew that you didn't.
The choice of language often plainly revealed an ideology that no public
employee's budget estimate could be trusted and that it was a self-serving
myth that some agencies, like parks, had been gnawing on the bone for years
and wouldn't know fat if they saw it. The door was shut and locked.

By the time the second year rolled around, I had developed a language
of my own that if nothing else made the budgeters listen for a few minutes.
My words were not lies and were backed up with the reality of expanded
constituencies, friends groups, corporate underwriting, private fund-raising,
volunteers, deteriorated resources, dangerous infrastructure, threats to public
health and safety, and the carrot of eventual self-funding for parks. The dialogue now began.

Clearly, dialogue had been the missing ingredient for years. Just as clearly, dialogue can't happen until you get the other party's attention—attention that in all fairness had been captured by the more eloquent pleas and urgent needs of others. To be successful, the dialogue between parks and the holders of the purse strings has to focus on three distinct and shared concerns. The first concern is obviously *economics*. The economic impact of parks in a tourism economy is a sure-fire attention getter. Just threaten to close a park for public safety reasons if you doubt its efficacy. The second concern is *constituency*. Parks need a vocal and organized constituency. The people who use parks, identify with parks, and love parks are also people who vote, have networks, and are willing to get organized and speak out. Viable parks' friends groups are not likely to be friends of the system, but they are friends of the land. The third concern is *relevancy*. Politicians are proud. They are proud of their mandate, proud of their legacy (or what they hope their legacy will be), proud of their districts, their State, and their history. Parks and historic sites are the caretakers of a great deal of that history, and parks can provide a powerful linkage for a political legacy. The door opens, and the plan unfolds.

There has to be a plan. The dialogue can't simply consist of a litany of declining resource conditions, deferred maintenance bills, and damaged tourism images; it has to include a plan for turning things around. The plan has to be realistic, leave room for others to buy into it, and it has to have a glimmer of permanence, sustainability, and a real solution to the underlying problems. In short it has to be a plan for success, and the architect has to be willing to give up ownership of the plan. Good ideas belong to everyone; it does take a team to make a difference. The dialogue expands, and more doors open.

All park systems have a mission, but how many have a *vision?* Taking the dialogue beyond the controllers of the budget to the public where real ownership resides is the immediate goal. The park system may have a vision that includes no deterioration of resources and infrastructure. It may have a vision for sustained and reliable funding and for an expanded role in areas of education, public health, and the economy. However, none of those visions are realistic without public support for a broader mandate. The test of that support comes through new legislative direction. The dialogue has to move to a public discussion through hearings with committees other than the budget watchdogs and into the media. This is good. Parks are being discussed as valued assets in their own right and are being considered as part of the solution to other social needs rather than just a cost to the taxpayer. Now the real language of the cost effectiveness of public parks can finally take place. The dialogue shifts, and candor is the currency of the day.

Candor is the only effective way to get beyond such flagrantly disingenuous and dismissive edicts as *"No new parks until we can take care of the parks that we've got now."* Expanding our parks and park systems is linked to expanding the concept of parks. If park systems are going to be viable, economically as well as socially, they have to be relevant to huge segments of a diverse public. They have to mean more than recreation, playgrounds, and the preservation of nature. It is probably not possible to adequately *"take care of the parks we have now"* without the infusion of a new generation of park concepts: corridor parks and greenways that provide a living connection between parks and between people and their parks; adopted mini-parks that are cared for by neighbors and volunteers; charter parks that are larger versions of the former; and interagency parks that combine the resources of park agencies with other organizations and nonprofits, such as industrial development commissions, schools, housing authorities, heritage preservation, water resources, and wildlife agencies. Parks can climb out of the cellar of budget priorities and achieve the level of "essential services" if the desire and the constituency is there. The questionable ethics of shutting down government for any reason does a huge disservice to the founding concept of "intelligent democracy." Is government of so little value? And what about the spin-off effects on the economy? Doesn't such an act alienate the citizen owners of that government?

The opposite of "essential services" is "nonessential services." Parks surely must have been viewed as essential when they were created. The reason for the slide to the bottom of public budget priorities is no longer the issue. At issue now is how long public parks can realistically survive at the bottom without dropping off entirely, while dropping out of the budget is being seen as increasingly plausible. In the language of public finance it is called *privatization*, and it offers a quick fix for those who would like to wish away the deferred maintenance issue that hangs like a black cloud over so many park budget discussions. Before the era of privatized parks is upon us, perhaps we need to ask ourselves if there isn't an ethical consideration to at least look at parks as essential for something more than recreation and income. In the blunt language of finance, if we fail to protect the investment nothing else will matter, and an investment in parks is an investment in the environment and in the economy that supports us all.

> *First, break all the rules. It's what the world's greatest managers do differently.*
> —M. Buckingham and C. Coffman

The Ethical Case for Fees as Dedicated Park Income

I like to be in America,
it's OK by me in America,
everything is free in America,
for a small fee in America.

—Stephen Sondheim

If fees are viewed as just another income source, or worse as an offset for a portion of appropriated funds, we miss their real value to a park and to a park system. User fees are an expression of support given in trust in the expectation that they will be used to meet park needs. As such, they express much more than the visitor's "willingness to pay" for value received; they can be seen as votes in support of assumed park goals that can constantly be re-earned by building confidence in the park's ability to convert revenue efficiently into meaningful accomplishments.

Most park visitors would probably be surprised to learn that there is no established principle for retaining the fees paid at the park. They might not think about it at all and few ever ask, but throughout my years of taking their money the assumption that fees stay in the park seems to be widely held. Some visitors even seem to think that their fees are earmarked for explicit purposes in the park and treated much like donations. While some park systems have made cautious moves in this direction, it still seems inevitable that appropriations get reduced by amounts that look suspiciously similar to the income generated by fees and donations. To simply collect fees and drop them in the revenue pot seems embarrassingly like prostituting park resources, a diversion of intent, or a violation of the "reasonable expectations law."

The case for parks as good social investments has always been a persuasive one over the years, but the integrity of that argument is compromised each time the park gates are closed in response to budget impasses and cuts. Today's sophisticated park users know that closed parks are vulnerable parks. They also know that the parks are not really theirs whenever somebody else denies them access. The return on the social investment never drops to zero, but it is hard to see it, touch it, and believe it when the gates are closed, especially when you always have paid your fees and your taxes. Of course, it makes it difficult to use the social investment argument when we need new parks, expansions, and improvements.

A park ethic for the 21st century needs to be grounded in the belief that the protection of parks includes the protection of park revenues. If we can have dedicated revenues for our highways, we certainly can have dedicated revenues for our parks. All it takes is desire and the commitment to a dedicated revenue source or combination of sources. User fees can be an important part of the revenue pool. In fact, it would be easy to link user fees with the costs of park operations. All of the nonoperational costs—those costs not directly incurred by providing user services—remain in the social investment category and can be covered by general funds. Park expansions and revitalization are obviously capital costs and clearly social investments.

The frequently heard call for government to operate more like a business has rarely extended far enough to encourage park agencies to experiment with businesslike approaches, including targets for cost recovery from visitors. Entrepreneurial management of state parks in Texas was experimented with in the 1990s, and New Hampshire initiated its (so far) successful self-funding experiment in state park management in 1991.

Most public parks generate four different types of income: appropriated funds, fees and charges, contributions and donations, and merchandise sales. Each represents a markedly different fiscal philosophy and is consequently handled differently.

Appropriated funds are essentially an advance, a debit account used to pay for park operations. Income from user fees, camping permits, and other charges is banked into the general fund account and a weekly cash report is filed. Contributions and donations are banked in a separate account and earmarked for specified uses at the park. Revenue from merchandise sales may be deposited in a revolving fund, used for restocking, and the profit over a certain amount gets transferred to the general fund. Since it is used locally, only income from donations and contributions offer any real incentive for maximization.

In an entrepreneurial system, we could provide encouragement to maximize campground and day-use income through a variety of incentives for extended and repeat visits. Retail merchandise sales could be tightly linked to more than simply meeting limited visitor needs and at the same time expand the wants of visitors. When opportunities for capturing park revenue to meet park needs are not there, the dominant incentive is to contract out the operations. When New Hampshire's state parks became entrepreneurial and the concessions were returned to the State, merchandise income rose dramatically despite the higher cost of public sector labor. Similarly, when fees for historic sites have been replaced by strategically designed donation systems, income usually rises dramatically despite the now free admission.

The focus on stewardship among park professionals has unfortunately been restricted to park resources. It is regrettable that we have failed to capitalize on the idea that good stewards of the land are also very likely to be good at applying the same principles of stewardship to a park's financial assets and to its public good will. Numerous studies of park visitor reaction to fees indicate that people want to support their parks at a higher level than is currently asked of them. That invaluable good will for the future of parks is being ignored and squandered in a hybrid system that is neither entrepreneurial nor public service.

Fiscal stewardship of a park, like resource stewardship, can be deferred or it can be accelerated. In either case, it is not stewardship when it is addressed piecemeal. Just as resource stewardship includes all the resources plus solid inventories and monitoring, fiscal stewardship is holistic and pays particular attention to cost control, revenue maximization, cost accountability, and cost sharing through partnerships. With such an approach to management, it seems likely that we might see a new era of park system growth rather than a continuation of past trends of cutbacks and closures.

Obviously, the entrepreneurial approach to park management includes both an income side and a cost control side. Just as obviously, parks have been addressing costs for years but often in the wrong ways such as cutting services, deferring maintenance, reducing seasonal employment, shrinking hours and seasons, and replacing the human touch with iron rangers and automated gates. Cost control too often results in a cyclical cutting of costs to predetermined levels at times of crisis rather than constant monitoring of cost-effectiveness. It is the rare park manager who knows the per-visit cost of operations, how that figure is trending over time, and how it compares with similar park operations.

Fundamental to any realistic entrepreneurial system for parks is an accurate cost accounting and monitoring system. The real costs of producing recreational experiences, park protection, maintenance, research, information, training, administration, and overhead are rarely the comparable line-item amounts in the budget because parks rarely assign their employees to such discrete categories. Even if such figures were available, they would have little meaning in the absence of additional knowledge of how they compare with other parks.

Meaningful cost accounting is impossible without a major change in the existing ethic of park management, which is unfortunate because cost control is an obvious credibility measure that parks could take. It would be refreshing to read in the annual report that the cost of producing recreational experiences had been reduced by seven percent this year with no reduction in visitor services. The owners of public parks might feel justifiably proud of their park management if it reported a reduction in the backlog of deferred maintenance as a result of corporate underwriting for the replacement of worn-out facilities. If that annual report along with the park's informational brochures were printed at no public expense, again through creative partnering, popular support for an increased budget would be greatly strengthened.

Partnering even without cost control initiatives is itself a strong credibility measure that any park can take. Sharing the costs of park operation and expanding the level of services offered through partnerships sends a powerful message that management is seeking creative solutions and is sensitive to current trends in providing satisfying visitor experiences. Sometimes whole properties, such as historic sites and natural areas, can be managed by cooperative agreements with historic associations and environmental groups while still retaining their identity as national or state "Partnership Parks." Such arrangements not only reduce costs, they also build the sense of parks being part of their communities. Expanding benefits through saving dollars can be the kind of forward-looking park ethic that expands park relevance for a new century.

Partnering with the visiting public can have immeasurable results in reducing operational costs. A park ethic is in essence saying that visitation is a privilege earned through responsible park behavior and can reduce the costs of waste disposal, vandalism, water usage, lifeguards, and even search and rescue. Experiments in trashcan removal in many states have increased the social control of littering. When parks are seen and treated as special places, the visiting public becomes a vast network of protective eyes and ears for management. The message that parks are special has to be reinforced by special attention to costs and to how visitor fee income is used.

Reinvesting in already profitable park ventures is yet another astute entrepreneurial move. When New Hampshire state parks enjoyed a twelve percent profit in their first year of self-funding, much of the overbudget income was used to expand the earning potential of one or two parks whose popularity had propelled them into becoming the "cash cows" of the system. Such an investment is bound to result in even greater future profits for use by other parks and in correcting past maintenance deferrals.

Probably nothing reflects the entrepreneurial spirit better than a focus on visitor satisfaction. No studies of park visitors have been more conclusive than those proving that satisfied visitors stay longer, spend more, come back more often, and tell their friends. The investment in satisfaction saves on the advertising budget while retaining a solid core of appreciative visitors who serve as an extended park staff. There is probably no more important component of visitor satisfaction than the power of personal contact. Iron rangers do not produce satisfaction nor can they respond to questions from a curious visitor; human rangers or volunteers are what visitors want and expect. Personal contact is far more effective than signs telling visitors "what not to do," which reduces visitor satisfaction. Do-it-yourself recreation is likely to be much less satisfying when information services, a visitor center, roving volunteer park interpreters, and human contact are lacking. Satisfied visitors tend to generate more satisfied visitors because of their energy and enthusiasm.

It is unrealistic to assume that even with a restructuring of the budget, a focus on cost control, and a partnership imperative that user fees alone can provide a reliable income stream for park operations. Park visits are heavily weather influenced, and visitation can be influenced by a variety of other unforeseen factors ranging from economic fluctuations to bad press. Parks need to have a supplemental funding source. Failure to provide this source is inconsistent with the idea that parks are a good social investment. Parks promote travel, so it would not be unrealistic to dedicate a small fraction of gas tax income to parks. Parks promote tourism and public health, so it is equally reasonable to seek support from a sharing of sales taxes, lodging taxes, cigarette and alcohol taxes. Ultimately, perhaps none of these supplements would be necessary if taxpayers were simply given the option of supporting their parks with a voluntary contribution when they pay their income taxes.

General Funding for Special Places?
Self-Funding State Parks

The Congress shall have the power to lay and collect taxes,
duties, imposts, and excises to pay the debts and provide for the
common defense and the general welfare of the United States.
— Constitution of the United States

The Need for Independence

The philosophy of the general fund—that enormous pool of tax revenue from
which we fund the majority of society's needs—is inimical to the long-term
protection of our parklands and nature reserves. Distribution of general funds
is overwhelmingly responsive to the urgency of the short-term. The result is
anything but a level playing field among the agencies competing for its attention. The needs for sustaining biological diversity, or simply for preserving
parklands for the future, cannot compete with the immediacy of law enforcement, hunger, illiteracy, prisons, and medical care for children and the elderly.
The potential for addressing these concerns by relating them to their many
obvious linkages with parks does little more than draw the line at selling off
parklands to help pay the doctor's bills. Since their benefits are perceived to
be either free-flowing or deferrable, we continue to go through long cycles of
parkland degradation interspersed with brief and infrequent periods of public
embarrassment and atonement for their condition. The level of vision that
created these showcases of our natural and social heritage deserves to be
matched by funding sources that are equally imaginative. Those funding
sources need to be protected with a tenacity equal to the protection of the
lands themselves.

The search for funding begins (and too often ends) with park visitors.
Their willingness to pay for the use of these lands has been the subject of
numerous studies and agency experiments with fees. The current range in
recovery of park operating costs from visitors runs from approximately ten
percent to over 100 percent of operating costs with an average of less than
50 percent among the fifty state park systems. While it is clear that a majority
of visitors are willing to pay a significant portion of the costs of their visits,
the jury is still out on whether or not total self-funding is desirable. Some significant degree of self-funding is probably requisite to securing a supplemental

dedicated revenue source. A variety of supplementary sources are currently favored in different states, generally in the form of a percentage of another tax such as real estate transfer, cigarette sales, tourism expenditures, a portion of lottery proceeds, and voluntary check-offs when filing personal income taxes. Often however, proceeds from the supplementary source are legislatively dedicated for specific park uses other than operations, and while a high rate of self-sufficiency (for example, 80 percent or more) might seem to increase the likelihood of securing a supplemental income source, it may in fact simply increase the pressure for raising fees to close the gap.

It has been amply demonstrated that Americans appreciate their public lands, want them to be protected, and are willing to pay for that protection through increased fees, taxes, and bond issues. What has been much less clear is whether their support for acquiring public lands carries over to support for managing those lands, or even if it is widely recognized that the job of protection carries on forever after the act of acquisition. It seems very unlikely, however, that the public's commitment to their parks would suffer if those parks had to be funded primarily from user fees. In fact park advocacy and stewardship might very well increase with the stronger sense of ownership that comes from paying directly for park services.

The Environment for Success

A test of these ideas became a reality in 1991 when the State of New Hampshire decided to legislatively mandate its park system to experiment with self-funding its operational budget. In many ways, New Hampshire was the ideal state for such a test. Having a mandate to maximize its revenue since its inception 56 years earlier, it had been averaging around 85 percent cost recovery for well over a decade and was consistently among the highest of the 50 states in recovery of park operation costs through user fees. The state also had a strong history of experimental management. The first to initiate differential campsite pricing nearly two decades earlier, New Hampshire was also first in monitoring the satisfaction of its visitors; first to adopt a policy of litter-free carry in, carry out trash removal; and first to enforce carrying capacity limits at its two state-operated ski areas. Relatively small in size, the system has 72 recreational, historical, and natural parks totaling about 55,500 hectares. Its several world-class attractions are located within a two-hour drive of the Boston metropolitan region, many of its natural areas are on the National Natural Landmarks Register, and many of its historic sites are on the National Register of Historic Places. Three of its major park attractions, totaling over 5,500 hectares, are totally surrounded by the added attraction and protection of the 300,000 hectare White Mountain National Forest.

The people of New Hampshire are proud of their park system and rally to its support with over 30 different parks' friends groups who during the first year of the self-funding experiment contributed an estimated $2.8 million in labor and private funds in support of the parks. Volunteer effort is clearly a vital component of any self-support experiment even though many volunteer programs are offered as extras. Volunteers have opened parks early in the season, kept them open late, provided interpretive services, hosted special events, raised funds, developed handicapped services and facilities, built and maintained hundreds of miles of trails, lobbied for increased park support and new parks, and provided a level of park protection that is invaluable just through their presence. If self-funding could not succeed in these circumstances, it is unlikely that it would succeed anywhere. While it is clear that this exact combination of favorable circumstances might not be found elsewhere, it is equally true that the elements of success, volunteerism, cost control, citizen support, and the availability of a mass market should help guarantee success.

The Measurement of Success

The state legislature's mandate was based on the park system's proven ability over the previous three years to generate revenue sufficient to cover its direct operating costs plus interest payments on over $12 million in capital development. What made the venture experimental in addition to the unpredictability of weather were the additional mandated charges for park system planning, recreation extension, and overhead charges. Conversely, the costs of major maintenance and new capital development were not initially charged to the parks bureau, but the success of self-funding has moved some of those costs into the system since 1991. The legislature created a nonlapsing fund into which all park income flows. Income in excess of budgeted expenses may be spent on any project or program with the approval of the legislature's fiscal committee, the governor, and Executive Council.

The two state-operated ski areas that were part of the state park system had been under separate management for two years and were therefore excluded from the fund. While these two areas were high-income producers (i.e., one-half of the park system's operating budget), they also tended to drain any excess revenue and legislative attention because of their constant demands for upgrading. For decades capital improvements in the rest of the park system languished and the deferred maintenance bills grew as the two ski areas competed for snow-making, lodge improvements, new ski lifts, a new aerial tramway, new sewer systems, and ever-rising energy costs.

With all of the success factors lined up, two critical elements were working against the experiment: a sluggish regional economy and summer weather that was wetter and colder than normal. The season started out with revenues 24 percent ahead of the previous year and ended barely seven percent ahead, but it was a success and the third-in-a-row new record income year.

In one respect the sluggish economy might have actually been an asset to the experiment in that New Hampshire state parks are ideally positioned to offer low-cost alternatives to people who might otherwise have gone farther for their vacations. In fact, camping, which had showed a slow but steady decline for a decade, suddenly rebounded with a ten percent increase. Ocean beach parks showed a remarkable fourteen percent increase in 1991 while inland beach parks actually declined by three percent. The bottom line for the first year of the experiment was a surplus of $640,000 for park improvements in a year when general fund budget cuts would probably have resulted in extensive cutbacks and lost income. Since 1991 the experiment has consistently produced significant annual surpluses for park reinvestment, even after allowing for the needed budget growth of an expanding park system!

Creating a Chain Reaction of Successes

Any system of public parks has three income classes of properties: (a) those few that consistently make significantly more than they spend, (b) those that might break even with a little help, and (c) those like historic sites that can never be expected to earn more than a small percentage of their needs. The temptation to use the added income for the first two categories of parks in order to generate even more income is understandable. However, two mitigating considerations make an argument against using all or even a large portion of the funds in this way. First is the need to maintain a reserve for use in the event of a subsequent poor weather year to cover fixed costs of the system. The second, the need for maintaining the integrity of the park system, has no easy answer. Should the fund be prorated between the needs for enhanced income and correcting deferred maintenance, or should it be between income-producing and nonproducing parks? For the first few years of the fund, the decision was made to reserve one-half of the income in case it was needed for the following year's operations. If not needed, it would be immediately put back in the fund for reinvesting in the parks. The second half of the surplus was earmarked for use in expanding facilities and correcting deferred maintenance at income-producing parks with a hope of a payback in subsequent years for sharing throughout the park system.

A number of other steps were taken to assure continued success and popular support for the program: increased promotion through partnerships, expanded in-park and off-park merchandising at the high end of park-related gifts, and careful cost monitoring. The New Hampshire park system has aggressive programs to seek corporate underwriting for park projects, to reduce operating costs through computerization and cooperative management of its historic sites, and to increase park visibility through cooperation and community involvement. Without resorting to continual fee increases, the opportunities for income enhancement throughout the system are extensive and exciting.

The success of the New Hampshire self-funding experiment is due to the cooperation of uncounted individuals and organizations, but perhaps the least heralded and most important contributors to the success are its employees—both career and seasonal. As a result of the experiment employee morale was palpably improved. Every employee became an outstanding ambassador for the program. They acted like, felt like, and were winners after decades of the negative effects of being a general fund agency. They were suddenly propelled from the bottom of the budget priority, with its cutbacks and deferrals, to the top. Correcting the backlog of deferred maintenance would still take years, but suddenly it seemed possible in our lifetime. In crafting this much-needed success, a set of ten principles emerged:

1. The value of a community's parklands is in no way related to the size of its budget or the size of its cutbacks.

2. Parklands are living parts of their community and their flow of benefits cannot be interrupted without adverse effects on the community.

3. The viability of a community's parklands is a reliable indicator of the viability of the community, its vigor, health, and pride.

4. Support for sustaining a park system's benefits cuts across all segments of the community and can be readily identified.

5. The only real obstacles to developing alternative funding sources for viable parks are the lack of will and the lack of know-how.

6. The number, quality, and diversity of potential park partnerships produces benefits vastly in excess of what might have resulted from "full funding."

7. Opening up park management to true public involvement not only benefits parks but can also be a model for reinventing government and reenergizing democracy.

8. The usually silent constituency for parks is emphatically in disagreement with frequent political demands for free or low-cost user fees.

9. There is no short-term, easy fix for the symptoms of park underfunding—the sooner we attack the problem and accept the complexities, the better for all.

10. As our concept of park management evolves, so does our understanding of the real meaning of parks to people, to communities, and to the economy.

If stewardship is the key to reigniting the public park movement and stewardship is limited by funding, we can no longer afford to let our park systems wither under general fund tokenism. Our park systems deserve to be funded as the important assets that they are rather than as wards of the state. The next generation of park users will not accept our excuses for allowing buildings to rot, lands to be eroded, waters to be polluted, vegetation to be destroyed, and infrastructures to be neglected simply because of insufficient funds. Their heritage demands the courage and commitment to aggressively seek alternative ways of doing the parks' business. If parks exemplify American values, a certain amount of freedom in their funding seems appropriate if not required. And, most significantly, an economically viable park system is able to provide many programs of positive assistance to economically disadvantaged citizens.

The Real Costs of Deferrals
The Un-Greening of America's Best Idea

To make us love our country, our country ought to be lovely.
—Edmund Burke

The General Accounting Office (GAO) estimate of $6 billion in deferred maintenance in the national parks in 2003 is but an indicator of a much larger problem. One way to assess the magnitude of that larger problem lies in recognizing that the GAO only considered park infrastructure. There are still other deferrals such as resource inventory, monitoring, and staffing, and of course the GAO did not look at the several other federal agencies with a stewardship mandate that collectively provide another five to six times as many recreational opportunities. The situation in the nation's state parks is equally grim. It is a well-known fact that maintenance delayed is maintenance magnified—the future costs can be staggering to contemplate.

We can each do our own estimates of the economics, but the real costs in terms of broken trust are probably beyond comprehension. Unfortunately, even if the National Park Service were to receive the $6 billion today, it would still be paying the real costs of deferrals more than a generation from now. Postponed stewardship insidiously erodes the public's trust in their park agencies and, by inference, in their government. A breach of trust is inevitably accompanied by a tarnished image, a loss in credibility, and a morale sink that it is not going to go away in response to yet one more temporary funding tourniquet to stop the most serious bleeding. Where's the guarantee that the cycle of deferrals won't start all over again if and when today's deferrals are corrected?

To say that the central mission of stewardship can be set aside until better times suggests that stewardship is a luxury and that it has no role in helping to create those better times. It also suggests that a sanctioned failure in the primary mandate of stewardship lowers the standard for performance across the board. Such a massive expression of low priority can only accelerate the downward spiral in support, leading to a massive lack of support for urgently needed new parks "until such time as we can take care of the ones we have." That lack of support among opinion leaders and policymakers readily transfers to the general public and to park visitors. Saying that we can wink at the big problems in parks seriously damages credibility among the visitors who are being asked to do what are individually "little things," such as *Tread Lightly, Leave No Trace,* and *Carry In–Carry Out*, that are collectively major savings for parks.

To suggest that stewardship is something deferrable is equivalent to saying that the park's mission is not a serious one. If we are not serious, what will make anyone want to partner or volunteer with us? In fact if our parks are not success stories, how viable is the partnering option anyway? The catch-22 of deferred maintenance spreads its tentacles into the community where parks are desperately seeking help!

If the ethic and philosophy of park management can be so easily compromised, the job satisfaction of agency employees plummets and recruitment of park professionals loses much of its luster for people who care. If we take an honest look at all of the consequences of deferrals, it is unmistakably clear that what once appeared to be a challenging and rewarding career for many could slip into being just another government job for some.

It is difficult to think of another profession where the major "assignment" could be so easily placed on the back burner. Not maintaining the parks is akin to the police, the doctors, and the educators not maintaining their skills. As a society, we would not allow it. To condone deferred maintenance of our national treasures is to suggest that they are not truly the treasures, the cultural assets, the quality of life necessities, and the tourism generators of a great nation.

Many months ago, I shelved my copy of the *Acadia National Park Business Plan* somewhere between outrage and despair. Returning to it a while back and getting beyond the obvious facts that Acadia is not a business and the *plan* is not really a plan, I experienced something akin to a eureka moment.

The Acadia business plan speaks of unfunded mandates in the field of personnel management totaling $386,859 as one of the many factors driving up the costs of operation. But what about the original unfunded mandate: *"to leave them [the parks] unimpaired for future generations?"* Stewardship seems to stand at the end of line in the government world of unfunded mandates. The epiphany came when I began massaging the figures within Acadia's 53 percent budget shortfall and realized that herein lies the stuff of successful class-action suits.

It turns out that a 47 percent funding level is the good news. The bad news is that resource protection—the very reason for the park's existence—is the lowest funded category at 34 percent of needs. Those of us who consider the unimpaired mandate akin to a sacred trust must ask ourselves what level of funding will cause us to reach the trigger point where underfunding and deferrals provoke legal action. If 34 percent of resource protection needs doesn't do it, add in park maintenance at 38 percent of needs for a total of annual deficit of $3.6 million in the park's primary mission. Finally, add to this an estimated $36 million in deferred maintenance and almost $6 million in resource management needs and it is easy to see how the Park Service has accrued a deferred nationwide maintenance bill of over $6 billion. Acadia's administration and management is funded at 45 percent of needs, which is also part of the bad news. The "good" news is that visitor services are funded at 58 percent of needs and park operations are at 65 percent.

Taking the parks into federal court is not an appealing prospect for the several nonprofit organizations that act as watchdogs for our parks, but then neither is standing by and watching a 34 percent level of funding for the unimpaired mandate dwindle even further. A class-action suit on behalf of generations to come seems less like an extreme action than a case of patience and tolerance lasting too long. Even so, a far better solution is readily available to Congress.

The results of the Congressional "fee experiment" of the 1990s would certainly justify requiring the parks to creatively fund the shortfall in visitor services while recommitting itself to fully funding the unimpaired mandate. If the data in the Acadia Business Plan are correct, then balancing the books at least at Acadia is suddenly in the realm of the possible. Full funding of resource protection, maintenance, and park administration would mean an additional $5.7 million in the budget (exclusive of the current deferred maintenance). Subtracted from the total shortfall, this leaves only $1.6 million to be creatively generated in support of visitor services and enjoyment. Interestingly, Acadia's nonappropriated revenue is reported as $1.76 million. Further, Acadia's current revenue figure of 30 percent of its budget can be viewed as a good beginning with 40 percent of its 2.5 million visitors still not paying. Major additional sources of revenue are currently untapped, such as Cadillac Mountain, and undertapped, such as the park's fair share of concessionaire gross income.

David Orr makes a powerful case in *Earth in Mind* that "complete human beings" (and by inference complete human organizations) are those "who know, who care, and who do." We have known for years (along with the Park Service) that our park assets are being passed on to future generations not only *impaired* but are also encumbered by a huge bill for *repairs*. For equally as long we have cared, and that caring has led to massive volunteerism and fundraising for park projects, but it hasn't been enough. The underfunding and the deferrals have grown apace with the giving.

The Congressional underfunding of its own "unimpaired" mandate is patently illogical. Perhaps if Congress were aware of the huge disparity in funding for resource protection (i.e., the future) versus visitor services (i.e., the present) a more realistic balance would be required, and perhaps if it required the kind of documentation provided by the Acadia Business Plan the discrepancy would be too obvious to miss. The declining stewardship of these sacred sites must be reversed by whatever tools are available to us. Let us challenge the Congress to fully fund the parks' future, and perhaps collectively and creatively we can fund the parks' present.

Just as "justice delayed is justice denied," the same is true of stewardship. It is time to start thinking in terms of justice for nature and justice for future generations. It is also time to start measuring park success by guaranteed tomorrows rather than ever-increasing numbers of bills for our children to pay.

Stewardship Delayed Is Stewardship Betrayed

When it becomes the norm to delay the public's major business of park management, it must also be acceptable to arbitrarily decide when or even whether to return phone calls, answer inquiries, or attend meetings. When it becomes acceptable to pass along the increased costs of deferred maintenance to future generations, it hardly seems important to build partnerships now to keep the costs down. As the price of broken promises in parks insinuates its sinister message to visitors, they are being asked to conclude, "If it isn't important to the park, why should it be important to me?" For a profession based on service and satisfaction, the costs of a loss of public trust are unacceptable!

Parks and the Ethical Use of Power

*You can have power over people as long as you don't take
everything away from them. When you've robbed a man of
everything, he is no longer in your power.*

— Aleksandr Solzhenitsyn

No one ever called him "Boss." To do so would have imposed a relationship that no one in his park wanted, including him. He was always simply "Charlie" and he was in every way the boss—one of those rare individuals who can lead without commanding. It was "his park" not because he claimed it but because everyone felt secure in knowing that he was in charge if someone got lost or injured or if there was a forest fire. Charlie was someone you wanted to please, simply because in doing so you knew that you had done the job to his standards—standards he exemplified by working alongside you whenever he could. Just as often he'd make it a little tougher by letting you figure out the right way to do a job. In the military he would have been, and during World War II was, someone you could trust with your life.

An organizational analyst might label him "a natural leader," but Charlie never thought of himself as a leader. In fact he declined to accept many leadership positions throughout his career. Charlie was a park manager, eventually a regional park superintendent, and a master at his job. I am sure that the concept of power never occurred to him. In his quiet unassuming way, the power of Charlie's personality and knowledge ran his parks and guaranteed memorable experiences for hundreds of thousands of visitors. It even created a cadre of dozens of seasonal workers over the years who went on to spread his work ethic in the fields of law, banking, medicine, teaching, commerce, and yes, even parks.

Very likely Charlie never considered himself a mentor, and yet he was to every person who ever worked for him. To him they were friends. Every person who ever worked for Charlie learned something about doing things right and doing the right things—fundamental organizational ethics. Decades later I had the opportunity to become Charlie's boss. The first thing I did, even before getting sworn in, was talk with Charlie. I had hopes of pulling him into the main office so that his style of leadership might spread throughout the organization. Charlie, of course, wouldn't consider it. I knew that over the years he'd been misused by the power structure so perhaps now he wanted no part of it. What I saw as his chance to use power in the right way he saw as a mismatch with his talents. While his refusal would make my job infinitely more difficult, it was reassuring to know that Charlie was still Charlie.

Today mentoring has become part of a professional's job description, something the professional does to help subordinates grow. Charlie saw it as something larger than what was required by his job—it was something that happened in the course of the job. For those who were truly alert, that's what their job was—a course in doing things right and doing the right things. Most impressively, he didn't draw the mentoring line at his employees; he was a mentor for visitors as well by helping them set up their camp, helping them pick the best trails for their ability, suggesting other places to visit for a more rewarding trip, and encouraging all in his quiet way to go beyond themselves. Far too often in recent years I have seen instances where the uniform, the badge, the book of blank citations, and the gun got in the way of effective mentoring for both employees and visitors. Charlie didn't need any of those things; he had the power of the smile, the power of knowledge, and the power of caring—and he understood the power of nature.

Professional training in parks and recreation began to include a required course in ethics only during the last decade or so. In creating such a course a few years ago at the University of Maine, I was struck by the paradoxical nature of power and ethics. By then Charlie had retired and was suffering from Lou Gerhig's disease. Of course, I never had a chance of getting him as a guest lecturer—It just wasn't his style. So, once again Charlie made my job tougher. I had to find other ways to convey his "message." He'd been my teacher, and now it was my turn to teach a little of his class to my classes. Luckily, I was able to find a lot of other park managers in Charlie's mold—The work seems to attract them. The message is a simple one, but it has to be taught by someone who lives it: *The only way that power is truly effective is when it is used with respect.* I came to realize that the best way to teach the ethical use of power was to use case studies of Charlie's opposites—those who respect power more than they do people. I recall one such example that occurred when one of Charlie's high-level bosses decided to call him on the carpet for "misappropriating government resources."

Charlie had decided to remove a large, dead, dangerous pine tree from one of his campgrounds in the off-season. Rather than leave the unsightly piles of wood to rot, he gave it to a needy family in the community. Charlie listened politely to the reprimand the boss had staged with some of his subordinates present and then quite simply pointed out that the tree had died of blister rust and that leaving the dead wood in the park would run the certain risk of infecting more of the handsome old pines that made the park so attractive. Also, to pay for having the dead wood hauled away would have really been a misappropriation of resources. His boss, not eager to back down, let the reprimand stand and Charlie returned to his park with his leadership undiminished and perhaps even enhanced. Charlie's approach to the problems facing every park manager can help us appreciate the paradoxical nature of power and leadership: *Power never conveys leadership. Power is the tool we use when leadership is absent.*

How do we ethically use power, and how is that we so often fail to act when it is in our power to do so for ethical causes? We are reminded daily in our newspapers and news programs that the misuse of power for personal gain is of epidemic proportions today. It is a curious fact of both human nature and the media that the misuse of power is far more interesting than the proper use of power. There are probably far more interesting stories about dedicated public servants (like Charlie) and ethical business people, but they seldom make the headlines. My own favorite example of using power in the very best way for the benefit of others is Theodore Roosevelt, a man who saw his presidency as an opportunity to save land, wildlife, resources, and the wonder of it all for future generations. It is of more than passing interest that President Roosevelt was influenced as much by his own beliefs in the necessity for wildlands as he was by his carefully chosen advisors. In an era when there were no presidential retirements, Roosevelt kept using his bully pulpit throughout his post-presidency years to earn an income, to make a difference, and to do the right thing.

If we hope to graduate parks and recreation professionals with an ethical foundation to support their mission and an ability to deal with the prevailing power structure, they need to have a clear understanding of not only the "right thing" but also the right way to do it. For the vast majority of park professionals the right thing isn't a matter to debate; it's a matter of conscience and an ability to seize the moment. Encouraging park visitors to get involved in their parks and to help keep parks attractive and inviting is the right thing to do. Picking up after them in a mistaken concept of "service" is never as worthwhile a service as is fostering the belief that littering is not acceptable behavior in special places like parks. Getting outside of the park in order to talk to schoolchildren and potential park partners is clearly the right thing to do even when it is not in the job description.

The right way to do it also means taking the time to make the message fit the audience. Doing the right thing in the right way may seem to come naturally to certain people like Charlie, but "natural" in this case means more than comfortable—It is a reflection of an underlying ethic about the purpose of parks. For example, when one of Charlie's parks was experiencing a wave of vandalism in the form of people peeling bark from the park's beautiful white birch trees which leaves unsightly black scars around the trees, he expected his employees to find a way to stop it. They tried using signs that read "Please do not peel the birch bark" but the problem only got worse—probably in response to long-forgotten memories from stories about all the things you can do with birch bark.

Even when the "Please" was replaced with a reference to a statute and fine for defacing public property, the problem persisted. Charlie's solution was to remove the signs and apply white paint to the scarred trees, and the problem immediately disappeared. In Charlie's world of parks you do not fill the park with negative signs, and you do not use threats to seek compliance from people who will almost always do the right thing if they know what it is. To him, the solution was natural and obvious because he respected his visitors, knew his responsibility for stewardship, and had no problem integrating the two.

The world of park management can be particularly difficult for the manager who lacks the ability to understand the various kinds of "authority" that impinge on the job. While organizational and political authority can be dominant to the point of being oppressive, there remains in the wings the authority of the resource (Blister rust will kill more pine trees!) and the authority of doing the right thing, at the right time, in the right way (Good stewardship is the best remedy for bad use of resources!). Fortunately, clashes between the various "authorities" are infrequent, but they do seem to occur with enough regularity that it has become necessary to establish laws to protect whistle-blowers and to create employee organizations that give voice in support of the ethical management of the public's resources. While for some the specter of organizational authority challenged by its employees is unacceptable, there clearly needs to be a better balance of power if our mandate to ensure the availability of unimpaired resources for future generations is to have any meaning.

While on the surface it would seem that we are still a long way from any kind of meaningful balance between the power of the bureaucracy and the authority of the resource, reality may actually be moving us toward that balance. Nature tends to have the advantage, and not just in the long run, because its power is real and holistic, whereas our Cartesian approach to managing nature has disaggregated it into artificially separated worlds of forests, wildlife, water, minerals, air, parks, and similar domains that we can deal with comfortably.

As the movement toward building park partnerships progresses, we are in fact beginning to put the pieces of nature back together again, along with an expanded constituency. More often than not, doing the right thing is a matter of having a holistic view and seeing the big picture—a focus that artificial bureaucracies often have trouble with because it is seldom in their mandate. The right thing done at the right time in the right way will seldom come across as righteous for the simple reason that if it is right it has to involve cooperation. Organizational ethics, like those of any other community, are based on the premise that the whole is only whole through cooperation of all the parts. The best answer for the land or for the park is always going to be found where there is mutual respect for the authority of the resource and that of the organization, and where power is used with respect.

> *Power has been the missing link in most of the work done in the field of ethics.*
>
> —*Journal of Power and Ethics*

> *We trained hard, but it seemed that every time we were beginning to form up into teams we would be reorganized. I was to learn later in life that we tend to meet every new situation by reorganizing, and a wonderful method it can be for creating the illusion of progress.*
>
> —Petronius

Training for Park Professionals
Ethics, Norms, and Paradigms

If we are successful, it won't be because of what we have, but because of what we believe.

—Lyndon B. Johnson

Nearly all graduates of four-year college programs in parks and recreation are now required to complete at least one course in ethics. Very likely, this is one course more than most of the people they will be working for and probably one more than many of their professors ever had. An ongoing ethical review of those same programs would seem to be a reasonable and timely requirement for the schools themselves. After parenting, there is possibly no greater ethical dilemma than defining the educational basics that young people need for rewarding careers and lives—a dilemma compounded by the realizations that it is a social contract paid by the student and lacking recourse if the advice is faulty or the selection of teachers is flawed.

Professional accreditation of college programs seeks to provide some minimal assurance that the right things are being taught, but it does so on the basis of norms (i.e., how one's program compares with all others). However, norms are not ethics. The review team may depart leaving behind a "feel good" evaluation and even a high ranking, but the ethical issues will probably have failed to get aired. Also, while it is unlikely that ethical issues might get re-solved, going as they do to the very heart of educational philosophy, can they ethically be ignored? What are the norms used to judge park and recreation training programs? Where did they come from? Are they similar to those in use by other disciplines such as medicine and law? What if the norms are outdated or self-serving?

Consider the following generally, though not universally accepted, academic norms. What is the origin of seven (in reality six) years to achieving tenure—that almost sanctified level of academic achievement? "Seven-year scholar" seems to have a distinctly artificial ring. What is the point of eligibility for sabbatical immediately following the obtaining of tenure? What is the merit of research-driven sabbaticals that send tenured faculty into even greater isolation from students? What is the ethical argument for teaching assistants so often taking over classes and adding a layer between the unschooled and the learned scholar? How often are approved courses regularly updated and not simply canned and taken off the shelf in order to create more time for research? In a field like parks and recreation, how evident is the ethic of service learning as a driving force in the curriculum? In a field where building partnerships is a major management initiative, how often are college courses being team-taught? Why is there no norm of a year's internship before graduation? Why has the four-year program of studies not changed in generations despite huge increases in the body of research and new knowledge to be assimilated by the student? Yes, these are imponderables, but don't we want them to be asked and asked again until we are sure that our norms are useful guides in the drive for excellence? Failure to do so is not just an ethical lapse in teaching; it is abdicating a professional responsibility with profound implications for the future of students, park health, and all of the recreational benefits we espouse.

Let's examine one of the norms, tenure, because ultimately they are all connected. To understand how tenure affects the curriculum, it is necessary to know the source of funding for many parks and recreation programs, particularly those in the land grant system of state universities. Oftentimes a large proportion of professors' salaries (commonly 50 percent or more) is provided by the federal government to support research in the professor's specialty. This educational partnership cuts the university's obligation and allows it to expand faculty and serve more people, but there is a price—the professor becomes a part-time teacher and a part-time researcher. This is in and of itself neither unethical nor a bad idea. In fact the underlying philosophy that "teaching and research are natural partners" seems almost unassailable. The logic that research generates new knowledge and that students will have immediate access to this cutting-edge knowledge is questionable, however. Where is the evidence that this is the knowledge students need? This is an eminently testable proposition. Further, how solid is the notion that good researchers make good teachers? Logic suggests otherwise, except in unusual people. Shouldn't we at least ask the students?

Enter the role of tenure and the ethical issues get more complicated. The professor's first goal is tenure. Tenure is given for scholarship, and scholarship is judged by the professor's peers on the basis of performance in three tasks: teaching, research, and service. Notice what is subtly happening here—the student's purchase of relevant instruction has become just one of three continuing demands on the professor because tenure once granted is never absolute. The roads appear to be diverging for professor and student and the relationship weakening, yet the professor continues to hold the keys to the student's future. Let's see if there can be a reconvergence. Peers evaluate research on the basis of published scholarly journal articles that have been reviewed by peers (i.e., other researchers, not park rangers or managers). This is usually done with quantitative guidelines, such as 1½ published articles per year. Meanwhile books seen as the highest mark of scholarship by the public fail to have the same impression on peers, possibly because most peers do not write books and consequently tend to undervalue them or at least to see them as syntheses of knowledge rather than as "new" knowledge. "Scholarship" is now defined as a number—a number granted by other number-oriented peers. Is it possible that this fascination for numbers escapes the students?

Since research can be quantified, albeit inadequately, it has come to be the surrogate for "scholarship." Teaching drops to a readily admitted second place in the tenure decision because its outputs, outcomes, and its benefits are down the road somewhere in the ultimate success of students. So, where would you place your priorities as a professor? Chances are that the students' needs, ostensibly the raison d'être for the program as well as for the university, are really far lower than second place. Of course peers could change the process by simply sitting in on a few lectures as peers and ranking them like an Olympic event, but they have no incentive to do so—first because research has already become the stand-in for scholarship, and second because their own teaching would then have to be similarly evaluated.

Now, with the students' needs safely tucked away in the back seat behind those of professorial tenure, we might take a look at the ethical dilemmas of selecting teachers in the first place. Not surprisingly, the selection process mirrors the tenure process. We select candidates on the basis of their likelihood of getting tenure—their research experience—not on the basis of any on-the-ground experience they might bring to the student. What's wrong with that? It tends to very obviously skew the selection in favor of the candidate with the strongest research skills, which is a logical bias if the students are seeking to become researchers rather than managers. It also means that faculties tend toward younger, more narrowly experienced candidates who are focused on their own careers rather than those of their students. The students' needs are moved from the back seat to the trunk of a vehicle that seems to be going in the wrong direction.

Could it possibly be that one of our basic educational paradigms is in need of adjustment? Do we have an ethical responsibility to periodically examine those principles by which we presume to guide the lives of others? Of course we do. The choices inherent in the relationship are life-changing. The fact that the student will pay many thousands of dollars for the right training becomes almost inconsequential in the face of the larger costs of a career and a lifetime. Are we not treating the educational contract almost cavalierly when we say that any publishable research is the professor's first priority, tenure the second, and teaching is a distant third? Have we not in a very real sense prostituted the traditional relationship of the unschooled student and the learned scholar, replacing it with that of two students who are each focused on their own very different agendas? Are we not also prostituting the teacher/researcher into a fundraising shill for the university? This is a prospect that is difficult to deny when we discover that every research grant carries an added "overhead" cost for administration, sometimes equaling the grant itself. Funding is always a nest of ethical issues but when the overhead norm on research grants and contracts escalates to the role of a "share the wealth" plan for the university, what is the ethical message?

Perhaps it is the application of the paradigm rather than the model itself that needs examination. To answer this we could take a look at the research flowing from the existing model and see how it helps the student. There are, of course, several genres of park and recreation research (e.g., social, physical, economic), but let's look at just one—visitor surveys—since it happens to be the single most common category. We do visitor surveys for a wide variety of reasons, such as to solve problems, measure management performance, better understand visitors, and to assess emerging trends. We also do visitor surveys because they just happen to be quantifiable, relatively quick to accomplish, and are well within the needs of the peer process, as opposed to long-term monitoring of a park's ecological health for example—also a major need of every park.

Over the years surveys have proven to be eminently publishable because they are meaningful statistically if not always applicable in the field, but how exactly is a descriptive survey of visitors of value to the student beyond the obvious advantages of a clearer understanding of visitor diversity? We know that visitors are diverse and changing and that they are in fact changing so fast that many of today's observations may be of little use by the time the student graduates. However, the more cogent question asks how the graduate will use that information to succeed in an entry-level job. Unless that survey is put into the larger context of visitors as a part of society, namely scholarship or wisdom in the application of knowledge, its discussion in the classroom simply adds to the already ponderous problem of research overwhelming practice.

Let's consider how two students, ten years after graduation, are approaching their new responsibilities as park managers. Student A was mildly imprinted by the major professor's descriptive studies of park visitors. Student B's imprinting was heavily influenced by the professor's ongoing studies of park decline in terms of infrastructure, biodiversity, erosion, and pollution. It isn't difficult to guess which student's memories will be the strongest and will reflect the most passion for parks, sustainability, and stewardship. The "half-life" of Student A's professional education was probably less than a year, whereas Student B's education will continue for a lifetime. However, the differences don't stop there. Student A will have a much more limited array of help to call upon when problems arise, whereas Student B is very likely to be calling upon the former professor. It is also reasonable to assume that the two students will have markedly different ways of viewing and solving problems. Now let's add Student C to the mix: a student who in addition to exposure to long-term studies of resource decline also learned—indirectly through team-taught courses and directly through service-learning and internship—about new methods of managing parks, using partnerships, coalitions, volunteers, and cooperation. Clearly accreditation looks not just at what is being taught but also at who is teaching it and how. Just as clearly, accreditation has no power to change the pervasive norms of tenure and peer review.

So, what's the answer? We must ask one more question first. Is the existing paradigm and its application damaging not only the student's preparation but also the profession as well? In the interest of service—that almost ignored third leg of the peer review process—to the communities of students, professionals, and academics, it might be enlightening to take inventory of our norms. Norms are behaviors that are on their way to becoming ethics. They can arrive at their destination by default or they can pass a more rigorous test of their validity—a test that we would expect of any group of researchers in search of truths. If the norms are flawed, the ethical researcher wants to know. Parks and the park movement have been around for generations longer than park and recreation research. With remarkably few exceptions, parks have stood the test of time without scientific justification. The park philosophy is much more of a philosophy of social values than of science. Ask yourself how many parks we would have if we had waited for science to prove the need. Or better yet, ask yourself if you want your parks put on the block of scientific decision making to determine whether they are the highest and best use of the land. The norm of tying research to teaching makes sense, but should it dominate the teacher's selection, time, and tenure? Given that this is the profession's major source of scientific research, is the process of identifying needed research entirely too peer-controlled? Is the profession getting the research it needs to be able to do a better job of stewardship, to fight the budget battles, to build partnerships, or to expand the vision?

So again, what are the answers and what are our options for getting out of the boxes we have created? First, faculties need to get concerned. Honestly, when are these questions ever discussed in faculty meetings? Second, students need to get organized; to ask questions; and to demand a meaningful role in the selection, review, and retention of their teachers. Third, the profession needs to get involved beyond the periodic need for academic program reaccredidation. Professional mentors for all entry-level positions could become a norm that would both help the graduate and give feedback to the institution.

Fourth, the academic administration needs to get out of the peer process or take it over, thereby giving teachers more time to teach. For the administration to both dictate the standards and have the final say on hiring and scholarly excellence makes a mockery of the peer system. Fifth, the tenure system has been widely considered obsolete for decades and research is done by contract. Why not have performance contracts for teaching? Tenure is a poor safeguard against arbitrary administrative actions. Teacher unions have become far more effective. Sixth, a safety net of instruction, in the form of a commitment to team-teaching service learning and internships, could serve to strengthen the present paradigm. Shouldn't teaching be at least coequal with research as the deciding factor in tenure decisions? Seventh, a high-level blue-ribbon commission could be chartered to undertake meaningful studies of the real costs and benefits of any funding that diverts the professor from the principal duty of teaching in a possibly self-defeating effort to sustain an underfunded educational program. Eighth, in the examination of our own norms, we should we take a look at those of others. For example, practicing physicians and surgeons teach our medical students, nurses teach aspiring nurses, and lawyers teach law students. Why not use experienced rangers and park managers to teach tomorrow's park and recreation professionals? Are park assets not as important as public health? Is the integrity of our parklands of less consequence than the integrity of the law? Wouldn't the ethics of future park rangers be better grounded in the holistic heritage of the land than in the disaggregating heritage of science? Are we really trying to balance park science with park literacy? Are not both teaching and research too important to be diminished to half-time activities—each getting half the attention it deserves?

The litmus test for any ethical issue is "Can we do better?" By addressing that question in our educational norms, we take it out of the realm of the hypothetical and ask, "Can we afford not to?" There can never be a guarantee handed out along with the diploma, but at a minimum we should make certain that the major ethical issues charting the lives of students haven't been swept under the rug of academic expedience. In so doing, we can be a bit more confident that the future stewards of our precious parks and recreation resources are qualified to ensure the sustained flow of parks' benefits well beyond the next generation. Expedience learned during professional preparation can only lead to expedience practiced in the managing of the public's resources—at the expense of excellence.

Beyond Principles
Exploring the Ethical Foundations
of Interpretation

A precedent embalms a principle.

—Benjamin Disraeli

"It simply seemed like the right thing to do," is how a legislator explained ignoring powerful special interest pleas and voting to provide for the humane treatment of animals to be slaughtered. In much the same way, the principles of environmental interpretation are grounded in ethical beliefs of rightness. While those principles could just as easily exist as the foundation for propaganda, what gives interpretation the force that it has is that it evolved from roots identical with our nation's beliefs. Democracy's respect for the individual is based on the belief that the informed individual will make the right decision and do the right thing for the nation. Similarly, the principles of interpretation proceed from the belief that the informed individual will make the right decision for the environment. It is these ethical foundations that truly make them principles. From time to time we need to go beyond the principles and cherish those ethical foundations by exploring ways they can take us into whole new realms of interpretation.

Relevance works well as an interpretive principle because it faithfully relates to the needs and interests of visitors, thereby demonstrating *respect for individuals*. Few among us are incapable of responding to respectful treatment. The principle of information as the raw material for revelation reflects a profound *respect for truth* and its meaning. Sound information logically presented is all but impossible to reject. The principle of holism *respects the whole* as something that is always more than the sum of its parts. Our *respect for nature* stems from knowing that nature is vastly more complex than its disaggregated wildlife, forests, soil, water, and air. Similarly, our *respect for past cultures* is more than the sum of all societies that have gone before us. The interpretive principles of artistry as a universal language and focused messaging flow directly from our *respect for diversity* among visitors—whole persons who are sensitive, special, and unique. The principle of provocation reflects a genuine respect for democracy—a belief that anyone can learn more, open doors, and make a difference if they want to.

There are many answers to the question of why we interpret. We do it to enhance understanding, to build appreciation, to assure protection, and to add value to experiences. We also do it because it works—interpretation is an effective way of building appreciation and, ultimately, the protection that only an appreciative public can assure. Even so, there is one answer that covers it all—*we do it because it is the right thing to do.* If interpretation is the right way to manage the public's resources, then the failure to interpret can only be the wrong way. We document the benefits of interpretation on the assumption that more of the public's resources will be interpreted. Perhaps failure to do the right thing should also be documented.

The failure to interpret is an ethical lapse, not a monetary one. It would be wrong to assume that the failure to interpret is a problem of the budget. It is remarkably easy to demonstrate that interpretation is a budgetary bonus for even the most cash-starved agency. Pointing out an ethical lapse has nothing to do with staking out the moral high ground. It simply means that the ethic of interpretation has never been adopted. However, the reasons for failing to adopt a powerful tool that has repeatedly been proven to be effective in protecting resources and enhancing visits might well be unethical if those resources are thereby placed in jeopardy. If the prevailing ethic is that people cannot be responsible stewards of their own resources—that Big Brother knows best—then interpretation is reduced to an extra and resource decline is inevitable.

What is an ethic of interpretation? What makes interpretation *the right thing to do* for managers of public lands and waters, tour guides, museums, historic sites, cruise ships, and even breweries? Right is not a matter of simple effectiveness—right is fundamentally respectful. To prove this you need only think about the interpretive failures you've encountered. In every case they were in some way due to a failure of respect—for individuals, for questions, for contributions, for beliefs, for diversity, for the bigger picture, or for the absolute necessity of preparation. Therefore, by inference the failure to provide interpretive services also reflects a failure to respect the owners of the resource, the users of the resource, the resource itself, and even the stewardship mandate to protect the resource.

Moving toward an interpretive value system requires an understanding that interpretation flows from a pool of respect as a river of principles and that those principles support the goal of spreading respect. This is the circle of interpretation. It follows, therefore, that the interpreter has a responsibility to not only use the flow but also to build the pool. Building that pool of respect means targeting a much wider audience than visitors and school children. Building an interpretive value system, or an ethic of interpretation, means developing a convincing argument that every single person from top to bottom in the organization must be an interpreter. No better argument can be made than that offered by Aldo Leopold in his *Sand County Almanac:* "The principal function of administration of recreational areas is to improve the quality of public use." Freeman Tilden, in *The State Parks—Their Meaning in American Life*, takes Leopold's conclusion further and equates the quality of public use with the quality and amount of nature interpretation that is provided. A few park systems, both public and private, have tried to mandate the end product of an interpretive value system by requiring training in interpretive skills for all employees who meet (or might meet) the public. But training for skills is little more than a band-aid for the lack of an interpretive value system. The skills alone make for very effective interpretation; however, the patient can still die unless there is also a modest attempt at imparting the beliefs behind those skills. Like any social value system, an interpretive ethic can exist only on the basis of widely shared beliefs. Those beliefs buttress the argument that interpretation is not just the right thing to do—It is the essential thing to do in a democracy.

For Leopold's conclusion to be useful it had to be interpreted. Tilden's conviction that the quality of public use can be improved through interpreta-tion is accepted at face value by those of us sharing similar beliefs. However, the evidence that such logic is not widely shared is all around us. Few park managers and system administrators have interpretation backgrounds. The budget for park law enforcement is vastly larger and remarkably more immune from cuts than the interpretive budget. Interpretation is regarded as a visitor service rather than a resource protector. In every case, a focus on principles to the exclusion of beliefs is the culprit. The beliefs that underlie both Leopold's conclusion and Tilden's conviction are profoundly evident in both men's writings. Both believed in the social necessity of heritage preservation, the importance of beauty in life, the power of the written word to effect change, and the effectiveness of enlightened self-interest. They shared a profound respect for what the land can do in shaping its people and for what people can do in shaping the land. Finally, their beliefs about democracy shaped their thoughts about our land.

Our roots feed our branches. Without a profound belief in the power of one, the principle of provocation becomes meaningless. Why bother to provoke someone to learn more, to care, to volunteer, to take action if one person lacks the ability to make a difference? Take away the belief that we are all connected—however loosely—to the land, to each other, to the future, and to the past, and what value is the principle of holism? This principle satisfies our need for intellectual understanding of the connections, but it is our belief that makes those connections come alive—and coming alive is what the prin-ciple of relevance is all about. If you believe that someone will care you empower them to care. Relevance is only of academic interest until someone makes it visceral. The belief that these resources will not be here for your children to enjoy is as relevant as it gets if you are still conscious. Whether or not they will be available to your children is, in the scientific sense, still debatable. The principle that an expanding universe of information is the essential raw material for interpretation satisfies our logic, but it is the belief that we must learn more, that research is essential, that the written word will make a difference that all combine to feed the fires of curiosity.

In the final analysis, everything we say or do, capture in song, on film, in words and through all kinds of artistic expression is interpretation. If we expect our interpretations to be adopted by others, we know that they must reflect reality in ways that are beautiful, appealing, attractive, challenging, and true. As senders of an interpretive message, we recognize the marketing values of it in our messages. If those same messages are to be welcomed, the receiver needs to believe in their beauty and in their truth and not in just in their strategic logic.

For interpretation to achieve its potential in preserving our heritage, it needs to expand the pool of respectful believers. Interpretation needs to be interpreted to the administrators, the budgeters, the policymakers, and the potential cooperators as the right thing to do. It needs to win converts not only for its efficacy but just as equally for its beliefs. If a nation can be built on the fundamental belief that informed individuals can govern themselves, its park systems must reflect and extend those same beliefs. It is logically, emotionally, and professionally the right thing to do.

Conscience is the perfect interpreter of life.

—Karl Barth

The Ethical Interpreter
Conscience, Courage, and Loyalty
at the Intersection

Beware of storytellers who are not fully conscious of the
importance of their gifts.

—Ben Okri

All ethical issues resist unraveling. They would not have become issues if they were easy to resolve, and because of their Gordianesque intransigence we tend to push them aside, saving our energies for things that are more readily achievable. However, for environmental interpreters the issue of loyalty is central to everything they do. Loyalty is linked to their credibility and their authenticity. For example, when science conflicts with the "official position" what is the interpreter to say? When stewardship becomes a matter of "do as I say, not as I do," how can the interpreter retain credibility? When the budget is grossly inadequate to protect the resource, does the interpreter have an obligation to speak out? How do interpreters sort out their often conflicting loyalties to their employer, to their profession, to their colleagues, to themselves, to the resources, to the public who owns the resources, and to future generations who will inherit the resources? Loyalty is not just a two-way street—at times it can be a traffic jam at the intersection. Yet, when the interpreter's credibility is on the line there has to be an ethical guide—a traffic cop—to merge these conflicting demands.

In *Change the World*, Robert E. Quinn says that we are authentic when we are congruent with our messages. If I am giving an in-park session on the need for stewardship and the park all around me shows signs of failing stewardship, the authenticity of my message suffers and my believability is the first victim while the importance of the message is the second. In another example, if it becomes clear at an interpretive session on the necessity for recycling that the visitor center is not a serious recycler, the result is similar. In both cases, the absence of credibility reflects an absence of passion and the interpretive message shrinks to simple information. There is an obvious ethical lapse that could be candidly addressed and thereby restore the talk to the level of interpretation. To do so, however, raises the issue of loyalty to the organization. Unless such incongruities are dealt with, the burnout rate for interpreters will probably rise to the level of an occupational hazard.

Coping with an imperfect world filled with conflicting loyalties is clearly not unique to the interpreter. We cope all the time with school sports programs that are more about winning than about learning and children getting hurt or even stigmatized as a result. We do it with friends who betray a trust and yet we still feel loyal to the friendship. We do it when our politicians and our prelates fail to defend our beliefs. We even do it when our families begin to act as less than family. We do it through the rationalization of situational ethics—a temporary setting aside of one loyalty in favor of preserving another. I might be distressed that my organization consistently fails to fully fund my program for protecting historic artifacts, but I can rationalize it by saying that what they are doing is better than no funding at all. If I speak out publicly, I run the risk of further reductions and the certainty of being branded as not being a team player. So I speak out professionally and passionately for my belief, knowing that parks cannot ethically be pro-diversity for the environment, for their clientele, and for the work force while stifling diversity of professional beliefs.

The first key to situational ethics is the ability to hierarchically arrange our loyalties, along with our ability to draw a bottom line we will not cross no matter how much pressure is exerted. It is that bottom line that is critical. Often we do not know that it exists within us until we are tested by hitting the traffic jam at the intersection. One of the standard questions that once was asked of applicants for officer candidate school created the uncomfortable position of having to choose between being loyal to one's spying mother versus loyalty to one's fallible country. Artificial as the scenario might appear to be, it forces the candidates to find and examine their bottom line—and it's not as simple as it seems. An ethics hierarchy works something like this: I believe in diversity, equality, and freedom, but I cannot accept a level of freedom or of diversity that compromises equality.

I once administered a totally self-funded state park system and its financial bottom line, which was critical to organizational survival, often abraded against the professional bottom line of appropriateness, fees, marketing, merchandising, and partnerships. In every instance, despite the self-funding ethic, it was the ethic of appropriateness that ruled the decision. If it was unseemly we didn't do it, and it never resulted in subordinating organizational loyalty to professional loyalty because the right decision always advanced the cause of both. Similarly, if the organization's leadership were to make a blatantly self-serving decision, it would be a mistaken sense of loyalty to feel a need to blindly support that decision—a decision that was ultimately bad for the organization.

Frequently it seems as if the only spokespersons for the resource are the interpreters who often find themselves at odds with administrative goals, policies, plans, actions, and in-actions. Their level of discomfort usually defines their strategy for dealing with such situations. An administrative proposal to charge for visitor center admission, expand visitation capacities, replace an old facility, or cut a program may be perceived as having a negative or even devastating effect on interpretive goals. A perceived reluctance of administration to address resource needs that conflict with political desires may lead to stressful cognitive dissonance for interpreters. By definition, interpreters speak for others who have no voice—the resource, the future, artifacts, and wildlife. Taking on the job of interpreter means assuming the sobering responsibilities of accurately and persuasively conveying those voiceless messages, and doing so with courage commensurate with the level of trust implied. Most principles of interpretation address the first responsibility only. Courage may be learned by example, but ultimately it must come from within.

The second key to dealing with the ethical dilemma at the intersection is to seek to change the setting. Organizations are changing all over the world in response to new ideas about how to be more effective. New organizations are beginning with a more progressive outlook and structure. Old-line and staff organizations find it much more difficult to change but are doing so. Organizations and agencies with a park mission—a mission of Parks for Life— should be in the lead. Let's face it, those organizations that fear change are doomed but interpretation can change them and save them. Changing the way our organizations do business may not be in anyone's job description, which means that they will never change from the inside. Who better to reshape the organization than those who work for it and are committed to its goals? Just look at the potentials for change and ask yourself which organizational style, old or new, has the best likelihood for success. Which is most likely to build teams, attract partners, accomplish its mission, and which would you prefer to work with? It is your organization, isn't it?

Give people curiosity. It is enough to open minds; do not overload them. Put there just a spark. If there is some good flammable stuff, it will catch fire.

—Anatole France

The New Park Ethic in the Workplace

From:	To:
Controlling	Empowering
Delegating	Relegating
Centralizing	Decentralizing
Hierarchies	Networks
Bureaucratic	Receptive
Boundaries	Communities
Process	Performance
Mistrust	Trust
Job Description	Job Satisfaction
Leading	Learning
Problem Creation	Problem Solving
Authoritarianism	Experimentalism
Pyramids	Teams
Solos	Symphonies

Parks and Sacred Sites
The Third Way of Thinking

States are not moral agents, people are, and can impose
moral standards on great institutions.

—Noam Chomsky

Belief is what this collection of essays is all about. Belief in the value of parks for every aspect of our lives, belief in the necessity for preserving undiminished parks for future generations, belief in the stewardship of professional park management, belief that we all can and must do a better job of that stewardship, and belief that all stewardship begins with a profound respect for the land and its spiritual quality. While on a national park project in Bulgaria in the early 1990s, I wandered away from a meeting and visited an Orthodox Monastery in the Rila Mountains. The monastery was just beginning its long road back from two generations under Communist rule. The only monk present was kind enough to visit with me and escort me around the grounds, showing me with enormous satisfaction how well the craftsmanship of his predecessors had withstood nearly a half-century of neglect. When I mentioned that I was assisting in the development of new policies for the national park system, of which the Rilas were a part, he gazed at the surrounding peaks and said with evident emotion that preserving the land was "sacred work" and that it was "too bad that the former government hadn't understood that." From that moment I began to see the discussion of park policies in a clearer, and inevitably, far more complex light.

The land becomes sacred in many ways—through its mystical past, like a Stonehenge; through its connections to high places, like a Mt. Olympus; through what it has witnessed, like a Gettysburg; and by way of its associations, location and features, like sacred groves and sacred trees. It might be argued that every park, simply by being designated as special, is a sacred part of our heritage. Advocates have often, and sometimes eloquently though always inadequately, sought to make the case that all land is sacred because it gives life. Certainly every person who feels a love for nature, for Mother Earth, has a special place that is sacred. Many parks have been consecrated, perhaps superfluously, but the way I see it the land needs every layer of protection it can get. In the final analysis, "sacred" is used best as an unofficial designation in response to an emotional connection to the land. Much like the words "love," and "mother," and "patriotism," it inevitably falls short of conveying the underlying emotion. Since "sacred" inevitably raises eyebrows and produces consternation among those unfortunates who do not have a sacred bit of nature of their own, perhaps the word "soulful" (i.e., full of soul) works as well. "Soul" somehow seems to be tolerable even to the most manifestly soulless legal mind. "Parks as food for the soul" might keep us out of pointless litigation and impart an understanding that will not invoke "whose soul?" and "whose religion?" To me, "unofficial" is an essential requirement of being sacred. Totally aside from the separation issue, it would be unseemly for government to designate and protect those lands already designated and protected by higher powers and by the individual, free-spirited, and capable soul.

Some of the most powerful writing about nature and parks that I know of is written not from the intellect of the mind or from the emotion of the heart but rather from the awakening of the soul. It is the prose and the poetry that comes closest to the visceral feeling of viewing an Ansel Adams photograph of Yosemite, or a Bierstadt painting of Yellowstone, or listening to Grofe's *Grand Canyon Suite*. It is the writing that makes us want to save land so that we too can savor similar experiences. Consider, for example, Norman MacLean's closing lines of *A River Runs Through It:*

> Eventually, all things merge into one, and a river runs through it. The river was cut by the world's great flood and runs over rocks from the basement of time. On some of the rocks are timeless raindrops. Under the rocks are the words, and some of the words are theirs. I am haunted by waters.

Having shared almost identical feelings, I am unable to forget Jim Harrison's words on seeing his first wolf:

> It took me twenty years to see a timber wolf in the wild. We stared at each other. From this single incident, I dreamt I found the wolf with her back broken on a logging road. I knelt down and she went inside me, becoming part of my body and skeleton.

In the world of environmental interpretation, we speak of establishing emotional and intellectual connections between that which is being interpreted and the viewer or listener. We also struggle with effective ways of blending the two—for the intellect rebels against the heart and the heart does not need the intellect. The connection that a few nature writers have been able to seize upon is writing from the soul. They are not writing for anyone but themselves, but their writing resonates with something within us that needs nourishing. Food for the soul from the soul of nature in sacred lands helps to fill that need.

Trying to analyze what comes from the soul, as opposed to the mind and the heart, is probably not a very good idea. It's a lot like beauty—you know it when you see it. However, after working many years with hundreds of students I don't believe a single one of them ever missed the point when I shared Aldo Leopold's account of killing his first and last wolf:

> We reached the old she wolf in time to watch a fierce green fire dying in her eyes. I realized then, and have known ever since, there was something new to me in those eyes—something known only to her and to the mountain.

Leopold was a scientist, with a huge heart, so what was new to him came neither from the mind nor from the heart. There are certain qualities that seem to be more commonly associated with food for the soul than with food for thought and for the heart. Among these qualities are humility and reverence and certainly silence and awareness. On this and many other occasions, Leopold appeared to be struggling with his scientific self and with the knowledge that scientific management of our parks and forests can only mean the seizing of control from nature and subordination of the sacred to the scientific.

If we hope to contribute to the need for sacred places in our lives, parks have a difficult role to perform. Some of the time we need to back away from our overwhelming propensity to control, to manage, to tinker, to improve, to regulate, and to protect. The problem is in knowing when. When the sacred tree in the sacred grove is severely damaged by lightning, we would like to believe that we have no compelling reason to interfere, to repair it, and perhaps install lightning rods. But can we control our urge to interfere? When New Hampshire's megalithic Old Man of the Mountain finally fell in response to the inevitability of gravity, we may have liked to believe that there would be no pressures to profane the still sacred site with a man-made replica. But, there were.

Managing sacred sites, like managing wilderness, may be a lot easier than we think. I for one would have no use for a *Field Guide to Sacred Places*. Sacred places are probably impossible to inventory anyway, and it also seems like a good thing not to identify them and classify them in categories of "Must See" and "Only If You Have Time." I have no desire to try to locate the spot where Leopold had his awakening or the exact canyon campsite where Terry Tempest Williams saw a lunar rainbow in

> *a sweep of stardust... the presence of angels... innocent and wild, privy to secrets and gifts exchanged only in nature. I was*

the tree split open by change. I was the flood bursting through
grief. I was the rainbow at night, dancing in darkness.

I like to think of these places as exemplifying Leopold's wise counsel: *"Of what avail are forty freedoms without a blank spot on the map?"*

In northern Maine, there is a peak named Katahdin that is sacred to the Wabanaki tribes of the region. Katahdin is surrounded by 200,000-acre Baxter State Park, a gift to the people of Maine by its erstwhile governor, Percival Baxter. The gift was wrapped in sacred trusts, making it impossible for future state governments to interfere with Governor Baxter's purpose. The Governor knew all too well that what one government creates another government can dismantle. Unable to call upon a higher power to protect the land he saw as sacred to the people of Maine, he did the next best thing—He took it out of the normal organization of government and created a trust to administer it. Probably very few of the thousands who annually visit Katahdin go in search of a soulful experience, but for those who do it is there and always will be.

If sacred places have the ability to awaken the soul to experiences that are denied us by the mind and the heart, we'd best not tinker with them. In ancient times, sacred sites were the domain of the Gods and all the rest of the land was profaned and available for the rest of us. Hopefully, the new gods of science will not find it necessary to use their magic to unravel the mystery of these special places. All that is necessary is to ensure that they be there.

Perhaps someday there will be a new and improved test for park administrators, consisting of three parts that match the three ways of thinking: scientific, emotional, and spiritual. Wouldn't you be a lot more comfortable knowing that your sacred sites were being overseen by someone who not only had to be credentialed in something called *park science* but who was also required to submit an essay called "Sacred Places I Have Known"? After all, it is a sacred trust, isn't it?

Through interpretation, understanding
Through understanding, appreciation
Through appreciation, protection
—U.S. National Park Service

Parks and Wildlife
Thinning the Herd—Diluting the Image

While stewards may stew,
and rulers may rue,
the laws of Nature always come through.

—WFL

Watching the little boy watching the Canada geese in the park, and watching the Canada geese watching the little boy for any sign that he might be bringing them food, proved to be an instructive experience. As the stale bread came out of the paper bag, a dozen geese converged on the source of food. The three-year-old stood his ground, throwing bread slices and even letting them take bread from his hand until—you guessed it—until the adults intervened. The child's sense of wonder changed to one of confusion as the unmistakable concern of his parents visibly revised his view of wild geese; the remaining bread slices were scattered in hasty retreat. Watchable wildlife has been a feature of parks for many generations, but only recently has it become an addition to the park management vocabulary, one that has taken off with jointly developed informational programs and construction of viewing sites, but not always with a set of ethical viewing guidelines.

Many of our ideas about wild creatures have, understandably, come to us in second-hand ways, from childhood fables to the sometimes equally fabled experiences of contemporary hunters and anglers. Unlike our forbears, most of us today will never hear the howl of a wolf in the wild, never see an elk or a bear outside of a zoo, and not be able to identify more than one or two species of birds. Wildlife, to the average urban and suburban dweller, is a growing collection of "problem" species, that adapt well to living among humans, such as skunks, squirrels, pigeons, coyotes, deer, and sometimes when we encroach into their territory even bear and cougar. Even so called "good" wildlife becomes a problem when it gets in the way of our vehicles and has to be cleaned off the roads. Businesses have sprung up to deal with problem wildlife, another new addition to wildlife taxonomy and management. Life was so much simpler when we just had good wildlife and bad wildlife, the "good" being those species that had a market value or we could sell licenses for harvesting, and the "bad" being varmints, disposables and "trash" species.

Without parks, most of us would have few chances to see wildlife in the wild, or at least near-wild, settings. Without parks, our understanding of wildlife habitat would drop from minimal to nonexistent. And, without park interpretation, the history of our interactions with wildlife would be little more than a subject in school. Wildlife legitimizes the wild nature of our parks in much the same way that books legitimize a library. But we have not always recognized wildlife as rightful park residents and visitors, as witnessed by early programs to eliminate wolves from Yellowstone, in an attempt to satisfy needs for more "watchable wildlife," and in the wildly mistaken assumption that the visiting public wanted its nature denatured.

The stories of wildlife in our parks are, by far, the single biggest item in the park interpreter's repertoire. Within that category, the "Everybody's somebody's lunch" theme, as my friend and children's book author, Cheri Mason, calls it, is probably the run-away favorite. The clusters of vehicles at wildlife viewing areas attest to the attraction that even a promise of seeing wild creatures holds for visitors. Attendance at campfire programs, visitor center presentations, and other special wildlife events, such as eagle watches, owl prowls, coyote calls, and elk bugles, should serve to clinch the fact that watchable, hearable, memorable connections to wildlife are what makes for a complete park visit. To simply have seen a bison, a wolf, a bear, a moose, an elk, or an eagle is as special for most of us as it is for a three-year-old to encounter a Canada goose or a squirrel in the park.

So, what are we doing for the wildlife? In parks having wildlife management programs, the focus tends to be on issues of population control, habitat improvement, protection of rare and endangered species, and protection of nesting and rearing sites. In most parks, the wildlife, like the visitors, are transients, so management of the wildlife is a form of visitor management; making it eminently reasonable to involve the human visitors in the wildlife programs. Human visitors make excellent tools for inventorying migratory birds and, since parks tend to provide superior aggregating sites, mountains for hawks, and marshes and water bodies for shorebirds and water fowl, the makings of a perfect management partnership for many parks. With people drawn to the same features that attract wildlife, it is only a small step to the understanding that seeing wildlife has to mean supporting wildlife.

In parks where small abandoned hydropower sites, such as mill ponds, have created valuable impoundments for wildlife, and where there is no money for maintaining dams, volunteers and heavy equipment donations have helped to maintain the resource for the benefit of both wildlife and visitors. Correcting streambed erosion and improving miles of spawning habitat has been a gift to the wild transients from their human counterparts in hundreds of parks. Nesting sites for rare and endangered species, like peregrine falcons, bald eagles, and piping plovers, have been respectfully and voluntarily off-limits to park visitors who enthusiastically share their parks in the recovery effort. The efforts of volunteers made the difference in successfully reintroducing wolves to the wildernesses of central Idaho. The voluntary contributions of millions of sportsmen to habitat preservation and restoration, over the past many decades, has helped to make the concept of watchable wildlife a reality all across America.

The issue now is what needs to be done, and what could be done, to ensure this vital connection to the wild in all of our parks? Perhaps, that's the first step—making the wild connection for every visitor at every park. Every community park, state park, and national park is the home of wild creatures. Every visitor, upon entering the park, needs to know whose home it is. Respecting the home of wild others is the first step to respecting the park for the human others who follow us. Parks, having the support of all visitors, do not have the burden of distinguishing between game and nongame species, between prey and predator, between charismatic megafauna and insects. Parks are in the enviable position among all public lands of being able, in fact, obliged, to treat wildlife holistically and ecologically. Parks can interpret and protect, if they choose to, major segments of the web of life; and provide truly wild visitor experiences.

What's presently missing, it seems, is not wildlife appreciation, but real appreciation of wild lives as the essential connection to parks for all of life. If wildlife were to be truly recognized for the incredible asset it is to parks, how might its management be different? What kinds of visitor alerts would be provided regarding pets in parks, disposal of waste, introduction of exotics, and areas to avoid? What messages would be given to visitors in the form of wildlife cycles and wildlife calendars in the park? What special sightings might visitors be alerted to in order to assist management in its wildlife stewardship efforts? What maps might be provided for the visitor to understand where else the transient species spend part of their lives, so that the really interested might be able to follow them on their journeys? What wild lives might be valuable indicators, even keynote species, of a healthy park?

Park boundaries mean nothing to wildlife regardless of park size. The vast majority of park boundaries reflect little more than the boundaries of opportunity when the park was created, so any meaningful planning for park wildlife must include a partnership with neighboring lands. In fact, any solid commitment to our wild connection for parks must have a long-range plan for converting those meaningless boundaries of opportunity into meaningful zones of necessity—necessary for sustainable wildlife populations, for their value added to the parks, if not for their intrinsic value. It is, in fact, real value added to the abutting lands.

When we fail to create these boundary partnerships, it isn't the wildlife alone that suffers. Thinning Yellowstone's bison herd also dilutes the park's image as a place where the preservation of a truly wild life is the mission. Seeing the panic and the fear in the eyes of these noble creatures as they are being herded, hazed, corralled, squeezed into loading chutes, and crowded into trucks for a disrespectful disposal leaves an indelible stain and raises an uncomfortable set of questions: How far have we really advanced in our thinking since the days when we eliminated Yellowstone's wolves? If the lives of the bison are not sacred enough to deserve a more respectful treatment, what does it say for the life of the park itself? What is the real significance of the bison image on the National Park shield? There are, of course, millions of acres of public lands where surplus bison could be successfully restocked. And, of course, a fair percentage of those lands are not all that public, having been locked into marginally productive grazing leases where tradition out-ranks the public good.

Bison are simply the most visible example of how we manage "problem" wildlife in parks. The list is extensive, with overpopulations of elk, beaver, deer, coyotes, wolves, numerous species of fish and birds, and yes, even Canada geese being treated, from time-to-time and from place-to-place as pests rather than guests. In every case, there is a better, more respectful, but admittedly more expensive, alternative. That difference in cost is precisely the value we currently place on park wildlife, whether it's the culled or the unculled, because the only difference between the two is the luck of the draw. If park agencies are not willing or able to pay the difference, the owner-public should at least know what that difference is. Parks are, after all, theirs.

What is a park for if it is not for life—a place where all of life is considered just a little more special? It seems hopeful that a Parks for Life ethic might force us to open many doors in search of management solutions that are more respectful than "thinning the herd." A qualified commitment to parks for human life alone will not work.

We do not understand that it is also vandalism to wantonly destroy or to permit the destruction of that which is beautiful in nature.

—Theodore Roosevelt

Part Three
EXPANDING THE FIELD

Successfully playing the game of parks today, and for the foreseeable future, requires a major increase in the number of players. To paraphrase an old saying about war being too important to leave to the generals, the very last thing our parks need is a layer of commanding generals. When park policy and park funding insists on arbitrarily restricting park programs to recreation facilities and services, it's time to build a new and enlarged stadium—one that can accommodate education, public health, human resources, peace and justice, jobs and the economy, and food for the body and the spirit. When the desire for control limits the number of players on the field by stifling opportunities to reach out and build partnerships, it's time to examine the controllers' agendas. When budget impasses shut down parks as "nonessential government services," our elected and appointed officials expose their one-dimensional view of the role of parks in society. Worse, their view of recreation is, itself, sadly out of step with today's understanding of the interconnectedness of work and leisure. However, whose fault is it if we have failed to invite all of the players onto the field and put them into the game?

The paradigm of stewardship as a job description has failed us. Stewardship cannot happen as an assignment for the few, only as a responsibility for the many. There can be no stewardship without partnership. Parks for Life is no small field. It embraces all of life. If our lives must be compartmentalized, with generals in charge of each compartment, here is where our lives can come together again. Here is where we can take charge, where parks can put the fragments back together. Here is where the connections become obvious, where play becomes work, and work becomes play, where learning becomes fun, and fun becomes learning. Parks For Life is not proposed as an expansion of the chain of command, but as a celebration of the chain of life. For any park, the links in that chain of life are called partnerships, the more links the stronger the chain.

Toward a More Perfect Union
Partnering, a Legacy, and an Imperative

I am truly sorry man's dominion has broken Nature's perfect union.

—Robert Burns

The philosophy of partnerships is to the park profession what "multiple use" is to the forestry profession. Though rarely recognized as such, this guiding principle is what makes parks a profession. In fact, some parks have gone way beyond partnerships and coalitions to organizational mosaics that begin to mirror nature's own way of operating. We take it for granted that our partnerships are an accepted precept of sound management. It isn't until we look at other professions that we realize how perfectly partnerships permeate all that we do. When we recognize the enormity of the stewardship responsibility, we know that there is no other way. If we were to do a complete balance sheet on the costs and benefits of parks, we would know that no amount of tax dollars could replace partnerships. The idea of subjecting partnerships to a cost-benefit analysis may be repugnant to some, but it is a guaranteed way to create true believers among the skeptics. While it is clear that no park experience is possible without the partnering of a visitor and a park in pursuit of the same goal, such as a litter-free park, it is often much less obvious that a few silent partners may have been critical to the success of that experience.

Throughout its history, America's public park movement has enjoyed a special relationship with its citizens and their institutions. Perhaps no other activity of government more clearly embodies the fundamentals of democracy than those public-private partnerships that create, sustain, and give meaning to millions of acres of public parklands. From outright gifts of land with no solid guarantee of stewardship to volunteer rangers and citizen advisory groups, America's public parks have moved us toward that "more perfect union" of people with their lands and their government. Nonprofit park protectors, corporate benefactors, and citizen advocates in the millions have joined forces in the "pursuit of happiness" at a dazzling array of our public parks, forests, trails, and historic sites at every level of government. A million-dollar visitor center built by park friends can only be compared with the reality of no visitor center and no improvement in park appreciation accruing from that visitor center.

The honor roll of friends of the park—that endless list of presidents and volunteers, industrialists and citizens, representatives and senators, artists and authors, teachers and students—has given real meaning to the ideal of participatory democracy. Their efforts are second only to the nation's defense, as Theodore Roosevelt, one of the most outspoken defenders of our public lands, insisted, *"Nothing short of defending America in time of war can be more important that of preserving these lands."* Teddy would be gratified by the growing army of defenders who have responded to his challenge. In fact, it would probably be difficult to find a park system or a park for that matter that does not appreciate volunteerism, friends groups, and park partnerships.

As other agencies of government struggle with mandates to reinvent themselves, many public park systems have known for years that they do not fit the conventional description of public administration. They were forced to become complex organizations before the term was invented. Even the word *organization* carries some baggage from out of the past that makes it difficult to view these affiliations for what they really are: revolutionary approaches to conducting the public's business and to discharging the public's mandates. If we are to fairly evaluate these partnerships against conventional styles of public administration, we need a new vocabulary for words like "staffing," "directing," "coordinating," "planning," and "budgeting." We also need some better indicators of success that aren't driven by inputs and measured by numbers. The real outputs of a partnered park go far beyond enhanced visitor experiences to include reduced tax burdens, extended life of resources and facilities, an involved public contributing to a stronger democracy, fuller lives and more rewarding careers for employees, and a new sense of community pride. And none of this appears in the annual report!

Trying to coordinate the workings of a traditional old-line public agency, constrained by its system of laws, rules, policies, procedures, budget, and fragmented authorities, with a comparatively unfettered advocacy group that is impatient for change, intolerant of red tape, funded, and staffed is probably an exercise in futility. Better to enjoy the creative tensions opposites produce and focus instead on a division of responsibilities between immediate and long-term projects, environmental and visitor service projects, easy and difficult tasks, and group and individual projects. With the possible exception of scheduling for public service, volunteer "coordination" is a misnomer at best. *Volunteer facilitation* is a much more accurate description of the essential tasks of developing guidelines and matching volunteer interests with park needs.

The richness of partnering opportunities in the parks and their almost unbelievable legacy of generosity conceals their relatively fragile nature. At any stage of development a partnership is highly vulnerable to the whims of park administration. Embryonic partnerships are easily left to wither by administrators who are too busy or too insensitive to nurture them. Even well-established partnerships may be derailed by being given largely symbolic and ritualistic functions. Friends groups face a constant risk of becoming too exclusive. Organizational and professional partnerships can easily become bogged down by the process of cooperation and the scarcity of budgeted funds. Corporate partnerships can succumb to a change in the economy or in leadership. Many partnerships, particularly in the early years, cannot weather the loss of a key player on either team. Perseverance, a willingness to experiment, and a commitment to objectives are the ideal qualities of a park administrator looking for partners. Quite fortunately they also happen to be the descriptors of most park professionals.

Tracking and reporting the accomplishments of partnerships is probably the most essential, and happily, the most rewarding aspect of the relationship. Accurate recordkeeping is not always easy for the park agency with volunteers, friends groups, interagency cooperation, corporate partners, and public partners. It's easy to miss something and hurt feelings can result. Similarly, in trying to portray a representative listing of the possibilities here, the omissions are overwhelming:

> In West Virginia, the Mountain State Railroad and Logging Historical Association laid track, restored railroad camp cars and an overhead tower log skidder, constructed and operated a railroad snack bar, raised funds for the purchase of equipment, installed track switches, and provided major maintenance on locomotives at Cass Scenic Railroad State Park.

> Over the span of several years, the Trustees of the Robert Frost Farm raised extensive funds to rescue, renovate, and provide programs and staff for the Robert Frost Farm Historic Site in Derry, New Hampshire.

> The Friends of the Rio Grande Nature Center State Park, in Albuquerque, New Mexico provide interpretive services for school groups, manage special events and field trips, provide funding for management of the park gift shop, pay speaker honoraria, and annually raise thousands of dollars for equipment for the center and protection of its riverine setting.

> Through a long-term partnership with PepsiCo, the New Hampshire state park system was able to develop learning materials for school children, concerts in the parks, an audio tape and CDs

of songs celebrating the parks and historic sites by the world-traveled Shaw Brothers, statewide parks promotion, a park mascot to deliver environmental messages, while becoming a nationally recognized model for corporate partnerships with parks.

In Wisconsin, the Seth Peterson Cottage Conservancy saved and operates a habitable work of art at Mirror Lake State Park. The cottage, that is said to have more architecture per square foot than any other building ever designed by Frank Lloyd Wright, a Wisconsin native son, continues to generate revenue for its upkeep and has gained national attention including a feature article in the *Architectural Digest*.

Partners for Pinnacle at Pinnacle Mountain State Park in Roland, Arkansas holds several fundraising events each year with its nearly 2,000 volunteers in support of a student conservation intern for the park and the Pinnacle Mountain Arboretum. The group has served as a model for the development of other volunteer associations throughout the Arkansas state park system.

At Maudsley State Park in Massachusetts, the friends association rents a van and provides tour guide service for mobility-impaired visitors to enjoy this spectacular former estate's rhododendron and azalea plantings.

In Hawaii, the Friends of Iolani Palace operate, maintain, and provide guided tours of the only royal palace in the United States.

In Connecticut, the Friends of Dinosaur Park Association provide funding and extensive volunteer support for programs, activities, events, and developments at Dinosaur State Park.

In New Hampshire, the Wentworth-Coolidge Commission fully restored and refurnished the only colonial Governor's mansion from the thirteen original colonies with researched attention to detail, including fabrication of the original wallpapers using completely original methods and materials.

Also in New Hampshire, a partnership with the visiting public resulted in America's first litter-free state park system. The replacement of litter barrels with "carry in, carry out" litter bags was facilitated by several additional partnerships that provided the bags imprinted with a park message on one side and the sponsor's message on the other.

In North Dakota, the Fort Abraham Lincoln Foundation spurred the reconstruction of General George Custer's command post and interprets frontier military life.

In Kansas, the Friends of the Public Lands raise funds and provide labor in support of wildlife projects, horse trails, handicap-accessible playgrounds, shelters, and the development of modern restroom facilities.

In Massachusetts, the Trustees of Public Reservations has served for over three generations as a quasi-public agency with the mission of acquiring and managing critical lands needing public protection.

Cumberland Falls State Park in Kentucky and Franconia Notch State Park in New Hampshire, along with uncounted others in many states, owe their origins to the dedicated activism of the Federated Women's Clubs, forest protection societies, and enormously generous private benefactors.

The Lutheran Brotherhood, a fraternal life insurance association, teamed up with Florida state parks to produce and distribute the state parks gift catalogue in hundreds of thousands of copies, drawing attention to the system's needs from computers to vehicles and boat docks and generating hundreds of thousands of dollars worth of donations to improve service to the public at no cost to taxpayers.

Through a long-standing partnership with the White Mountain National Forest and the state park system, the Appalachian Mountain Club (AMC) maintains and operates a world-famous hut-and-shelter system on state and federal lands in New Hampshire. On the summit of Mt. Washington, highest point in the eastern United States, the operation of a 56-acre state park are overseen by a unique partnership, including the AMC, the Mt. Washington Observatory, three public agencies, and two private corporations.

The Friends of Arizona's Site Stewards provides funding and technical assistance in support of the state's park and historic site stewards who both help protect and document the area's archeological treasures.

In Idaho, the Old Mission Associates devotes its energies and resources to the restoration, protection, and interpretation of the oldest standing building in Idaho, the Old Mission at Cataldo.

The Society for the Protection of New Hampshire Forests has partnered with the state in buying critical tracts of land and cooperatively managing several tracts including the lands of Mt. Monadnock and Mt. Kearsarge State Parks and the John Hay estate on Lake Sunapee in southwestern New Hampshire. In addition, the New Hampshire Audubon Society and the Friends of Odiorne Point State Park helped to raise construction funds and operate the park's $1 million visitor center.

In New Hampshire, the complete infrastructure of Mt. Cardigan State Park was replaced by local volunteers and donors; and the Friends of Pisgah purchased lands critical to Pisgah State Park, obtained staffing for the park, and dismantled and moved a historic farm house into the park for use as a visitor center.

The Telephone Pioneers of America have provided handicap access in parks all across America, such as accessible trails and fishing piers in Vermont, Wisconsin, New Hampshire, and South Carolina; park adoptions and fundraising programs in Michigan and New Hampshire; accessible play equipment, cabins, telephones, captioned videos, brochures, and an endless variety of work projects in these and other states.

Finally, prior to its collapse on the night of May 2, 2003, New Hampshire's trademark natural feature, the Old Man of the Mountain, had been expertly maintained by two generations of the Neilson family at great personal risk and no cost to the state, with no formal agreement and with no insurance.

Any attempt at a complete listing of partnerships for America's parks would be an encyclopedic undertaking. The dollars, the hours, the devotion, the battles fought, the acres protected, the visits enhanced, and the dreams realized could only be characterized as unbelievable anywhere else but here. Here, where the parks inspire and the volunteers see their role as just part of being a citizen, the accomplishments may be heroic in scope but they're also a way of doing the public's business. Often lacking any kind of legislative authorization, executive order, charter, nonprofit status, mission statement, or even formal recognition by the park, they epitomize a famous line by Jonathan Winters: *"I couldn't wait for success, so I just went ahead without it."*

Beyond a doubt, the single most important thing that the park profession could do to help sustain its vital partnering movement is to document and publicize it size, accomplishments, trends, and value to the parks. Professional research in park partnerships would inevitably highlight barriers to even greater accomplishments through partnering, such as the many issues raised in the 1987 President's Commission on Americans Outdoors: leadership, insurance and liability problems, needed legislation, improved recordkeeping, and support for training staff and volunteers.

Perhaps equally important to publicizing partnering accomplishments is the setting of challenging goals. Every park in America needs an endowment. When the Friends of Acadia challenged their membership to raise the millions necessary to create the national park system's only endowed trail system, they challenged us all. What facet of your park would you like to see protected with a trust fund for all time? Now, thanks to the Friends of Acadia, you know it can be done.

If you believe you can or if you believe you can't, you're right.
—Henry Ford

Inviting Involvement
Tapping into the Energy of Partnerships

Coming together is a beginning. Keeping together is progress.
Working together is success.

—Henry Ford

Few among the all-too-small group that call themselves park professionals
would dispute the necessity for park partnerships, yet relatively little is provided in professional park training on the subject of how to do it. What are the
building blocks and who are the players in this vital enterprise? While there
can be no formula or blueprint for successfully crafting a partnership, it is not
illogical to expect some guidelines drawn from the vast pool of partnering
initiatives over the past many decades.

Partnerships can range from handshakes to formal agreements, from the
individual volunteer to the multinational corporation, from the local elemen-
tary school to the university, and from highly focused friends groups to
adoptions by the local Kiwanis club. They can be unspoken, as in the social
contract to not litter. They can be highly specific and limited in scope to
helping to plan, staff, and operate the park. They can also be open-ended or
terminated when their task is completed. With such diversity in tools, it becomes clear that each partnership has to be crafted to fit the situation and that
a partnership is a living thing that can grow from one arrangement to another.
At least the range of potential players is identifiable, beginning with that group
that has the largest stake in the outcome—the visiting public.

Beginning in the latter half of the past century, many decades after the
gates to the parks were thrown open, the public's involvement in park planning
became a requirement of management. What was previously a good idea for
any careful planner now became the law. Inviting the public to help plan
their parks is clearly just a step away from asking the public to help manage
their parks. Most of the partnerships that parks have with their visitors can
be thought of as relatively nonbinding social contracts.

However, the public's acceptance of park rules as a condition of admission
is clearly a legal contract. Similarly, the use of a variety of financial incentives
and discounted admission benefits to the public in return for their patronage
is a solid economic contract—a limited partnership. So, parks have been in

the partnering game with their visitors for years. What is of interest now is converting those passive partners into active partners with park watch programs, park promotion programs, and park appreciation programs.

Partnering with the public for the purposes of good stewardship simply means creating an ambassador out of every visitor. Encouraging greater awareness, familiarity, and knowledge of public parks is a natural outcome of rewarding and memorable visits and is probably the single best way of countering threats to a park's integrity. The ultimate protection for any park is an appreciative clientele. The National Park Service's passport program (with a different stamp for every park) and West Virginia's Very Important Parks Person (VIPP) program are clearly designed to produce ambassadors for parks. Many parks have Junior Park Ranger programs with similar goals.

Any enhancement in park visibility is bound to pay results indirectly through greater involvement and membership in environmental organizations, tax check-offs (where possible) for parks, and increased public awareness of park needs; and directly in terms of an enormous increase in the eyes and ears of park protection. The fact that these partnerships tend to be informal, spontaneous, and ad hoc makes it easy to take them for granted. However, these are the partnerships that create the fertile field for all the others to grow in, such as the often-silent partners and private benefactors that have given parks life.

The contributions of thousands of committed individuals and families in the development of our state and national park systems are legendary and have made spectacular differences. From the well-known contributions of the Rockefeller family to national parks all across America to the forgotten deeds of a national park superintendent who, during a budget-slashing frenzy in the early years, retained his entire staff at his own expense for a year, and the California congressmen who used his own money to preserve a stand of threatened coastal redwoods.

Very often the success of private friends groups and corporate partnerships are closely tied to the dedication of an individual or a family who funnels their generosity through the group, often through a bequest because they know it will strengthen their gift (perhaps in perpetuity). Parks do not have to promote such giving themselves; they only need to produce benefits and their friends will do it for them.

Less spectacular, but often the difference between a visit and a memorable visit, are the countless opportunities for individual volunteerism that can be promoted by parks. Campground hosts (now a standard in most park systems), marina hosts, visitor center hosts, self-appointed litter police, trail builders, interpreters, and storytellers are just a few of the ways people choose to become involved in their parks. In doing so they make parks come alive in very special ways. No one has yet compiled their stories, but they are every bit as much a vital part of our park legacy as are the spectacular scenery and the quiet places by the stream. Hopefully someday these stories will be written as incentives to others and as training for future park professionals. How much more useful might they be as graduate student theses than just one more survey of visitors?

The fragmentation of responsibility for our public lands gives different agencies different jurisdictions and responsibilities for forests, water, air, minerals, parks, wildlife, and fisheries and has made interagency partnering an absolute necessity. With state, federal, county, and local parks often abutting each other and sharing identical clientele, the necessity for compatible rules, access, and interpretive programs can only happen in a spirit of professional cooperation.

The National Park Service, the founder of the National Conference on State Parks, continues today to assist the states with their park programs in stunningly effective ways with the Land and Water Conservation Fund Program and through such innovative park partnerships as the Lowell State and National Historical Park in Massachusetts and the Lyndon Johnson Historical Park in Texas.

In recent years the interest in corridor-type parks, greenways, and long trails for jogging, cycling, cross-country skiing, walking, bird-watching, and all-terrain vehicles has resulted in physical linkages and partnership agreements between a great variety of public land managers and private landowners. The Great Western Trail that runs from Canada to Mexico through Idaho, Montana, Utah, Arizona, and New Mexico unites numerous federal and state land managing agencies in a common effort. The 230-mile Heritage Trail, to run the length of the state of New Hampshire, links five different state agencies, two federal agencies, and over 40 community agencies in a multipurpose trail/greenway program. Similar greenway programs all across America herald both a new way of meeting recreational needs and new ways of interagency cooperation. Interagency information centers in several western cities provide one-stop shopping for the public lands visitor needing information. Rails-to-Trails conversions inevitably link a multiplicity of public agencies and nonprofit organizations as they zip us all together in common interests.

However, professional partnerships with natural resource agencies are but a small part of the potential that exists for knitting a fabric that binds parks to the rest of a community. Parks are providing unparalleled sites for agencies charged with environmental monitoring, weather forecasting, and scientific studies of all kinds. Corrections departments are providing a valuable source of labor in return for skills training in numerous park systems. Schools and state departments of education are linking up with parks to provide enhanced learning opportunities, such as Florida's Parknership program that matches state parks with hands-on learning opportunities in environmental education. Few park agencies have adequate budgets to conduct their own needed research, but partnerships with universities are answering the needs with studies of visitor behavior trends and visitor impacts on resources. National Guard units and parks are often natural partners for construction and restoration projects.

One of the most obvious and perhaps least developed partnerships is that between parks. The idea of sister parks across state and national boundaries and across the world has been with us for decades, but the number of such ventures is but a fraction of the opportunities. Partnerships for excellence such as the one between Mt. Rainier and Olympic National Parks, partnerships for training between island parks and between mountain parks, and partnerships for cross marketing between state and national historic sites are little past the infancy stage. Adding a small innovation fund to park budgets could do wonders for paying the start-up costs of travel and meetings to bring these potentials along. Is it any wonder that so many partnering efforts have focused on corporations rather than with other underfunded agencies?

Several states have developed very successful corporate partnerships with electric power companies. In recognition of North Carolina State Park's 75th anniversary year, Carolina Power and Light sponsored regional symposiums on The Future of State Parks and the Environment while also committing $144,000 toward that future. The CP&L program also included an Adopt-A-Park program of challenge grants, engineering assistance, and an information and education program about parks. Virginia and West Virginia are among other states that have similarly strong corporate partnership programs with utilities.

As often happens, a one-time corporate "bailout" during a budget crunch to keep a neighboring park open may not seem like a partnership, but it is certainly an open door to developing something of a longer-lasting nature. The images of a park and a partnership can be valuable corporate assets. Similarly, the image of a closed park or a rundown park in the corporation's neighborhood is very likely to be a corporate liability. Similarly, local businesses that happen to share the same name as a nearby park are ideal candidates for partnering. Their image is the park's image. The park can be a great asset to them in focusing visitors on their services and businesses can often field a volunteer work force for the park.

For years, Sea & Ski tanning lotion underwrote the Miss Mississippi State Parks beauty pageant. Pepsi underwrote an effective promotional and educational campaign for New Hampshire state parks for several years. Off! insect repellent and Florida state parks have successfully collaborated for years. In 1991, the S.C. Johnson Company, makers of Off! Deep Woods, underwrote a campaign called "Take Off! to a Florida State Park" and provided over $200,000 in free advertising annually and $40,000 in support of special projects.

Given their impacts on parks, automobile manufacturers and energy corporations should have become global park partners decades ago. Since its earliest years, the National Park System has worked with the railroads to get people to the parks and with hotel developers (often one and the same) to keep them there longer. Railroads have become corporate partners with state parks by making their abandoned lines available for trails, as the Burlington Northern did in South Dakota. The National Guard became a partner by assisting in developing the trails. Finally, communities along the line joined the partnership to provide trail maintenance. Today, measuring conservation victories is done not simply by celebrating each new acre of parkland but rather by snowballing park alliances.

The number, variety, and influence of nonprofit organizations that can be counted on to support our public parklands is impressive by any standard. At the national level, groups like the National Parks Conservation Association, The Nature Conservancy, The Wilderness Society, the Sierra Club, the National Parks Foundation, the National Recreation and Parks Association, the Audubon Society, the Student Conservation Association, and many others are strong advocates for the mission of parks and wildlands. Many of these same organizations have state and regional chapters. Some states have their own state park foundations that raise funds and lobby to protect park budgets and boundaries. Still other state conservation groups raise funds and acquire properties to be protected and donate them to park agencies.

Individual parks and historic sites are similarly supported or adopted by an endless array of groups that may have no obvious connections to park missions. A local service club, such as the Kiwanis, may adopt a roadside rest area or an unstaffed natural area to maintain it and encourage civic pride. Local unions and employee associations have taken on the responsibility for improving handicapped access in many park facilities. A local civic improvement association, a lake owner's association, or a garden club might make park beautification their permanent project. State and local historic societies have adopted and staffed state historic properties as volunteer projects under contract with park agencies.

Recognizing the legal limitations of park agencies, legislatures have established commissions, foundations, and boards to oversee specific park functions, raise funds, or otherwise support the parks. The accomplishments of these groups in any state are an unending source of pride.

Nonprofit organizations purchase, hold, manage, and donate land to parks. They lobby, promote, and research park causes. They are the activist arm that every park organization needs. They are always there and have often been described as the future of the park movement in America. Their energy and their accomplishments have been responsible for the creation of many of the groups that we know as friends of the parks—the front line of defense for any threatened park. Friends of the parks are the most dedicated of organizational partners because they exist for one reason only—the park.

Typically a friends group is formed to fill an unmet park need, often making them the equivalent of an auxiliary park staff. Since park appreciation is the lifeblood of a friends group, they often focus their energies on providing interpretive services, visitor center staffing, cultural and natural history projects, beautification of park grounds, and restoration of park structures. Friends groups can perform activities that are proscribed for park employees such as fundraising and lobbying. Those parks having friends groups are visibly more vibrant, more vigorous in their outlook and in their grassroots support. Every park needs at least one friends group.

While it might be impossible to find a park without friends, the park with an organized and active friends groups continues to be the exception. Given that paradox, an understanding of how friends groups are born might be helpful. Some are self-starters in that they see a need and come forward to fill that need. Many, however, owe their origins to a crisis in the park—either a threat of a park closure or the potential loss of a park program or feature. Oftentimes the threat may only be perceived, but it is enough to mobilize a group in support. In such cases, the group may quietly disappear, but it is reassuring to know that it will surface again if the need arises. Sometimes an astute park manager may take advantage of the mobilization and put them to work on other park needs.

Friends groups are as diverse as their parks and the functions that they perform. Highly structured or loosely knit, with or without dues, large or small, broadly or narrowly focused, open or closed memberships, their one common denominator is commitment to the park. There are no uncommitted friends groups. How they activate that commitment can mean millions to their park and to its visitors. As a social movement across America's parklands, the friends of the parks carry the torch of the park tradition that was ignited long before our first national park was dedicated and even before our freedoms were enunciated. They are dedicated to keeping alive the spirit of the land.

Fostering partnerships is critical to the very survival of parks.
—Marie Rust

Parks, Paradoxes and Partnerships
The Search for Logic in the Parks

*Individual effort to a group effort— that is what makes a team
work, a company work, a society work, a civilization work.*
                                                        —Vince Lombardi

Short-term budgets or long-term resource protection? Public safety versus
personal responsibility? Minimal fees or fiscal viability? Efficiency versus
diversity? Resource protection or customer service? In a field beset with
contradictions, perhaps the most inexplicable paradox is that the elegant
harmony of nature that inspired America's public parklands has failed to foster
a complimentary administrative ethic based on partnerships—meaningful
linkages with other parks and with every aspect of a society that needs, uses,
and believes in its parks. Often, and appropriately, characterized as a confusion
of agencies, mandates, jurisdictions and philosophies, our public parks have
nonetheless met the changing needs of their publics for several generations.
Legitimate concerns can be raised, however, as to their continued ability to do
so given the ever-growing gap between public demands and organizational
limitations. With almost clockwork regularity we call for blue ribbon evaluations and reorganization of resource agencies as ways to deal with impending
crises, yet rarely do we look at the real reasons for resource decline: the gaps
between our beliefs and our practices.

For a glimpse at just a few of the daily paradoxes that park professionals
live with, consider the following inconsistencies between our principles and
our routine administrative practices.

- Almost by definition, park agencies are committed to the fundamentals of accountability for and stewardship of the resources and
  assets entrusted to them; yet their "stockholder" reports rarely
  comment on the condition and trend of those resources and assets.
  By managing to account for the budget at a very high level, the
  security of the treasures is assumed.

- Every public park agency subscribes to the principle that our public
  lands belong to all and should be available for the enjoyment of
  all. In practice, this usually translates into minimal fees and general

fund subsidies. In turn, the general fund dictates the level of park management with the inevitable result that there are temporal, spatial and staffing restrictions, and closures that result in significant barriers to enjoyment by all.

- Most public park agencies have a policy, written or unwritten, of avoiding competition with the private sector. Public park pricing practices, expansion practices, and promotion practices undercut those of their potential partners in the private sector. A noncompetition policy lacks the teeth of a positive policy of partnering.

- In principle, most park agencies are committed at the policy level to empowering their employees as a way of fostering job satisfaction and more fully utilizing available talent. Empowerment is a fundamental characteristic of public administration in a democracy, yet it is rarely translated into a meaningful partnering relationship with employees, volunteers, or in contracts.

- Every park agency has policies to ensure that people with disabilities are not denied the benefits of their parks, yet few have successfully dealt with the issue beyond partial provision for the mobility impaired. Viewing parks from the vantage of a partnership with all users is a better way of seeing the barriers and the benefits parks could deliver for mental and physical disabilities.

- All public park agencies subscribe to the democratic principle of public involvement in decision making. Involvement in practice, however, tends to be limited to the planning function with little or no encouragement to participate in the equally vital administrative functions of operations, staffing, monitoring, organization, and research.

The second greatest paradox of the park management profession is that while seeming to support the goal of improving the quality of public use, as advocated by Aldo Leopold, it actively engages in practices that increase the quantity of use while diminishing the quality of that use. For example, do lifeguards at a natural beach build personal responsibility or serve as a substitute for it? Do trash cans throughout a park promote a quality of use that is consistent with park values? Are fences around hazards an overzealous attempt at public service? Do extreme recreational pursuits in a park, with their attendant search-and-rescue risks, promote an appreciation for the respectful use of that park? Do automated entrances and iron rangers serve the visiting public as well as a volunteer or partner might? Finally, does the almost automatic focus on closures and limiting visitor services at budget-trimming time reflect a commitment to improving the quality of use?

If the underlying philosophy of management is anything close to the concept of "improving the quality of public use," are these the practices to use? The direct costs of locking up a resource, and enforcing that lockup, can easily be higher than some of the alternatives. Disenfranchising people from their resources or failing to give them needed information is not only a professional inconsistency but also sacrifices long-term resource appreciation (i.e., quality of use) for short-term expedience. The rewards for failing to improve the quality of public use can only be more restrictions, more deferred maintenance, more loss of heritage, less diversity, and a reduction in the public's feelings of pride and ownership. Conversely, the commitment to improving the quality of public use and expanding the public's responsibility for its own resources can provide real assurance of park perpetuity.

The third great paradox of the park profession is that while parks are managed under an assumption of the public trust to ensure park assets for the enjoyment of future generations, we still have not committed to a true accountability reporting system. Had that commitment happened decades ago, we might not now be facing the national embarrassment of a deferred maintenance bill on our stewardship in the *billions* of dollars for park infrastructure alone. Further, a strong commitment to asset accountability would have led us to create meaningful measures of accomplishment in areas of ecological protection, biological diversity, cultural resource stabilization, quality of use, levels of maintenance, and public appreciation. Collectively, such a commitment would have guaranteed the reality of an annual State of the Parks report to the American public. The progression from resource inventories to management plans to accomplishment measures is still achievable even at this late date, but only with an extensive network of public park partners.

We seem to have done a poor job of persuading most political and administrative transients that accountability for park resources is the first order of business for a park. No one questions the need for a daily cash report or an annual equipment inventory, but we never seem to have the budget to inventory natural resource conditions and only rarely for infrastructure assessment. Recognizing that the assets are valued in the billions and the cash and equipment in the millions, the partial accounting ends up looking much like a smoke screen. True accountability goes well beyond the simple tracking of inputs — It addresses missions. We have remarkably accurate records of dollars and staffing but seem to be also remarkably silent on biodiversity, lost species, pollution levels, erosion, plant and animal diseases, and other threats to park integrity until a crisis appears, which it does on a fairly regular basis. However, crisis reporting is not the same thing as accountability—it is an admission that accountability has been missing—and crisis reporting that is laid at the feet of public overuse of resources may be politically persuasive but professionally simplistic.

The fourth great paradox is the huge gap between the public's support of their parks and that of their elected representatives. It is also apparent in the distinction between legislative support for designating new parks and the evaporation of that support when annual appropriation time rolls around. This is symptomatic of a larger problem of park relevance. Clearly there is a difference in the relevance of parks between the public and their elected representatives and just as clearly the difference is one of perspective. It seems fair to say that elected representatives, facing an endless array of budget demands, tend to see parks as meeting a relatively narrow range of social needs that are almost, but not quite, limited to the ideas of open space and pleasuring grounds, whereas for the public, parks fill a much broader band of needs and wants. It would seem to be the ethical responsibility for the park profession to interpret those benefits to the elected representatives. The conventional view of parks as "islands of permanence in a changing world" is neither very realistic nor very helpful in that interpretation. We know that parks are constantly changing in real terms as well as in the ways that they are perceived by a changing public. Parks proven roles as economic engines for the community, sources of creative inspiration, outdoor classrooms, health assets, crime fighters, and builders of pride can be documented and become part of that interpretation.

Although parks can provide relevant answers to a host of social problems, perhaps what is most convincing in the budget crunch for human services is the understanding that relevancy is also a fiscal matter. Parks can offer far less costly preventive solutions to many social problems, but they need to do so in partnership with other human service agencies. Fiscal relevance does not have to be linked to self-funding but rather with adequate and stable funding from a variety of sources. Park systems that are fiscally relevant can be far more responsive to society's needs than those that are understaffed, closed, and poorly maintained. Charging cost-based fees and abating those fees where necessary can provide a pool of funding to address the wider array of public expectations from their parks. Clinging to the feel-good philosophy of underwriting the 90 percent who can afford to pay so as not to be criticized for the ten percent who can't is hardly relevant to the times. Parks and park systems that can provide demonstrable social benefits while simultaneously eliminating subsidies and reducing the backlog of deferrals cannot fail to generate powerful political relevance and advocacy. Getting on the political agenda and staying there should be a professional ethic of the highest order, fully as important as improving the quality of public use and providing full accountability. Relevance is probably the greatest asset any profession can nurture.

The fifth great paradox of our public parks is that their attractiveness has had so little influence on development standards at their borders and beyond. Does our philosophy of parks as a source of enrichment in our lives change or cease to exist beyond formal park boundaries? Do we create parks as special places only, or are they also demonstrations of a land ethic? Do we create parks as an expression of our civility toward nature and as a counter to our many excesses against nature? If so, shouldn't our parks have radiated some demonstrable measure of respect for the land? To free the parks profession from the constraints of park boundaries would inevitably lead to exciting new levels of personal and professional growth, yet the "reservation mentality"— a hangover from earlier days when park protection was the primary mission— continues. We continue to draw boundaries not just on the land but in job descriptions as well. Park outreach needs to be part of every employee's job, not just the responsibility of the information and education specialists. The growth of greenways linking people to parks and parks to parks is just one of the ways we can move out of the reservation model. Bringing parks into schools and making every park a classroom is another way.

Outreach does not mean a shifting of goals from park protection to park evangelism but rather a commitment to park appreciation as the ultimate means of protecting parks and land. Past failures to follow up on needed land acquisitions within park boundaries and assisting in the establishment of buffer zones around parks are a failure of outreach as much as they are a failure of the budget. A park's appreciation, like a park's infrastructure, needs to be built and relevance is the foundation for that structure. The best way to make parks relevant to people is to get involved beyond park boundaries. The perennial and curious observation that our parks are being "loved to death" seems to suggest a growing shortage both in the quantity of parkland and the quality of life outside of parks.

Two facts and a challenge constitute the sixth parklands paradox. The facts are that every park has a story to tell and yet rarely is that story heard, even though it may be a key to the park's ultimate protection. The challenge is to reverse this situation and make appreciation the fundamental reason for a park's existence. To accept this challenge might also involve a reversal of current priorities in which park interpretation is in a distant second place to law enforcement or, at the very least, a combining of both activities under the mission of park protection. Such an alliance not only recognizes the value of aligning short-term and long-term protection but it can also have the added effect of strengthening the hosting role of law enforcement. No longer would mandated budget cuts be able to zero in on park interpretation as an "extra" that can safely be shelved in hard times.

For the administrator faced with a mandated cut in the budget, temporarily silencing a park's message in order to keep the park open may seem eminently preferable to closing the gates. But is there really any difference? The doors of the opera house, the theatre, and the cathedral can also be open, but if there is nothing going on and no message, is the experience remotely the same? The park may be both medium and message for some visitors, but it certainly isn't for those who need the message the most.

In the crush to balance a budget and save a few dollars it's possible to forget that those national symbols that we cherish so much here become the real thing and that the land is more than a recitation of its resources. It's also a collection of states of mind, adventure, opportunity, nostalgia, freedom, pride, and wonder. Parks embody that and more because they are showcases of pride in our heritage. A park's existence is proof that someone once cared deeply about that piece of land, and hopefully its condition similarly demonstrates that someone still cares. The way in which the park was developed demonstrates our sensitivity to its values, and how it is maintained demonstrates our commitment to stewardship of those values. Its programs demonstrate our desire to build appreciation of those values. In short, every park, trail, historic site, and natural area is a classroom that teaches its lessons and tells the world something about us.

Only history can say whether the current generation of Americans were able to rise to the challenge set forth by its predecessors in acquiring public lands, protecting them, and making them accessible. Today's challenges of building appreciation may be even more difficult than those of the past because they don't have the glamour of acquiring and developing land. However, the idea of finding ultimate protection for parks through an appreciative and concerned public could be the most successful conservation strategy we have ever embarked upon because it is a democratic strategy for a practicing democracy.

The seventh major paradox facing parks is that we continue to highly value our public lands for utilitarian reasons while seemingly not being able to appreciate their intrinsic value. Labeling them and managing them as "resources" somehow keeps us from seeing their value as assets. Resources, almost by definition, are to be used while assets are to be preserved with only the "interest" being used. While it is obvious that only current generations vote, it is equally obvious that future values of a shrinking land base may vastly exceed today's uses and those values may be seriously compromised without an advocate. A categorical listing of parks as cultural assets, recreation assets, historic assets, natural assets, and economic assets guides their planning and helps to identify needed management skills. Carving up the parklands pie has made it possible to focus attention on the parts, but a park's real value has little to do with categories or even the sum of its parts. Its value is in the beauty of the functioning, living, whole park—the very reason for its designation as a park.

It has been said that good park systems preserve the cultures from which they grew while a great park system extends them. Great parks are more than resources for their communities to draw upon—they are part of the community and inseparable from who and what we are. What makes Lowell Industrial Heritage Park so successful is its elegant fitting together of past and present, state, national, and local. Physically and culturally, the city and park are one. The popularity of river walks and heritage trails in urban areas is a profound endorsement of the asset management approach to park management. For such linear parks to be successful, the bureaucracy must relinquish control to the partnership. The disassembly of a park into its component parts, like the bureaucratization of nature, makes no sense if it isn't going to be put back together again. Attempting to manage wildlife without habitat control will ultimately fail.

Perhaps the best example of the difference between resource management and asset management is in the inspiration value of parklands for enriching lives and inspiring creative expression. The artist, in capturing a scene in nature, puts together again that which we have taken apart to manage—the woods, the wildlife, the grasslands, and the water bodies. In recent years, the reality of this has led us to talk about integrated resource management, viewsheds, environmental planning, and holistic concepts. What we are trying to do, of course, is to emulate nature. When we see parks as part of a larger community, we do not arbitrarily close them; and when that larger community includes the next few generations, we do not blithely colonize their future with our preferred alternatives.

The flow of benefits between a park and its larger community is not something to be turned on and off like a faucet. Once we divest ourselves of the regulatory mentality, we see that the flow actually goes in both directions. When that happens, the sign at the gate will be changed to read "This Park Never Closes." Must the sights, sounds, feel, and beauty of a park be forever off limits during those times when we feel that the risk to the park and to the visitor is unacceptable, or do we find ways to reduce the risks and keep the benefits flowing? One of the biggest differences between managing assets and resources is an absolute commitment to protecting the capital. Since the "capital" and the "interest" of a public park are difficult to separate, protecting the capital becomes a matter of reinvesting annually to compensate for the normal attrition and wear and tear of park visitation.

After generations of public park management, we still lack the basic guidelines for reinvestment either on a per capita attendance basis or as a percentage of the operating budget. Successful private parks can tell you what their figure is because they know that the capital is their attraction. They also know that deferred maintenance of the attraction will put them out of business. However, tax dollars are not the only or even the best way that parks can reinvest in their park capital. Corporate and civic revitalization programs, volunteers, coalitions, and creative partnerships can spur whole new growth cycles and facelifts for tired parks, often resulting in expanded hours, increased services, and a new look! The "Under New Management" sign may be a frightening prospect to some, but it may be the logical next step in a park's growth. It is certainly better than the "Closed" sign.

Asset management also recognizes the good sense of a land bank approach to public lands by converting surplus lands to cash for new park acres, or to an infusion of accelerated maintenance dollars. Given the land values involved in park systems, it is ironic that so many find themselves operating at the poverty level while being surrounded by billions in assets.

The eighth, and perhaps the ultimate, park paradox is that all of these inconsistencies have come to be an accepted part of the territory of parks and recreation management rather than being seen as the paralyzing professional challenges that they are. If escaping from the maze of paradoxes, contradictions and ambiguities were easy, we would have done it before now. While there are no easy answers to any ethical issue, two questions invariably come up whenever these paradoxes are discussed: "What are our professional positions?" and "Where does the leadership stand?"

But, that's another subject.

The Paradoxical World of Parks

Conceived in Pride but forgotten in Priority.
Born of Emotion but managed by Numbers.
Adopted by Many but fostered by Few.
Dedicated to the Future but maintained in the Past.
Storehouses of Treasure lacking in Accountability.
Regarded as Special while treated as Replaceable.
Nature's Perfect Whole administered in Bits and Pieces.
Committed to Preservation but lacking in Effective Tools.
Showcases of Heritage tarnished by Neglect.
Prized Economic Engines deprived of Fuel.
Owned by All but stewarded by Few.
Protected by Law but vulnerable to Apathy.

Thinking Outside the Paradox
A New Century and a New Ethic

We must learn to live together as brothers or perish together as fools.

—Martin Luther King, Jr.

The popular image of leaders as charismatic Pattonesque figures, charging across the desert in the lead tank, exposed, confident, audacious, and invincible is hardly the model we can expect to appear from the ranks of most professionals—parks and recreation being no exception. Parks leadership is not about winning battles but rather about building constituencies, promoting greater public appreciation for parks, enhancing professional credibility, moving parks toward a broader definition of accountability, skillfully addressing issues of broad contemporary relevance, demonstrating a deep commitment to parks as cultural assets, protecting parks against the numerous threats they face, and successfully resolving competing and contentious demands for the use of park resources.

While it is not entirely unrealistic to view each of these elements as battlefields in a war on many fronts for parks, it is far more reasonable to look at leadership as the ability to navigate and coordinate the many other "ships" in the park fleet: partnerships, stewardship, salesmanship, craftsmanship, scholarship, and statesmanship. Such a view of leadership calls not for heroics as much as for a quiet, understanding, reliable, relaxed, affable, informed, and believable professional, someone who can be counted on to take a strong, defensible position for the park and for its constituents. Parks offer numerous impregnable positions for defense; abandoning those positions to go on the offense for parks, however tempting, makes it relatively easy for the leadership to get knocked off. Leaving parks vulnerable is hardly the role of a leader. However, there are times when, even in parks, a good offense may, in fact, be the best defense. The varied assaults facing parks at the beginning of the 21st century as well as the many paradoxical interpretations of park philosophy may be evidence that this is one of those times. If it is, the entire fleet of "ships" will be needed.

Put bluntly, the battle for a new park ethic that will address the paradox of not having an advocacy team—a pervasive partnering ethic that can match the strength of diversity in its parks—will require real statesmanship to put park values ahead of organizational constraints. Few would deny that many of our park systems are in a rut when it comes to trying something new like partnerships, particularly when all response to the idea comes as mumbled negatives of "It won't work here," "We lack the authority," "We need to develop policies first," and "We'll lose control." Wasn't it Mark Twain who noted that the only difference between a rut and a grave is their depths?

Real leadership encourages partnerships from the bottom up as a solid way to grow park staffs. A belief in the superiority of partnerships of all types, but particularly partnerships with the public, provides sound encouragement for breaking down some of the barriers and sharing both the challenges and successes. This can only happen where there is a sense of teamwork, willingness to experiment, true empowerment, and the explicit right to make mistakes. An equally important step is to assure that park staffs are reflective of the public that they serve. Gender and ethnic relevance offers not only a better fit with the public but also an expanded network for partnership building. Partnerships with the general public include the obvious kinds of litter reduction and park watch campaigns, but they can also take the form of appeals to search the family photo files for old pictures of the park, historical anecdotes, and connections with early park employees.

Perhaps the most essential element of the partnering ethic is its experimental nature. By definition not all experiments succeed, and the right to fail means the same as the right to learn. Learning how to partner is not an easy assignment. If it were, we wouldn't have any need for marriage counselors. However, we do not avoid marriage and we cannot avoid park partnerships just because they might not always have storybook endings. Real leaders will not only empower their staffs to build partnerships but also will provide them with the help of written case studies and guidelines and with their presence at exploratory meetings with potential partners. Real leaders will recognize and reward employees for their partnerships initiatives—both failed and successful.

Leadership that develops out of the second paradox of failing to commit to improving the quality of public use also requires a change in attitudes, roles, and beliefs about what is possible. The belief that existing public use patterns are nearly impossible to change conveniently ignores the fact that most of our existing park use patterns are the product of park designs and park management. The difficulty in changing user behaviors is, therefore, less with users than with management. Numerous recent experiments with litter-free parks have repeatedly proven that the public's habit of leaving trash is far easier to change than is park management's behavior of picking it up. Despite public support there still may be political resistance from a public service perspective, from an environmental perspective, and even from employees who might fear loss of jobs. Building the quality of public use can only succeed if it is approached as a partnership with the visiting public, the employees, and all parties having a stake in the outcome. The time to begin is now—before existing patterns of use and administrative practices become legal expectations. The number and variety of potential improvements in the quality of public use is limited only by the ability of the park profession to look at problems from a different perspective and the profession's willingness to experiment.

Leadership emerging from the third paradox, the absence of true resource accountability despite the mandate for preservation, again requires a major shift away from long-standing practices. Basic resource inventories may not be perceived as research, but without baseline data our ability to assess trends in species composition or biodiversity (and to use those trends to guide management) is nonexistent. If research institutions are not interested in developing such data, management clearly has to develop its own capability for inventorying and monitoring their assets, and if there is no line item in the budget for such assessments, it becomes the responsibility of professional leadership to secure the necessary budget approvals. Probably no item in the budget is more important to discharging the legislative charter for "preservation for future generations." However, even a failure of the budget is not a barrier because the option of using volunteer partnerships to develop and analyze the data still exists. Volunteer water quality monitoring in lakes, rivers, and bays has been a reality in many parts of the country for years as have partnerships with the Audubon Society to conduct bird surveys.

The thought that the dollars for making true accountability a reality are as close as a clientele willing and able to pay realistic fees opens many doors for leadership within parks and legislative bodies as well. Legislatively, it is time to demand minimum accountability requirements. In the parks of the 21st century, neglect of infrastructure and loss of diversity may well be seen as dereliction of professional responsibility. It has long been assumed that professional management was the equivalent of faithful stewardship; however, in recent years public understanding and scrutiny of all government activities has been much more knowledgeable and intense. Today and in the fishbowl of tomorrow, complete and timely accountability will be demanded by a concerned public and their elected representatives.

Leadership from the fourth paradox, of managing traditional parks in traditional ways for a changing society, takes the idea of accountability to the next step of reviewing park operations in the same way that we might inventory park assets.

For years we have conducted surveys to find out who is using our parks. Today we need to know more about the people who are not using public parks and why they do not use them. Like any consumer service, parks have to be relevant. If they are not being used, we have to ask if it is because they are not relevant, not accessible, not responsive, not friendly, not usable, or simply not where they are needed? Wouldn't we like to know, for example, whether we are serving 37 percent of the population today as opposed to 41 percent ten years ago? If that is a trend, what would it mean for the future?

Parks are one aspect of government that should be seen as fun, rewarding, exciting, and valuable. Don't we want 100 percent of society to see them that way?

Leadership from the fifth paradox and into the world of extra-park cooperation shouldn't have to wait for assessing park relevancy. Parks have much to offer their communities and all that is needed is to reach out with an invitation. The health values of parks and their opportunities for learning and self-discovery alone would draw sufficient attention from countless other agencies, organizations, philanthropies, and potential corporate underwriters to keep a full-time staff person exploring the options for a year. Many groups have profound needs for ready access to the resources of parks and would probably be pleased to see parks become a little more approachable. Positive encouragement of staff to pursue such opportunities through sanctioned use of official time, recognition, and rewards could enhance the image of parks overnight. Similarly, the encouragement of park teams to volunteer to help in related community projects, such as trails, would constitute a powerful statement of professional commitment to not just the project but also to the necessity for community.

Leadership to fully utilize the story that created the park to help sustain the park requires a fresh new look at the role and value of interpretation for every park and historic site. There is no better way to enhance the quality of public use than to build appreciation for the foresight of a park's founders. Preserving and extending the geologic, biologic, and social history of parks is as much an interpretive function as it is a law enforcement responsibility. Reaching out for cooperators to help tell those stories is not only budget-wise, but also it is professionally superior to involve those people who already have a linkage to the park in their hearts and their minds. If leadership means recognizing limitations and doing something about them, sharing responsibility is the highest order of park leadership.

Finally, leadership for managing parks as financial and cultural assets requires the freedom to search out a broader set of talents than that which exists on most park staffs. If park professionals are restricted from such activities because of organizational constraints, it may make sense to give parks their independence from traditional departments in exchange for a greater level of cooperation with a multitude of partnerships and alliances that have shared goals and objectives. If independence can help reduce the ambiguities between park principles and park practices, shouldn't we at least experiment with the idea? The problem with partnership as an alternative management style—as Peter Block, author of *Stewardship: Choosing Service over Self-Interest*, tells us—is that it hasn't been seriously tried.

The building of park partnerships has both practical and philosophical roots. From the practical view, the enormity of the park management task, coupled with its low public budget priority (far less than one percent of most public budgets), makes partnering the only sensible option. Philosophically, the partnership approach offers exciting opportunities for making parks the model of democratic involvement. Ultimately, it is this broad base of appreciation that will provide enduring protection for the land while extending public budgets—the perfect win-win solution for park management.

Leadership in the park profession is the ability to move freely among the rest of the ships in the squadron with the sure knowledge that the course will not falter. Only by helping to develop a permanent team of leaders is this likely to happen. Leadership may in fact connote exactly the wrong image of what is needed. A more realistic set of qualities is probably that which is evoked by the word *advocate*. Some of the people who created yesterday's parks were leaders, but all were advocates. Advocacy for today's and tomorrow's parks requires that the promises be kept, the paradoxes minimized, and the deferred maintenance eliminated.

> *Each is given a bag of tools,*
> *A shapeless mass,*
> *A book of rules;*
> *And each must make—*
> *Ere life is flown—*
> *A stumbling block*
> *Or stepping stone.*
>
> —R. L. Sharpe

Suggested Best Management Practices for Parks and Heritage Sites

Practice	Implemented by
Partnering	Policy statement on the importance of partnerships and at least one ongoing partnership that is viewed as such by the partnering organization
Heritage Appreciation	Policy statement endorsing heritage appreciation, hiring of a heritage interpreter, an active heritage-focused friends group, heritage appreciation programming, documented heritage protection accomplishments
Friends Groups	Written guidelines for friends groups or legislation authorizing and/or protecting volunteers, one active friends group for fundraising and/or adoption of the park or of a park feature
Accountability	Policy or budgetary guidelines requiring regular reporting of the condition and trend of all park resources and guidelines requiring continuing staff development, recent published report on park conditions and threats, plus current training plans for all staff
Asset Inventory/ Monitoring	Contract or cooperative agreement or an assigned position for assessing the state of the park, budgeted program for inventory/ monitoring of any aspect of park natural resources, or a recent published report on resource conditions, trends, and threats
Good Neighbor	Policy guidelines or personnel evaluation criteria requiring community involvement, service on community committees, park outreach programs, or cooperative agreements with local agencies for mutual assistance or joint projects
Advocacy and Activism	Policy guidelines or personnel evaluation criteria encouraging advocacy through organizational memberships or personal initiatives, or the absence of guidelines discouraging such involvement, or a record of recognition for advocacy
Planning	A comprehensive mandate and approach to planning for resource protection, development, staffing, cooperation, emergency preparedness, risk assessment, financial management, acqui-sitions, in-progress or adopted plans, planning staff, contracts, implementation, and progress reporting.
Experimenting	A clear commitment to finding better ways of doing business; supporting research; challenging existing policy, practices, and procedures; rewarding innovation; and accepting failure

Afterword
A Park Is How Society Writes
Its Poem on the Land

Someday, somewhere, somehow, a park will be conceived without a fight, without animosity, without anger, without name-calling, stridency, and rancor—simply because a park is not ugly, or threatening, or warlike, or exclusive, or a blight on the landscape—simply because it does not cut down, dig up, flood, or pave over.

Although the word *park* may be flung aside with disdain or hurled like an insult, it will remain untarnished because *a park is*

how society writes a poem on the land,

a stage with endless theatre,

freedom and refuge,

wild, untamed, natural, pure, and simple,

beauty expressed by nature for all,

a living history of who we are,

music on the wind and in the sky,

art and artistry and inspiration,

a challenge, a dare to find ourselves,

spirit, vitality, and renewal,

hope and dreams,

an idea that grows with its community,

for life—all of life—for all time!

Although the idea of a park may be ridiculed and denigrated, it can never be dismissed because *a park is*

for children, all children, always,

for family, yours, mine, and theirs,

for community, for bonding, for caring,

for jobs, rewarding, earning, building,

for extending yesterday into tomorrow,

for learning and connecting,

an incubator of pride, esteem, and confidence,

for everyone—every one!

Although the promise of a park may be challenged and debated, it cannot be denied because *a park*:

promotes peace, and understanding,

preserves a child's sense of wonder,

rekindles reverence and awe,

encourages generosity and sharing,

breeds thoughtfulness, and humility,

fosters caring and stewardship,

captures the imagination of those it touches,

interprets itself to those who listen,

returns its investment over and over,

embodies ideals of life, liberty, and the pursuit of happiness,

is a billboard for our belief in ourselves,

is democracy's dream spread upon the landscape.

Source Notes

Beyond Principles: Explorations into the Ethical Foundations of Interpretation was published in 2005 by *The Interpreter, 1*(3), 18–21. Reprinted here, in part, by permission of the National Association for Interpretation.

"Conversation with a Mountain," which appears at the end of Parks and the Purpose of Life, was originally published in February 2005 by *Monadnock Adhoc*, an online magazine of the Monadnock Writers Guild.

Parks and Inspiration: Artists, Tourists, and the Elusive Sublime is based on a 2001 article published by the *Journal of Interpretation Research, 6*(1), 49–54. Reprinted with permission of the National Association for Interpretation.

Parks and Pride: The Land Defines Its People was previously published in 2006 by *The Interpreter, 2*(1), 14–16. Reprinted with permission of the National Association for Interpretation.

Parks and the Economy: The Essential Environmental Partnership is based, in part, on Best Management Practices – It's Time to Certify Our Public Parks, Natural Areas, and Historic Sites was published in 2001 by *Legacy, 12*(1), 10–12. Reprinted with permission of the National Association for Interpretation.

Ethics and the Health of Public Park Systems was previously published in *Parks and Recreation, 40*(2), 8–13. Reprinted, in part, with permission of the National Recreation and Parks Association.

Parks and the Pursuit of Happiness: An Exercise in Lateral Thinking is based, in part, on a 2005 article published by *Parks and Recreation, 40*(4), 8–13. Reprinted with permission of the National Recreation and Parks Association.

Parks and Wonder: Interpretation and the Eureka Moment is based, in part, on a 2002 article published in the *Journal of Interpretation Research, 7*(1), 25–29. Reprinted with permission of the National Association for Interpretation.

Parks for Beauty in Our Lives: Wilderness and Cultural Identity is based on a July 1988 paper, Wilderness—The Heart and Soul of Culture, published in *Parks and Recreation, 22*(7), 24–31. Reprinted here with permission of the National Recreation and Park Association.

Parks for Hope: Homeless and Hopeless in the Parks is based on a 2005 article published in *Parks and Recreation, 40*(8), 8–9. Reprinted, in part, with permission of the National Recreation and Parks Association.

Parks for Life: An Emotion-Based Park Ethic is based on a Jan/Feb 2005 article published in *The Interpreter, 1*(1), 16–19. Reprinted, in part, with permission of the National Association for Interpretation.

Parks for Meaning: Senior Park Volunteers—Working at Their Leisure is based, in part, on a 2005 article published in *Parks and Recreation, 40*(5), 8–12. Reprinted with permission of the National Recreation and Parks Association.

Self-Funding State Parks: The New Hampshire Experience is based on a 1994 article published in *Parks: The International Journal for Protected Area Managers, 4*(2), 22–27. Reprinted with permission of IUCN The World Conservation Union, Gland, Switzerland.

The Essays: Parks and Inspiration and The Art of Park Management are based on a two-part series, Conversations with Creative People and Implications for Management, published in 2000–2001 by *Legacy, 12*(5), 18–23 and *12*(6), 28–32. Reprinted with permission of the National Association for Interpretation.

The essays Parks, Paradoxes, and Partnerships: The Search for Logic and Thinking Outside the Paradox: Leadership for a New Century and a New Ethic were based, in part, on the article "Parklands as Paradox" published in 1995 by the *Journal of Park and Recreation Administration, 13*(4), 1–12.

The Ethical Case for Fees as Dedicated Park Income is based in part on a paper from *Recreation Fees in the National Park Service – Issues, Policies, and Guidelines for Future Action, 1997* (pp. 29–31). St. Paul, MN: University of Minnesota.

The Ethical Interpreter: Conscience, Courage, and Loyalty at the Intersection was originally published in 2006 by *The Interpreter*, 2(3), 10–12. Reprinted with permission of the National Association for Interpretation.

The Real Costs of Deferred Maintenance: Neglecting America's Best Idea is based, in part, on essays published in *Parks and Recreation* (Aug 2002); and the *Friends of Acadia Journal, 7*(5), (Winter 2002–2003).

The two essays, General Funding for Special Places and Toward a More Perfect Union, are based on a booklet, *Partnerships for Parks*, published for The National Association of State Park Directors, by the New Hampshire Division of Parks and Recreation in March, 1994.

For Further Reading

Abbey, E. (1968). *Desert solitaire—A season in the wilderness*. New York, NY: Ballantine Books.

Acadia's business plan—An assessment of the park's operational needs. (2001). Washington, DC: National Parks Conservation Association.

Altman, N. (2000). *Sacred trees: Spirituality, wisdom and well-being*. New York, NY: Sterling.

Americans outdoors—The legacy, the challenge with case studies: The Report of the President's Commission. (1987). Washington, DC: Island Press.

Belanger, P. (1999). *Inventing Acadia: Artists and tourists at Mount Desert*. Rockland, ME: Farnsworth Gallery.

Block, P. (1993). *Stewardship: Choosing service over self-interest*. San Francisco, CA: Berrett-Koehler Publishers.

Brandon, K., Redford, K., and Sanderson, S. (Eds.) (1998). *Parks in peril—People, politics, and protected areas*. Washington, DC: Island Press.

Bryant, W. C. (1821). In H. Dana and E. Channing (Eds.), *Poems*. Cambridge, MA: Hillard and Metcalf.

Callicott, J. B. and Nelson, M. P. (Eds.). (1998). *The great new wilderness debate*. Athens, GA: University of Georgia Press.

Cahn, R. and Ketchum, R. G. (1981). *American photographers and the National Parks*. New York, NY: Viking Press.

Carr, G. I. (2000). *In search of the Promised land: Paintings by Frederick Edwin Church*. New York, NY: Berry Hill Galleries.

Carson, R. (2002). *Silent spring, 40th anniversary edition*. New York, NY: Houghton Mifflin.

Chase, G. (1966). *America's music*. New York, NY: McGraw-Hill.

Csikszentmihalyi, M. (1990). *Flow: The psychology of optimal experience*. New York, NY: Harper Periennial.

de Bono, Edward. (1973). *Lateral thinking: Creativity step-by-step*. New York, NY: Harper & Row.

Driver, B. L., Dustin, D., Baltic, T., Elsner, G., and Peterson, G. (Eds.). (1996). *Nature and the human spirit: Toward an expanded land management ethic.* State College, PA: Venture Publishing, Inc.

Edward, B. (1986). *Drawing on the artist within.* New York, NY: Simon and Schuster.

Everson, W. (1981). *American bard: The original preface to Leaves of Grass by Walt Whitman.* New York, NY: Viking Press.

Frost, R. (1962). "The Gift Outright" for John F. Kennedy at His Inauguration. In *In the clearing* (pp. 28–31). London, UK: Holt, Rinehart, and Winston.

Gardner, J. (Ed.). (1998). *The sacred earth: Writers on nature and spirit.* Emeryville, CA: New World Library.

Gilb, C. L. (1996). *Hidden hierarchies—The professions and government.* New York, NY: Harper and Row.

Gilman, C. (1938). *The poetry of travelling in the United States.* New York, NY: S. Coleman.

Goodenough, U. (1998). *The sacred depths of nature.* New York, NY: Oxford University Press.

Gottlieb, R. S. (Ed.). (1996). *This sacred earth: Religion, nature, environment.* New York, NY: Routledge.

Harrison, J. (1991). In D. Henley and D. Marsh, *Heaven is under our feet: A book for Walden Woods* (pp. 64–67). Stamford, CT: Longmeadow Press.

Huth, H. (1990). *Nature and the American: Three centuries of changing attitudes.* Lincoln, NE: University of Nebraska Press.

La Page, W. and Ranney, S. (1988). America's Wilderness: The Heart and Soul of Culture. *Parks and Recreation, 23*(7), 24–31.

Leopold, A. (1948). *A Sand County almanac and sketches here and there.* New York, NY. Oxford University Press.

Louv, R. (2006). *Last child in the woods.* Chapel Hill, NC: Algonquin Books.

Lowry, W. R. (1995). The Capacity for Wonder: Preserving National Parks. *American Political Science Review, 89*(1), 210–211.

Machlis, G. and Tichnell, D. L. (1985). *The state of the worlds parks: An international assessment for resource management, policy and research.* Boulder, CO: Westview Press.

MacLean, N. (1976). *A river runs through it*. Chicago, IL: University of Chicago Press.

Nash, R. F. (1989). *The rights of nature—A history of environmental ethics*. Madison, WI: University of Wisconsin Press.

National Park Service. (2001). *9.11.01 remembrance*. Washington, DC: Author. Retrieved December 15, 2006, from www.nps.gov/remembrance

Newman, C. (2001). Welcome to Monhegan Island. Now please go away. *National Geographic, 20*(1), 92–109.

Nyerges, A. L. (1999). *In praise of Nature—Ansel Adams and photographers of the American West*. Dayton, OH: Dayton Art Institute.

Orr, D. (1994). *Earth in mind: On education, environment, and the human prospect*. Island Press: Washington, DC.

Peace Parks Foundation website. http://www.peaceparks.org

President's Commission on Americans Outdoors. (1987). *Report of the President's Commission on Americans Outdoors*. Washington, DC: Island Press.

Quinn, R. E. (2000). *Change the world: How ordinary people can accomplish extraordinary results*. San Francisco, CA: Jossey-Bass.

Roosevelt, T. (1912). *Confession of Faith speech*. Progressive National Convention, August 5, Chicago, Illinois.

Russell, R. (2000). *The vast enquiring soul: Explorations into the further reaches of consciousness*. Charlottesville, VA: Hampton Roads Publishing.

Schama, S. (1995). *Landscape and memory*. New York, NY: Alfred A. Knopf.

Taylor, J. C. (1976). *America as art*. Washington DC: Smithsonian Institution Press and U.S. Government Printing Office.

Taylor, P. W. (1985). *Respect for Nature: A theory of environmental ethics*. Princeton, NJ: Princeton University Press.

Tilden, F. (1962). *The State Parks—Their meaning in American life*. New York, NY: Alfred A. Knopf.

Tobias, M. and Cowan, G. (Eds.). (1994). *The soul of nature: Visions of a living earth*. New York, NY: Continuum Publishing Company.

Trimble, S. and Williams. T. T. (1996). *Testimony: Writers of the West speak on behalf of Utah wilderness*. Minneapolis, MN: Milkweed Editions.

Turner, F. J. (1935). *The frontier in American history.* New York, NY: Henry Holt and Co.

Turner, J. (1996). *The abstract wild.* Tuscon, AZ: University of Arizona Press.

U.S. General Accounting Office. (2003, September 27). *National Park Service efforts to address its maintenance backlog* (#03-1177). Washington, DC: U.S. Government Printing Office.

Watkins, T. H. and Byrnes, P. (Eds.). (1995). *The world of wilderness: Essays on the power and purpose of wild country.* Niwot, CO: Roberts Rinehart Publishing in cooperation with The Wilderness Society.

Williams, T. T. (2002). *Land that we love: Americans talk about America's public lands.* Salt Lake City, UT: The Cultural Olympiad.

Willis, N. P. (1840). In H. Huth (1990), *Nature and the American—Three centuries of changing attitudes.* Lincoln, NE: University of Nebraska Press.

Other Books by Venture Publishing, Inc.

*21st Century Leisure: Current Issues, Second
Edition*
by Valeria J. Freysinger and John R. Kelly

*The A•B•Cs of Behavior Change: Skills for Working
With Behavior Problems in Nursing Homes*
by Margaret D. Cohn, Michael A. Smyer, and
Ann L. Horgas

*Activity Experiences and Programming within
Long-Term Care*
by Ted Tedrick and Elaine R. Green

The Activity Gourmet
by Peggy Powers

Advanced Concepts for Geriatric Nursing Assistants
by Carolyn A. McDonald

Adventure Programming
edited by John C. Miles and Simon Priest

Assessment: The Cornerstone of Activity Programs
by Ruth Perschbacher

*Behavior Modification in Therapeutic Recreation:
An Introductory Manual*
by John Datillo and William D. Murphy

Benefits of Leisure
edited by B.L. Driver, Perry J. Brown, and
George L. Peterson

Benefits of Recreation Research Update
by Judy M. Sefton and W. Kerry Mummery

*Beyond Baskets and Beads: Activities for Older
Adults with Functional Impairments*
by Mary Hart, Karen Primm, and Kathy
Cranisky

*Beyond Bingo: Innovative Programs for the New
Senior*
by Sal Arrigo, Jr., Ann Lewis, and Hank
Mattimore

*Beyond Bingo 2: More Innovative Programs for
the New Senior*
by Sal Arrigo, Jr.

*Boredom Busters: Themed Special Events to Dazzle
and Delight Your Group*
by Annette C. Moore

*Both Gains and Gaps: Feminist Perspectives on
Women's Leisure*
by Karla Henderson, M. Deborah Bialeschki,
Susan M. Shaw, and Valeria J. Freysinger

Client Assessment in Therapeutic Recreation Services
by Norma J. Stumbo

Client Outcomes in Therapeutic Recreation Services
by Norma J. Stumbo

Conceptual Foundations for Therapeutic Recreation
edited by David R. Austin, John Datillo, and
Bryan P. McCormick

Constraints to Leisure
edited by Edgar L. Jackson

*Dementia Care Programming: An Identity-Focused
Approach*
by Rosemary Dunne

*Dimensions of Choice: Qualitative Approaches to
Parks, Recreation, Tourism, Sport, and Leisure
Research, Second Edition*
by Karla A. Henderson

*Diversity and the Recreation Profession:
Organizational Perspectives*
edited by Maria T. Allison and Ingrid E.
Schneider

*Effective Management in Therapeutic Recreation
Service, Second Edition*
by Marcia Jean Carter and Gerald S. O'Morrow

*Evaluating Leisure Services: Making Enlightened
Decisions, Second Edition*
by Karla A. Henderson and M. Deborah
Bialeschki

*Everything from A to Y: The Zest Is up to You!
Older Adult Activities for Every Day of the Year*
by Nancy R. Cheshire and Martha L. Kenney

*The Evolution of Leisure: Historical and
Philosophical Perspectives*
by Thomas Goodale and Geoffrey Godbey

*Experience Marketing: Strategies for the New
Millennium*
by Ellen L. O'Sullivan and Kathy J. Spangler

Facilitation Techniques in Therapeutic Recreation
by John Datillo

*File o' Fun: A Recreation Planner for Games &
Activities, Third Edition*
by Jane Harris Ericson and Diane Ruth Albright

*Functional Interdisciplinary-Transdisciplinary
Therapy (FITT) Manual*
by Deborah M. Schott, Judy D. Burdett, Beverly
J. Cook, Karren S. Ford, and Kathleen M. Orban

*The Game and Play Leader's Handbook:
Facilitating Fun and Positive Interaction,
Revised Edition*
by Bill Michaelis and John M. O'Connell

*The Game Finder—A Leader's Guide to Great
Activities*
by Annette C. Moore

*Getting People Involved in Life and Activities:
Effective Motivating Techniques*
by Jeanne Adams

*Glossary of Recreation Therapy and Occupational
Therapy*
by David R. Austin

Great Special Events and Activities
by Annie Morton, Angie Prosser, and Sue
Spangler

Group Games & Activity Leadership
by Kenneth J. Bulik

*Growing With Care: Using Greenery, Gardens,
and Nature With Aging and Special Populations*
by Betsy Kreidler

*Hands On! Children's Activities for Fairs, Festivals,
and Special Events*
by Karen L. Ramey

Other Books by Venture Publishing, Inc.

Health Promotion for Mind, Body and Spirit
by Suzanne Fitzsimmons and Linda L. Buettner

In Search of the Starfish: Creating a Caring Environment
by Mary Hart, Karen Primm, and Kathy Cranisky

Inclusion: Including People With Disabilities in Parks and Recreation Opportunities
by Lynn Anderson and Carla Brown Kress

Inclusive Leisure Services: Responding to the Rights of People with Disabilities, Second Edition
by John Dattilo

Innovations: A Recreation Therapy Approach to Restorative Programs
by Dawn R. De Vries and Julie M. Lake

Internships in Recreation and Leisure Services: A Practical Guide for Students, Third Edition
by Edward E. Seagle, Jr. and Ralph W. Smith

Interpretation of Cultural and Natural Resources, Second Edition
by Douglas M. Knudson, Ted T. Cable, and Larry Beck

Intervention Activities for At-Risk Youth
by Norma J. Stumbo

Introduction to Outdoor Recreation: Providing and Managing Resource Based Opportunities
by Roger L. Moore and B.L. Driver

Introduction to Recreation and Leisure Services, Eighth Edition
by Karla A. Henderson, M. Deborah Bialeschki, John L. Hemingway, Jan S. Hodges, Beth D. Kivel, and H. Douglas Sessoms

Introduction to Therapeutic Recreation: U.S. and Canadian Perspectives
by Kenneth Mobily and Lisa Ostiguy

Introduction to Writing Goals and Objectives: A Manual for Recreation Therapy Students and Entry-Level Professionals
by Suzanne Melcher

Leadership and Administration of Outdoor Pursuits, Second Edition
by Phyllis Ford and James Blanchard

Leadership in Leisure Services: Making a Difference, Second Edition
by Debra J. Jordan

Leisure Services in Canada: An Introduction, Second Edition
by Mark S. Searle and Russell E. Brayley

Leisure and Leisure Services in the 21st Century: Toward Mid Century
by Geoffrey Godbey

The Leisure Diagnostic Battery: Users Manual and Sample Forms
by Peter A. Witt and Gary Ellis

Leisure Education I: A Manual of Activities and Resources, Second Edition
by Norma J. Stumbo

Leisure Education II: More Activities and Resources, Second Edition
by Norma J. Stumbo

Leisure Education III: More Goal-Oriented Activities
by Norma J. Stumbo

Leisure Education IV: Activities for Individuals with Substance Addictions
by Norma J. Stumbo

Leisure Education Program Planning: A Systematic Approach, Second Edition
by John Dattilo

Leisure Education Specific Programs
by John Dattilo

Leisure in Your Life: An Exploration, Sixth Edition
by Geoffrey Godbey

Leisure Services in Canada: An Introduction, Second Edition
by Mark S. Searle and Russell E. Brayley

Leisure Studies: Prospects for the Twenty-First Century
edited by Edgar L. Jackson and Thomas L. Burton

The Lifestory Re-Play Circle: A Manual of Activities and Techniques
by Rosilyn Wilder

Marketing in Leisure and Tourism: Reaching New Heights
by Patricia Click Janes

The Melody Lingers On: A Complete Music Activities Program for Older Adults
by Bill Messenger

Models of Change in Municipal Parks and Recreation: A Book of Innovative Case Studies
edited by Mark E. Havitz

More Than a Game: A New Focus on Senior Activity Services
by Brenda Corbett

The Multiple Values of Wilderness
by H. Ken Cordell, John C. Bergstrom, and J.M. Bowker

Nature and the Human Spirit: Toward an Expanded Land Management Ethic
edited by B.L. Driver, Daniel Dustin, Tony Baltic, Gary Elsner, and George Peterson

The Organizational Basis of Leisure Participation: A Motivational Exploration
by Robert A. Stebbins

Outdoor Recreation for 21st Century America
by H. Ken Cordell

Outdoor Recreation Management: Theory and Application, Third Edition
by Alan Jubenville and Ben Twight

Planning and Organizing Group Activities in Social Recreation
by John V. Valentine

Planning Parks for People, Second Edition
by John Hultsman, Richard L. Cottrell, and
Wendy Z. Hultsman

*The Process of Recreation Programming Theory
and Technique, Third Edition*
by Patricia Farrell and Herberta M. Lundegren

*Programming for Parks, Recreation, and Leisure
Services: A Servant Leadership Approach,
Second Edition*
by Debra J. Jordan, Donald G. DeGraaf, and
Kathy H. DeGraaf

Protocols for Recreation Therapy Programs
edited by Jill Kelland, along with the Recreation
Therapy Staff at Alberta Hospital Edmonton

*Puttin' on the Skits: Plays for Adults in Managed
Care*
by Jean Vetter

*Quality Management: Applications for Therapeutic
Recreation*
edited by Bob Riley

*A Recovery Workbook: The Road Back from
Substance Abuse*
by April K. Neal and Michael J. Taleff

*Recreation and Leisure: Issues in an Era of Change,
Third Edition*
edited by Thomas Goodale and Peter A. Witt

Recreation and Youth Development
by Peter A. Witt and Linda L. Caldwell

*Recreation Economic Decisions: Comparing
Benefits and Costs, Second Edition*
by John B. Loomis and Richard G. Walsh

*Recreation for Older Adults: Individual and Group
Activities*
by Judith A. Elliott and Jerold E. Elliott

*Recreation Program Planning Manual for Older
Adults*
by Karen Kindrachuk

*Recreation Programming and Activities for Older
Adults*
by Jerold E. Elliott and Judith A. Sorg-Elliott

*Reference Manual for Writing Rehabilitation
Therapy Treatment Plans*
by Penny Hogberg and Mary Johnson

*Research in Therapeutic Recreation: Concepts and
Methods*
edited by Marjorie J. Malkin and Christine Z.
Howe

*Simple Expressions: Creative and Therapeutic Arts
for the Elderly in Long-Term Care Facilities*
by Vicki Parsons

A Social History of Leisure Since 1600
by Gary Cross

A Social Psychology of Leisure
by Roger C. Mannell and Douglas A. Kleiber

*Special Events and Festivals: How to Organize,
Plan, and Implement*
by Angie Prosser and Ashli Rutledge

*Stretch Your Mind and Body: Tai Chi as an
Adaptive Activity*
by Duane A. Crider and William R. Klinger

*Therapeutic Activity Intervention with the Elderly:
Foundations and Practices*
by Barbara A. Hawkins, Marti E. May, and
Nancy Brattain Rogers

Therapeutic Recreation and the Nature of Disabilities
by Kenneth E. Mobily and Richard D. MacNeil

*Therapeutic Recreation: Cases and Exercises,
Second Edition*
by Barbara C. Wilhite and M. Jean Keller

*Therapeutic Recreation in Health Promotion and
Rehabilitation*
by John Shank and Catherine Coyle

Therapeutic Recreation in the Nursing Home
by Linda Buettner and Shelley L. Martin

*Therapeutic Recreation Programming: Theory
and Practice*
by Charles Sylvester, Judith E. Voelkl, and
Gary D. Ellis

*Therapeutic Recreation Protocol for Treatment of
Substance Addictions*
by Rozanne W. Faulkner

*The Therapeutic Recreation Stress Management
Primer*
by Cynthia Mascott

The Therapeutic Value of Creative Writing
by Paul M. Spicer

*Tourism and Society: A Guide to Problems and
Issues*
by Robert W. Wyllie

Traditions: Improving Quality of Life in Caregiving
by Janelle Sellick

 Venture Publishing, Inc.
1999 Cato Avenue
State College, PA 16801

Phone: 814-234-4561
Fax: 814-234-1651